Mikak and her Tutauk in London, 1760s

While other Inuit may have been taken to Europe previously, the visit of Mikak, a clever and attractive woman, is especially significant because of her impact on the highest reaches of English society in the eighteenth century. On her return she played a key role in early relations between aboriginals and Europeans in Labrador.

Donald Smith with Innu, early nineteenth century

Donald Smith, the man who was Sir John A. Macdonald's emissary during the Red River Rebellion and who drove the last spike in the CPR, was the same canny Scot who built up the eastern edge of the Hudson's Bay Company's empire in Labrador in the nineteenth century. One of the most prominent Canadians in history, he had his start in North West River.

Moravian Mission, Okak, northern Labrador, 1903

Some of the first prefabricated materials ever used in Canada were shipped over by the Moravian church to build their structures in Labrador. The station was built at Okak in 1776. The Moravian church, a Protestant church that originated in what is now the Czech Republic in the middle of the fifteenth century, was the first Christian church in what is now Arctic Canada.

Joseph Jacque, English River, Kaipokok Bay, early twentieth century
Most white settlers in Labrador came from the British Isles but some, like the Jacques, came from Quebec in the nineteenth and early twentieth centuries. They married aboriginal women and combined their wives' skills with their own to survive and flourish in a harsh northern land.

Gilbert Blake, 1905

A trapper from the age of thirteen and the product of a unique trapping culture that had grown up in Lake Melville, Gilbert Blake knew the rivers of northern Labrador like the lines on his palm and spoke the language of the Innu. Mina Hubbard showed the good judgment that ensured the success of her historic trek across Labrador when she chose him as a guide.

Bridgetta Piwas and cousin, Davis Inlet, 1940s

Although life was not always easy, in the 1940s the Innu were by and large happy treading the interior woods of Labrador in search of the caribou and furs for the traders. Young and old lived and laughed together. Only later, after relocation to settled communities, would they begin to suffer from family violence and social disintegration.

Newfoundland fisherman, southern Labrador, 1940s

Every summer during the first half of the nineteenth century, thousands of hardy Newfoundland fishermen sailed "down on the Labrador" in search of the lucrative cod. Most returned to the island in the fall with full hatches and faces lined with memories; but some stayed to add their presence to the established Inuit-European population.

Labrador City, 1960s
Carved out of the wilderness of
the Labrador interior in the 1960s,
Labrador City and Wabush shipped
their high-grade ore to the St.
Lawrence over one of the modern
construction miracles of the twentieth century, the Quebec North Shore
and Labrador Railway. The towns
would become model towns in modern Canada, still thriving today with
the resurgence of the market for iron.

Battle Harbour, 1970s
Known as the "capital" of Labrador
in the nineteenth century, Battle
Harbour was so popular with fishermen that it was said one could walk
across its narrow tickle on the decks
of schooners. Because of its Grenfell
hospital, its Marconi station, and its
Ranger post, this storied community
was sought out by others, too, such
as Robert Peary, who sent from here
his message of triumph on reaching
the North Pole.

Churchill Falls

"The noise of the fall has a stunning effect…can be heard as a deep, booming sound." When A. P. Low made these remarks at the turn of the century, he could not have foreseen the stunning effect that the deal with Quebec in the 1970s would have on the people of Newfoundland and Labrador. The harnessing of this cataract higher and mightier than Niagara continues to be a contentious issue to this day.

From the Coast to Far Inland

collected writings on Labrador

edited and with an introduction
by William Rompkey

NIMBUS
PUBLISHING

Nimbus Publishing Limited

PO Box 9166, Halifax, NS B3K 5M8

(902) 455-4286

Printed and bound in Canada

Design: Margaret Issenman

Map credit: Joel Trojanowski

Library and Archives Canada Cataloguing
in Publication

    From the coast to far inland : collected writings
on Labrador / edited and with an introduction
by William Rompkey.

Includes bibliographical references and index.
ISBN 1-55109-559-9

1. Labrador and Newfoundland. 2. Labrador and
Newfoundland—History. I. Rompkey, William, 1936-

FC2193.4.F76 2006   971.8   C2006-901493-0

Canadä   The Canada Council | Le Conseil des Arts
for the Arts | du Canada

Excerpt from *The Vinland Sagas*, translated with an introduction by Magnus Magnusson and Hermann Pálsson (Penguin Classics, 1965). Copyright © Magnus Magnusson and Hermann Pálsson, 1965. Reproduced by permission of Penguin Books Ltd.

Excerpt from *The Merchant Princes* by Peter C. Newman. Copyright © Power Reporting Limited, 1991. Reprinted by permission of Penguin Group (Canada), a Division of Pearson Penguin Canada Inc.

"One of the Grandest Spectacles in the World," from *Brinco: The Story of Churchill Falls* by Philip Smith. Used by permission of McClelland & Stewart Ltd.

Excerpt from *Remembering the Years of My Life: Journeys of a Labrador Inuit Hunter,* by Paulus Maggo, 1999. Reproduced with the permission of the Minister of Public Works and Government Services, and Courtesy of the Privy Council Office, 2006.

All other material used with permission.

We acknowledge the financial support of the Government of Canada through the Book Publishing Industry Development Program (BPIDP) and the Canada Council, and of the Province of Nova Scotia through the Department of Tourism, Culture and Heritage for our publishing activities.

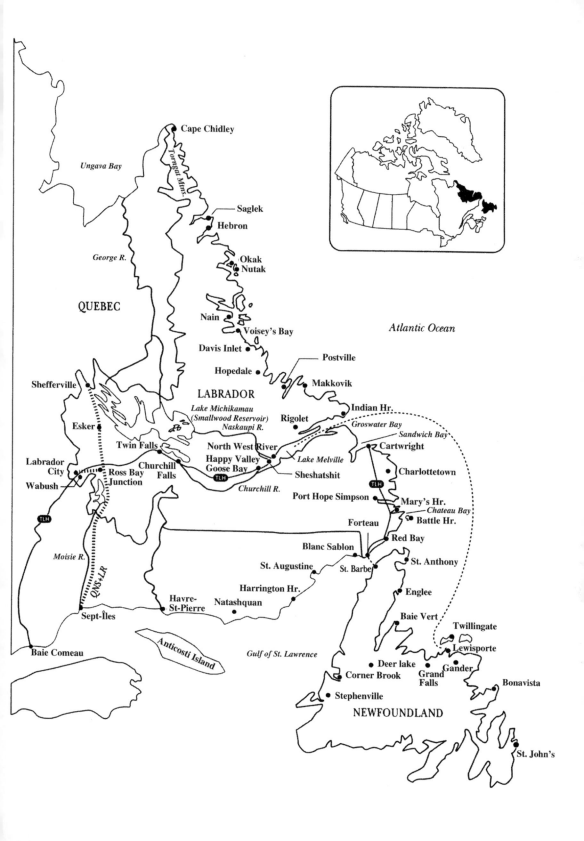

Boyd Chubbs

Away To The North: A Landscape Is Singing, 1997

Sivullivinivut uvannenginnatut.

Anitsataujuk ilonnainut ujakKanut innanullu;

Kaumagutauluk aKittuni piggapijanni;

takutsaujuk inglulialunni;

tusatsaujuk ikummalammi kallumilu anuggaumijanimmilu;

napvatausok nunaup atani ivuluvvalaningani, sivullita uKausingit piusingillu.

Natsataujuk tutsianginnut ananauninginnulu Kupanuat, natsivuk ommatikkut
niaKukkulu, tunggavittalunga apvitannisamma pitsatunitsanganik,
mitsiKattumik, isuKanggitumik angiggasaganik.

Una nunak, Labrador, aninniminik itsasuanitamik tuniggutiKavak minggui
siKullugu tarnigani; tigullalvuk ilonnainik piusikkanik sulijotillugillu
suliagijakka.

Una nunak itjunaigivage.

(Inuktitut)

The Past is always with me.

It breathes through every stone and cliff; is illuminated
in the soft, wild moss; is seen across the heavy swells
of sea; heard in the pitch and tone of thunder and lashing wind; is found in the
    low and slow murmur through the ground, the ancestral sound and story.
And carried in the song and glory of birds, it settles
through my heart and head, anchoring me with the
liberating power of a true, eternal home.
This land, this Labrador, brings the breath of its long age
to rest in my soul; engages all I do and insures my labours. This place is my
    Holy Land.

Neme utat nantem nikunuenten nin.

Nete ut nenemikan kassinu ashinit mak
Nete estashekat utshiti nete ut uasteu ne
enushkast uapitsheuska muk; kie kassinu nete
Nuken nete uinupekut; kasinnu nete petakanu
Nete ut nanamisut tshetutau mak ne niutiki
Kie tshipa mishken nete minaush pietakuak e
nutik netu assit mak ne tshiashinut kaeitit mak utipatshamunaua.
Mak nete ispanu nete nikamunt mak nete ispatentakushit peneshishat nete
    isteu nete
enteit mak nistakuant. Kie ne ispish
Shutshian e tapian. Nete ntshisk nitshit.
Ume assi, nitasinat, kie mue kheipish iniuimikak tshikeisteu ute nteiti kie
    kassinu tshekuau
ispish tutaman mak itusian.
Umue assi ekun tshiatuauentiman assi.

(Innu-aimun)

Contents

Introduction

Over the centuries, different peoples have appeared on the Labrador stage. Some stayed; others did not. Some retreated to the rear of the stage for a while, though we were still aware of their presence and waited for them to emerge once again in the full glare of lights. Some learned from others, competed with others, or learned to work together. Some fought. Some tried to dominate, and did. Some cared for and protected others and helped them make the best of their lives and their land.

Those who are still there have made it their place, whether or not they are entirely satisfied with it. For as the following stories show, there have been clashes, mostly between aboriginal and non-aboriginal, from the time of the Vikings up to the present day. While some have found reconciliation, others are still far from it. Moreover, there has been an uneasy relationship between Labrador and the Island of Newfoundland, like that of two stepsisters who have yet to fully resolve the tensions and conflicts that exist when siblings are forced to share the same space.

Recently the name of the province was changed to Newfoundland and Labrador, reflecting an understanding on the Island that there is a need for inclusion. Yet attitudes remain and will take some time to change. Throughout the history of Labrador, there has been adventure and hardship and beauty and challenge, met sometimes with greed and animosity and sometimes with generosity and love by both men and women.

All of these are found in the following stories of Labrador, a big, beautiful land, sometimes bitter, sometimes challenging, always varied, always stimulating—a land that grips you and won't let go.

This is an anthology about Labrador's people and their places. The stories have been chosen not only because they are some of the best writing on Labrador but also because they trace, to some degree, its history. As well, they serve as a backdrop to the emergence of the Labrador identity. The excerpts are arranged chronologically, from the arrival of the Vikings to the flowering of a unique political movement, the New Labrador Party.

The first excerpt is from the Viking Sagas. In his translation of the sagas, Magnus Magnusson, a well-known and respected Norse scholar and writer, recounts how the Vikings encountered and fought people they called "skraelings," likely the Innu. The Viking sagas were the first recorded meeting between Europeans and the aboriginals of Labrador, setting the stage for the tensions and conflicts that were to follow.

Early contact between Labrador's aboriginal people and Europeans is explored further by the Canadian anthropologist Garth Taylor, who tells the story of the Inuit woman Mikak and her encounter with Europeans, both in Labrador and in Britain. An attractive and compelling figure, she captivated the highest reaches of London society in the eighteenth century and played an important role in the advent of the Moravian Church in Labrador. With its origins before Luther, and a presence in eighty-three countries in the world by the eighteenth century, these Transylvanian Protestants were the first Christian church anywhere in the Canadian Arctic. They radically changed Inuit society in Labrador and were the *de facto* governor of northern Labrador until the early decades of the twentieth century.

The next piece records George Cartwright's relationship with the Inuit, which was mostly benign, and in particular the visit of a group of them who, like Mikak, visited London and charmed its high society. Cartwright was a British army officer who became one of the earliest, and certainly the best known, British trader on the Labrador. An adventurer of great courage and appetite, he established trading posts along the southern Labrador coast, one of which bears his name. His *Journal*, one of the few comprehensive publications on Labrador at that time, found favour with, among others, Coleridge and Southey.

Jens Haven visited Labrador around the same time as Cartwright but for quite a different reason: He was the leader in establishing the Moravian Church among the Inuit in Labrador. In this account from his journal, we see the imperatives that drew him to Labrador. It is also clear that Mikak exerted a great influence in convincing the British to sanction Haven's efforts and the support he received from the Newfoundland governor, who found that Haven's purposes meshed with his own. We are reminded, as well, of the difference that language makes in bringing two peoples together.

Donald Smith was a clever man of ambition and imagination who led the Hudson's Bay Company to dominance of the fur trade in Labrador in the later decades of the nineteenth century and witnessed the growth of the Scottish-Inuit trapping culture that evolved during his stay. This culture is explored and captured in the later piece by Elliott Merrick, who, with his Australian wife, the nurse Kate Austen, spent time on the trap line in the wild with the trappers, setting down with such charm and affection the life of these mothers and fathers of present-day Labradorians. Peter C. Newman, the eminent chronicler of the Canadian establishment and the Hudson's Bay Company, paints a picture that shows both the warts and the astonishing achievements of Donald Smith, Lord Strathcona, one of the most striking figures of Labrador and Canadian history. The same canny Scot, whose bearded presence is shown driving the last spike for the CPR, started his career with the Bay during his almost 20 years in North West River, near Goose Bay.

By the turn of the twentieth century, Labrador was one of the last frontiers, and several adventurers and explorers, mostly from the U.S., tried to discover its secrets. One of those secrets was the Barren Ground Innu, hitherto largely undiscovered and unknown by the outside world. It was this nation, whose children today are sadly struggling for survival against the demons of cultural dislocation, poverty and abuse, that Leonidas Hubbard, an American writer and outdoorsman, hoped to encounter in his tragic trek across the Labrador Peninsula. Where he failed, his wife, Mina—surely a unique woman in Canadian Arctic history—succeeded in 1905 after a dramatic race with Hubbard's surviving companion, Dillon Wallace. In her diary Mina recorded her "discovery" of and encounter with the northern Innu, particularly the women. She also brought back up-to-date maps of the area she traversed. A young Canadian woman who had little experience in the wilderness met aboriginal women who had spent their lives on the isolated sub-Arctic tundra. The 100th anniversary of Mina's historic trek was celebrated in 2005, replete with events in Labrador and a new biography.

Elliott Merrick is perhaps the best writer on Labrador, not simply because of his extraordinary way with words but also because he lived Labrador in different ways at different locations. The son of a wealthy American businessman, he eschewed the smoky cities of industrial America for the unspoiled and the untouched. He found it in Labrador, sponsored by the Grenfell Mission, first at Indian Harbour, where he was a jack of all trades at one of the first Grenfell hospitals, and later at North West River, where he was a teacher and would-be trapper. He lived with the men and women of the long trap lines, their quest for the fur that was their gold, and their encounters with the Innu, their bittersweet companions and rivals in the occupation and use of the Labrador Peninsula. No one has captured this confluence of cultures with such sensitivity and charm, albeit in happier times than those experienced by the Innu of today.

Lydia Campbell was the first woman to publish her experiences in central Labrador near the turn of the twentieth century. She was the daughter of one of the area's earliest settlers, who passed on to her literacy and a faith that provided her with the skills and motivation to tell her story. It captures, as nothing else has, life and labour in Labrador at that time.

Elizabeth Goudie's is a singular account of the hardships and joys of a trapper's wife in the early decades of the twentieth century. Of British and Inuit ancestry, all that is best in the character of both are drawn upon as she struggles to make a life and care for her family in spite of the natural and man-made vicissitudes of a harshly beautiful land.

Norman Duncan, the Canadian writer who, like so many others, was captivated by the magnetic personality of Sir Wilfred Grenfell, captured in charming prose the character and personality of those thousands of Newfoundland cod fishermen who, in the early twentieth century, sailed to the Labrador coast each summer. In search of a staple food that fed the world, they encountered those who were already in Labrador, settled and struggling to survive. Again, the relationship was bittersweet, as it always is with those who seek to share a common place.

The ship that bound them all together for twenty-six years in the 1930s and '40s, both Newfoundlander and Labradorian, was the *Kyle*: a legend, a lifeline, a conveyer of goods and people, a village green, a meeting place. Merrick captures her with all her sights and sounds and all she meant to those hardy souls rooted on the rocks of the Labrador coast.

Michael Crummey is an established Canadian novelist and poet. Growing up in Western Labrador, he nevertheless heard the tales of his father's experiences on southern Labrador in the days when Newfoundlanders chased the cod. His knowledge may be secondhand but his writing is first class.

Tony Paddon, the Labrador-born son of Dr. Harry Paddon, a Grenfell contemporary and the man who brought medicine and community development to the Labrador coast, is a natural raconteur, whose own signal accomplishments were recognized by his appointment as the first Labrador lieutenant-governor of the province. His love of Labrador and his love of life shine through in this recounting of one of his many adventures in the forbidding reaches of the North Atlantic.

Philip Smith's admirable account of Brinco, the international consortium Joe Smallwood created to develop Labrador resources during his early years as premier, traces in pristine prose the story of Churchill Falls. Here are those who experienced it and used it: the Innu hunters whose woods were later bulldozed and flooded, the boatmen of the Hudson's Bay Company and the trappers of Lake Melville who built along its river an extensive chain of trap lines, the explorers and adventurers who braved raging rivers to witness the grand spectacle, the economic giants of Britain and America who harnessed its vast potential to the enormous benefit of Hydro Quebec and the enormous loss of its owner, Newfoundland and Labrador. The icon of our province's economic misfortune, Churchill Falls is, ironically, the romantic heart of the Labrador Peninsula and a classic industrial accomplishment.

The modern twentieth-century machine, which first touched Labrador at the Goose Bay air base, moved west when markets and money were available for digging out the iron ore that lay there in abundance—ore that had been identified by Catholic curés, by Donald Smith, and later by that great explorer and documenter of northern Canada, A. P. Low. The building of the Quebec North Shore and Labrador Railway, encouraged by Canadian industrial giants such as Jules Timmins and C. D. Howe, and backed with American money, was a seminal engineering achievement. It is captured here in the rich prose of Pierre Berton. He describes his journey on the railroad from Sept-Îsles to Knob Lake, later the

Quebec community of Schefferville, north of Labrador City, all the while taking us back through a natural and social history of Labrador.

Yet few Innu or Inuit found jobs either in the iron mines of Labrador West or in the great powerhouse at Churchill Falls. Compelled to leave their traditional homes and way of life by church and government authorities on whom they had become dependent, they struggled to cope with the ways of the whites and with modern life. Both the Innu and the Inuit were at various times hustled into new communities without adequate consultation or preparation. The uprooting and the social dislocation that came from it had, and still have, their effect on once proud and self sufficient peoples. Carol Brice-Bennett has described with great care, sympathy and skill the traumatic move of the Inuit by church and government authorities from Hebron and Nutak. In "Reconciling with Memories" her voice is joined by the voices of those who felt the anguish of the move and their descendants.

Brice-Bennett has also edited the memoirs of Paulus Maggo. In 1993, when asked to conduct research for the Royal Commission on Aboriginal Peoples, she immediately chose him for a family history. He was 83 at the time, highly respected in Nain and living in a modest cottage at the northern end of the village. As his age advanced he had come to symbolize, Brice-Bennett says, "traditional Inuit customs and values in the uncertainty of the present community environment." The era that Paulus experienced ranged from Inuit hunting from kayaks and dogsleds to the communities of today linked by satellite communication and aircraft and abuzz with the whine of speedboats and snowmobiles. In the last chapter of his book he reflects on the present and the future.

From the arrival of the Europeans, Labrador's Innu have struggled to maintain a place for themselves in a land that they and their ancestors had occupied for thousands of years. Their way of life, their customs and traditions, their religion, and their very culture were ruptured and supplanted by a white society that believed its own ways to be superior. Loss of hunting grounds, the bewilderment of adapting to new social norms, the onslaught of technology and modernity, and living with a white society that did not understand or appreciate them led to family and community breakdown, loss of identity, dependency, and substance abuse. The personal account of George Rich is that of one who has experienced and yet survived the valley of the shadows.

The Labrador identity, developed over the decades, had its political flowering during the late 1960s and early '70s in the New Labrador Party. Along the rugged coastline, in the north, among the new society that grew up around the air base at Goose Bay, and in the west, feelings festered of neglect and indifference on the part of a far away capital that had little knowledge of Labrador's problems and little resources to do anything about them anyway. These feelings burst into the open with the upstart New Labrador Party. Led by Tom Burgess, an Irish soldier of fortune and labour leader, it held the balance of power in a perfectly divided legislature after the 1970 provincial election. But through his personal ineptitude, Burgess was unable to realize the long-held dream for power of many Labradorians. Here Richard Gwyn, one of Canada's finest writers and an adopted son of Newfoundland and Labrador, chronicles the last days of Joe Smallwood's government in the province and the rise and fall of Tom Burgess.

The origins of Labrador are lost in the mists of antiquity. Eight hundred million years ago, forces deep within the earth formed Labrador as part of the Canadian Shield. It is some of the oldest rock in the world. Over millions of years, it has been torn and shorn by wind, rain, and ice. It has been covered by the sea and ripped by the rifting of the continents. Glaciers moved across it, scouring and scraping the land and carving its surface into majestic mountains and rocks, leaving it a land of endless variety. The glaciers dug trenches and ravines that filled with water to create lakes and rivers. When the ice melted about 12,000 years ago and the sea rose, deep fiords appeared. In time tundra shrub and forests provided a habitat for wild game and fuel and shelter for the humans who found their way there.

Over these thousands of years, various groups and individuals have trod, sailed, paddled, and flown the Labrador. Whether lasting or temporary, in spite of or because of the tides of history, these peoples have left an imprint. The earliest of these may have been Paleo-Indians that moved across what is now Canada as the ice retreated, but so far no evidence has been found of their occupation of Labrador. Between 8,000 and 9,000 years ago, early Maritime Archaic people arrived. Their occupation of the coast was extensive, with campsites dotting the interior as well as the coast. Not far from the place where two prospectors recently found the richest nickel mine in the world, the Maritime Archaic people found Ramah chert, what for their time was an equally rich substance. It was easily flaked into tools and thin symmetrical weapons. About 4,000 years ago, Paleo-Eskimos, or Pre-Dorsets, made their appearance; they were replaced about 2,500 years ago by the Dorsets. This group shared the coast with Groswater Eskimos and with the Intermediate and Point Revenge Indians. Nobody is sure where the latter came from, but they lived mostly in the forests and away from the sea.

About 1,200 years ago, a new people inhabited Labrador who were likely the immediate ancestors of today's Innu. Although they hunted caribou, they were primarily a coastal people. There they made their living until the Thule Eskimos pushed them into the interior, where they turned more and more to the caribou for sustenance. Skirmishes with the Inuit are still remembered in the Innu oral tradition. Recent archaeology appears to support the contention that the Innu are the descendants of almost 2,000 years of uninterrupted Algonkian presence in Labrador. The coming of the Europeans, particularly the fur traders, had a profound effect on the lives of the Innu. Hunters who had previously tracked caribou for sustenance were now enticed to trap beaver to satisfy the demands of the European fur market.

The Thule Eskimos, ancestors of today's Inuit, arrived in northern Labrador about 700 years ago. They arrived with dog-drawn sleds, large skin boats (umiaks), and kayaks. They were well prepared for the harvest of the sea and the land with their toggling harpoons, bows and arrows, dogs, and spears. They hunted—cooperatively—bowhead and white whales, walrus, seal, and birds. The coming of the Europeans changed their lives as well. Over time the influence of the Europeans grew as their goods became objects of great desire. Gradually the Inuit moved farther and farther south along the coast. Baleen, oil, ivory, and sealskins were traded for European goods. The people who practised communal sharing were harshly punished when the Europeans caught them "stealing." Relations between the two became characterized by hostility and treachery.

It is difficult to say for sure which aboriginal peoples were the "skraelings" (people who wear the skins of animals) the Vikings encountered during their stay in northern Newfoundland. "Indians" and "Eskimos" are often confused in early records. Whoever they were, the eventual relationship was not peaceful. Leif Eiricsson sailed past a wooded land he called Markland, undoubtedly Labrador, and continued south to spend the winter at Vinland, now L'Anse aux Meadows. Later Thorvald Eiricsson sailed north to Markland, where he was killed by the Innu. How long the Vikings had contact with the aboriginal peoples of Labrador we do not know, but they had proved there were rewards to trans-Atlantic voyages, and they did leave a lasting impression on the aboriginal peoples.

Centuries later, other Europeans arrived. The Basques operated a whaling station at Red Bay from the 1530s onwards; thousands worked there and elsewhere along the Straits shore. Iron tools were traded for the furs of the Innu, who also helped process the whale oil. The Inuit, on the other hand, were hostile and attacked with bows and arrows. The aboriginals also encountered Dutch traders in the early seventeenth century. Gaspar Corte Real of Portugal made voyages in 1500 and 1501, capturing about sixty Innu and taking them back to Lisbon. Indeed, it was a Portuguese, Joao Fernandes, who gave Labrador its name: *lavrador,* a farmer or landowner in Portuguese, became Labrador. Later, in 1534, Jacques Cartier found Labrador to be a land of rocks and stones, calling it "the land God gave Cain," an unfair and much overused appellation. In the same century, Martin Frobisher described it in much the same way. During the sixteenth and seventeenth centuries, other explorers, some searching for the North West Passage, sailed the coast: Davis, Weymouth, Knight, Gibbons, Henry Hudson, and Thomas Button who went to find him. Most of them refer to encounters with aboriginals, although it is difficult to tell exactly whom because they often confused the Innu and the Inuit.

By the early 1500s, French fishermen were going ashore to trade. The Innu welcomed Champlain, who likely would not have been able to survive the early years without them. It was he who called them Montagnais, after the mountains at the mouth of the Saguenay River where he met them. Over time life changed for the Innu. By the early 1600s, they were using copper kettles and iron axes and wearing European clothes. But other Indians to the west intruded upon their territory and forced them eastward. With the traders came the church. Both the Recollets and the Jesuits advocated "civilizing" the Innu while supporting their role in the fur trade. From 1627 French military men, merchants, and bureaucrats were awarded seigneuries (tracts of land) by the French crown, and many trading posts sprang up along the southern Labrador coast. One of these, Louis Jolliet, the discoverer of the Mississippi, was a seigneur at Mingan, trading as far north as Lac Nascapis, the present day Ashuanipi, where Fort Nascapis was established as early as 1696. He made trips up the Labrador coast as far as Zoar and kept a journal of his travels. Until the Treaty of Paris in 1763, the French controlled the Labrador trade at L'Anse au Loup, Chateau Bay, Forteau, Red Bay, Cape Charles, Pinware, West St. Modeste, Brador, Isle aux Bois, and L'Anse au Clair. In 1743 Louis Fornel led an expedition north, establishing posts at North West River and Rigolet and leaving the first Europeans to winter there. In Esquimaux Bay (now Hamilton Inlet) was Eskimo Island, where the Inuit acted as middlemen for the trade north and south in cod, salmon, and seals. Even though the Treaty ceded control of New France to the British, the French continued to be a presence for some years.

But the Inuit had encroached on the territory of the Innu, and animosity and bloodshed resulted. After Palliser made his peace with the Inuit in the 1760s, they confined themselves, mostly under the patronage of the Moravian Church, to the north coast. The hostility remained for some time and didn't really end until about 100 years ago, when starving Innu arrived at Zoar, about 65 kilometres south of Nain, and were cared for by the Inuit. Over time relations improved, particularly in recent years, when negotiations with governments and multinational companies brought them a common cause.

After the Treaty of Paris, the English tried to limit the French fishery to the French Shore, around the northern tip of Newfoundland, and to give as much sea room as possible to the fleets of Devon and Dorset. This forced more and more Newfoundland fishermen who had fished off that shore to move north to Labrador. It also angered the New England captains who continued to fish there for cod, trading with the French and destroying shore facilities. Consequently, legal control of Labrador, which had been passed to Quebec in 1774, was returned to Newfoundland jurisdiction. But British fishing interests realized that some wintering over was necessary to protect fishing grounds and installations, and in the early nineteenth century, a number of British and Channel Islands firms set up operations on the Labrador coast, bringing with them some of the early settlers. These caretakers acquired more and more independence. In 1834 a man named Buckle became one of the first planters in the Straits with his own gear and account. But settlers were still at the mercy of merchants who supplied them and bought their catch. They were also in conflict with the Newfoundland fishermen who only came to Labrador for the summer. Disputes about fishing berths arose that helped set the attitude of resentment of some Labradorians toward the Newfoundlanders.

Perhaps the most prominent British trader to set up on the Labrador coast was George Cartwright, largely because of the journal he kept and published. He came over with Governor Palliser in the late 1700s and liked what he saw so much that he set up trading operations, first at Cape Charles and later at Cartwright. His publication, *Journal of Transactions and Events, during a Residence of Nearly Sixteen Years on the Coast of Labrador,* is valuable for his observations on natural history and his account of the Inuit, with whom he had good relations. However, his establishment was ruined by John Grimes, a Boston privateer, and he was forced into bankruptcy.

Meanwhile, because of the conflict that existed between the Inuit and the British fishermen who frequented the coast, Governor Palliser struck an agreement with the Moravian Church to convert the Inuit to Christianity and confine them to the area north of Cape Harrison. The establishment of the Moravians' first station at Nain in 1771 started the process of displacing the market networks of the Inuit leaders and traders—a process helped by the collapse of the market for baleen, the depletion of whale and walrus stocks in Labrador waters, and the effect of new weapons such as the rifle and the animal trap. Although the Moravians supplanted Inuit governance, their records are extremely important to Labrador history. They started the first schools in Labrador and did their best to keep the Inuit healthy. Indeed, it is fair to ask how many Inuit there would be north of Hamilton Inlet today if it were not for the Moravians. However, while they did the lion's share in preserving the race, there is no doubt that they brought about permanent change. In the first three hundred years of their occupation of Labrador, the Inuit had been an aggressive and opportunistic people, willing and able to exploit resources, initially for subsistence but later for trading. With the increasing presence of the Europeans, their settlements were moved and their lives changed forever.

While the British may have had jurisdiction over Labrador from the early nineteenth century, they regarded it as a huge coast with marine resources to be harvested for businesses and interests elsewhere. Those who settled, the Labradorians, could expect no help from the British government. Such help as was given, and the authority that was exercised, was by substitute patrons and non-governmental organizations, chiefly the Moravian Church, the Hudson's Bay Company, and the Grenfell Mission. They filled the void left by a government that pursued and promoted the interests of others.

Labrador had been outside the original territory granted to the Hudson's Bay Company, but in the 1830s, Governor Simpson turned his attention to the extreme east coast. Traders who already had operated in the Lake Melville area were bought out as the Bay sought to control the fur trade with the Innu who travelled from Hamilton Inlet to Ungava Bay to the St. Lawrence. While the concept of a connecting series of posts between Fort Chimo and Lake Melville turned out to be impractical, the investigation of the idea did lead to John McLean's "discovery" of the Grand Falls (later Hamilton and, still later, Churchill). Nevertheless, more and more entrepreneurs were bought out, and HBC posts were established as far north as Saglek and Killinek.

It was the coming of Donald Smith that brought the Bay in Labrador its golden age. In 1848 he was appointed assistant to the chief trader. Steady, shrewd, and imaginative, Smith quickly rose to control not only the Labrador territory but eventually the Hudson's Bay Company itself. During his time in Labrador, a unique culture developed in the Lake Melville area. More and more men, mostly from the Orkney Islands but some from other parts of Britain and Quebec, settled in Lake Melville as planters and took wives and partners from among the Inuit women there. While initially the Bay hoped that the Innu would be their main source of fur, the Innu continued to be more interested in the caribou hunt, which was for them a means of sustenance that also had great spiritual significance. They were reluctant trappers, fur being for them a means of emergency supplies of food and ammunition. So it was that the settler Labradorians became the chief suppliers of the Bay. Through the late nineteenth and early twentieth century, they built an extensive network of family trap lines and tilts hundreds of miles from home. The settlers and the nomadic Innu learned from each other and often kept company. Over time, though, as more and more pressure was exerted on the trapping grounds both of them used, tensions arose—tensions that were exacerbated once the bottom dropped out of the fur market and the Innu were settled in communities at the urging and under the guidance of the Catholic Church. While the settlers were able to find alternative employment in the cash economy, brought about particularly by the building of the great air base at Goose Bay, the Innu became more and more dependent on government assistance. Their loss of occupation and dignity would lead over time to great social ills, abuse, alcoholism, and family violence.

The coming of the second non-governmental benefactor, the Grenfell Mission had different origins. Wilfred Grenfell was a young British doctor, full of adventure and religious zeal. Working with the British Mission to Deep Sea Fishermen, he was sent over to determine how best to meet the needs of up to twenty-five thousand Newfoundland men, women, and children who sailed annually to Labrador in search of cod. They somehow survived there until October with no administration, no law and order, and no relief or medical care. Experiencing such unbelievable poverty and such squalid conditions, Grenfell scarcely knew where to begin. As support from the Newfoundland Government was nominal, he searched elsewhere for financial support and found it in, among others, Donald Smith, who was by this time president of the Canadian Pacific Railway and the Bank of Montreal. In 1893 Grenfell opened a hospital at Battle Harbour and later another at Indian Harbour. From there he would go on to establish a far-flung medical organization in northern Newfoundland and Labrador that lasted well into the twentieth century. Grenfell was so much more than a doctor; he also was a social activist who established fishermen's co-ops, schools, orphanages, and local craft industries, but who also found time to be an agent of change and a politician.

Harry Paddon was another young British doctor who followed Grenfell to Labrador. Encountering the many settlers in the Lake Melville area, he established a hospital there and began a regular service to these people and to the coast by sailing ship in summer and dog team in winter. In 1915 he moved to North West River and the hospital that became the centre for medical services along the north coast and much of the south. He built a house there and began to raise a family; his eldest son, Tony, replaced him as medical officer shortly after his untimely death. Harry Paddon was not only a medical practitioner, but a social activist who, in co-operation with Rev. Henry Gordon of Cartwright, initiated dormitory schools in Labrador and was a political spokesperson for people who had no other. After his father's untimely death in 1939, Tony Paddon replaced him as the Labrador doctor and saw the medical mission enter the age of radio, aircraft, and nursing stations. His outstanding work was recognized in the 1980s when he became lieutenant-governor of the Province of Newfoundland and Labrador. Led by the Paddons, in its time the Grenfell Mission brought innovation and change to Labrador. In its heyday it too was a political force, its leaders filling the vacuum left by absent politicians.

Without any real help from government, the foundations had been laid for schools, medical services, and churches, and traders big and small had established themselves. Challenging though it was, the Innu who ranged through the woods of the Ungava Peninsula, like the Inuit and part-Inuit, settled around the Moravian compounds in the north, and, like the trappers in Lake Melville and the British and mixed bloods of the south coast, whoever they were, they held to their communities and cared for each other as best they could. They had little choice but to rely on benefactors near at hand, for the government that was nominally theirs was far away and inaccessible.

It was the Earl of Carnarvon, a secretary of state for the Colonies, who mused that in the far reaches of the Empire there were "races struggling to emerge into civilization....To them it is our part to give wise laws, good government, and a well-ordered finance....This is...the true strength and meaning of imperialism." Clearly he did not have Labrador in mind. For a long time the situation on the coast was virtual anarchy. In 1820 a civil court judge was appointed, but the position was short lived. Nevertheless, the government continued to exact customs duties and other revenues. After 1832, when Newfoundland achieved representative government, this constituted taxation without representation. Yet in 1863 Prime Minister Hoyles rejected representation for Labrador. For him it was merely a venue for Newfoundland fishermen. As a result, Labrador had no political recognition for at least eighty years.

After resources were discovered, both Quebec and Newfoundland eyed the territory hungrily. Following a dispute over a wood's licence, both Quebec and Newfoundland submitted the question of jurisdiction to the British Privy Council. Where was the Labrador boundary and who had jurisdiction over what part of the Ungava Peninsula? In 1927 the Privy Council decided that the case for Newfoundland had been "made out." The height of land became the north-south boundary while the fifty-second parallel served that purpose from west to east. The Romaine River was set as the western limit. Newfoundland was exultant. It was predicted that the decision would close off Canada from access to the North Atlantic, but in fact the opposite has been true. Because the market for resources is in the heart of North America, Quebec blocks Newfoundland's access. Her resources, whether iron ore or water power, have had to pass through Quebec, and the toll has contributed substantially to the growth of the Quebec treasury.

Ironically, by giving up responsible government to a commission in 1934 Newfoundland gave Labrador its first government. The commissioners began to develop forest resources, specifically at Port Hope Simpson, as well as the iron ore potential in western Labrador, and the rationalization of fish buying and selling. Perhaps their most effective social measure was the creation of the Newfoundland Ranger Force, giving Labrador not only policing and welfare assistance but a contact with St. John's that it never had before. In 1942, when the Hudson's Bay Company announced the closure of its northern Labrador trading posts, the commission took over the operations. For the first time, the government was taking a direct role in Labrador.

The Second World War was a transforming event for Labrador. Once Goose Bay was designated as the jumping-off place for planes and materials headed for Britain, people all along the coast came to take jobs for cash. Until then, Labrador had been a land of parts operating on the "truck" system, where patrons would outfit supplicants at the beginning of the season and deduct returns from their accumulated debts at the end. In the north were the Inuit and part

Inuit, along with the Innu at Davis Inlet (now Natuashish); on the south coast were settlers, some from Newfoundland and some not; in the Lake Melville area were the Orkney Islanders and part British. Each group had remained more or less on its own ground. The building of Goose Bay changed all of that. Drawn away from the shrinking markets for fur and fish, people came to Goose to find new lives for themselves among Canadian and American servicemen. Over time, a modern community would grow up in Happy Valley, five miles from the base. It was a construction company that started the radio station and the Americans who began the television station, but not until 1971 was a permanent communication link established with the Island. So for the first thirty years after Confederation, one part of the province did not hear from the other on a regular basis. With the exception of those who read the Newfoundland papers and those who had shortwave radios, the two parts of the province existed in splendid isolation from each other. After the war, Happy Valley continued to grow and develop, with the base as its main economic support, as it is today.

In 1945 the British government, wishing to divest itself of its oldest colony, called a national convention to discuss options. Lester Burry, a United Church minister at North West River, was elected to represent Labrador. It was the first time the people of that territory had ever voted in a proper election. Burry brought Labrador's concerns and the Labrador point of view to the convention. However, the presence of the Innu and Inuit was barely mentioned, and after Confederation their special needs, unlike elsewhere in Canada, were met by the province with special subventions from Ottawa. In a close referendum vote, Confederation with Canada carried the day, and the Island of Newfoundland, with Labrador as demarcated by the British Privy Council, became the tenth province of Canada. Canadian social programs brought an immediate and lasting improvement to life in Labrador communities. Many smaller communities would be relocated to growth centers where bigger schools and medical facilities could be built. The Innu would be persuaded to turn from the nomadic life of hunters and gatherers to settle in communities at North West River and Davis Inlet in order to adapt to a more modern North American lifestyle in the process. Their lives would be fraught with difficulty and tragedy as increased dependency encouraged alcoholism and social dislocation. Grouped around the Moravian communities in the north, the Inuit fared better. In the south settlers still relied for a living on the fishery with all its vicissitudes, but here, too, Confederation brought improved social services.

Labrador's second major demographic shift came with the development of the iron mines in the west. The major population influences now came from the Island of Newfoundland and Quebec rather than from Labrador itself. The Quebec North Shore and Labrador Railway, a huge and imaginative project for its time, was built to link Schefferville and eventually Labrador City and Wabush to the North Shore. These were no ordinary Labrador or Newfoundland towns. Young people came from all over the world, and they soon realized that they had to be their own grandparents, quickly bonding to build unified and vibrant communities. From the beginning, although Premier Smallwood kept a tight rein on development, the government was a marginal player. The company was all things to all people, building modern facilities that made the towns second to none in Canada.

Gradually the companies withdrew much of their support from the communities, forcing them to turn to the provincial government; but Labrador was far away from the centre of power and too often out of sight and out of mind. What's more, requirements in Labrador were very expensive for a government that had so much catching up to do all across the province. Still, the residents of Labrador West knew that they were contributing substantially to provincial coffers. Like the fish being taken from the Labrador coast and the wood being shipped from Goose Bay, the ore they dug from the ground was, in their view, being sent out in a relatively raw state, primarily for the benefit of someone other than themselves with too little return to the area. Even those who had come from the Island sensed the gulf that existed between Labrador and Newfoundland. Closing the gap in infrastructure would be formidable. Even more serious was the communications gap. The English station that Labrador West received originated in the Maritimes and rarely covered Newfoundland news. The newspaper of choice, because it was readily available, was the *Montreal Gazette* and not the St. John's *Evening Telegram*. Smallwood knew the problem and tried to assuage feelings, but mostly with gestures that he felt he could afford.

The next major development that caused a population movement in and to Labrador was the construction of the great power project at Churchill Falls. Struck by the awesome magnitude of the waterfall, Smallwood incorporated the British Newfoundland Corporation, which included the Rothschilds, Rio Tinto, and English Electric, among others. This would be the largest industrial project in Canada since the construction of the Canadian Pacific Railway, and at the time it spawned the largest hydroelectric project in the world. Old wounds such as the 1927 boundary decision were reopened, and Quebec, which was being asked to buy the power generated, was a tough, intransigent bargainer. In the final agreement, they reserved the right to buy all of the electricity produced by Churchill Falls for a period of sixty-five years and committed to doing so. The contract provided for a fixed price for the first forty years, after which it required a slightly lower price for the remaining twenty-five years. This provision, beyond anything called for in the bond financing, would inevitably lead to the insolvency of the project and the Quebec takeover of Churchill Falls. For the people of the province the contract was unmercifully severe and grossly unfair. Quebec would take in something like eighty times the return to Newfoundland and Labrador. It has been the prime cause of resentment all across the province.

While modern communities had grown up in Labrador, they were single-industry towns, vulnerable to the vicissitudes of distant markets. In the absence of rural economic development on the Island and on the coast of Labrador, men and women had flocked to Labrador attracted by the opportunities it offered for a new start. However, the economic security they began to enjoy did not blind them to the vulnerability of the communities they shared or to the fact that they had moved farther away from the centre of power to a territory that had an identity all its own.

In tandem with changing attitudes across the country, during the 1970s there was social and political change in Labrador, helped by a scheduled air service and progress in electronic communications. Perhaps the most dramatic change was the birth of the New Labrador Party. The feeling of alienation from and dissatisfaction with the government in St. John's came to a head in 1969 in Wabush. Tom Burgess, an Irish union leader, fired the resentment of his audience, and the New Labrador Party was born. After a dramatic provincial contest that ended in a tie, Burgess, the lone NLP representative in the House of Assembly, was heavily courted by both the Liberals and Conservatives; but his ineptitude squandered the unusual bargaining position he held, and the Party, strapped for funds, retreated to Labrador. The emergence of the NLP, and the new policies espoused by Labrador members of the House of Assembly, such as Melvin Woodward of the Liberals, and later Mike Martin of the NLP and Joe Goudie of the Conservatives, had a salutary effect—especially among those who held the reins of power. It was clear that the people of Labrador would no longer be taken for granted and were no longer willing to be quiet.

Between 1970 and 1975, many of Labrador's communities were incorporated, regional development associations were formed, heritage societies were founded, and a new Labrador flag was flown. The same decade saw the creation of a Royal Commission on Labrador, which confirmed that the industrialization of Labrador had not brought a proportionate increase in the availability of wage labour for longtime Labrador residents. It recommended, among other things, a greater use of federal funds and moving some of the functions of government out of St. John's and into the affected regions. Electricity was provided, but many communities still did not have water and sewer systems. The Canadian Salt Fish Corporation provided infrastructure and marketing expertise to coastal fishing communities.

In 1986 the Labrador Metis Association was formed to protect the traditional, constitutional, and aboriginal rights of the Inuit descendants in southeastern and central Labrador. While the Labrador Inuit Association had developed in the communities of the north coast, the people whose ancestors had settled on the south coast found themselves without a voice and without access to the funds for aboriginals that had been provided for the Innu and Inuit of the north coast. Thus what is now the Labrador Metis Nation was born. Although it has not been successful in getting either level of government to entertain a land claim, through hard work and a determined voice it has made significant progress in accessing federal funds in other ways to enhance the lives of its members in the Lake Melville area and along the south coast.

A roll on-roll off ferry service was begun from the Island to Goose Bay. The CBC expanded its services, helping to establish a real consciousness of Labrador on the outside. Led by the federal Department of Regional Economic Expansion, a number of shared-cost programs were put in place. In the north, the Labrador Inuit Association had grown in strength, spawning co-operatives and a broadcast voice, the OK (OkalaKatiget) Society. In 2005 Inuit land claims were settled and the new territory of Nunatsiavut was created. A passengers-and-vehicle ferry ran across the Strait of Belle Isle. Also in that area, the Labrador Shrimp Company, a fishermen's co-operative, was formed for harvesting deep sea shrimp. In the 1990s, $345 million was announced for the extension of the Trans-Labrador Highway. As well, a strong private sector had emerged in almost all regions of Labrador, and small business would continue to create long-lasting jobs. Change was readily apparent.

Now there was a growing awareness that the various peoples of Labrador must work together toward a future in which all of them could share. The Inuit in the north and the Innu in Sheshashiu and Natuashish had overcome their historical animosity, particularly when the world's richest nickel mine was discovered at the intersection of their respective land claim areas. They had partnered with some existing businesses in the Lake Melville area in order to successfully bid on the contracts they knew would be offered. In the western mining towns and in the fishing villages of the south coast, through improved communication and mobility, there was a consensus that only through co-operation and joint effort could progress be made. In June 2002 an agreement was reached with Inco to develop the nickel mine at Voisey's Bay. For the first time, all racial groups had supported a project for which they could all see benefits, as had their partners on the Island. If it could be done for nickel, then why not for fish, wood, tourism, or oil and gas?

The founding of Nunavut also opened new horizons for that territory's southern neighbour. Many skilled people moved from the province to work in Nunavut. It became apparent that if goods and services were coming over the road from Quebec to Goose Bay, they could go on from there by sea or air to Iqaluit. Could connections be made not only in trade and commerce but also in education and research? For some time, the Labrador Inuit had been part of the Inuit Circumpolar Conference, and since the creation of the Arctic Council, the bonds among countries and territories around the pole, including Labrador, have strengthened. Like Janus, Labrador looked both forward and backward, north and south.

The challenge in the future, as in the past, is how these different people in different places, with different skills and expectations, can find a way of living together. It was the challenge of the Inuit and Innu; it was the challenge of the ancestors of today's aboriginal people when they met the Europeans; it was the challenge of the early Labradorians who encountered the Newfoundland fishermen; it was the challenge of Canadians and people from other parts of the world as they came to work side by side with settlers; it was the challenge of the French and English workers in Churchill Falls and Labrador West. Today, in the wired world and the global economy, Labradorians are better informed and confident of their ability to articulate their needs and aspirations.

VINLAND

The Vikings were the first Europeans proven to have trod the soil of what is now Newfoundland and Labrador. Bjarni Herjolfsson sailed from Iceland to Greenland in 986 but was blown off course, sighting the coasts of Labrador and Newfoundland before making his way to his original destination. Leif Eiriksson, who followed him around 1000, sailed past what is now Nunavut and then proceeded south, going ashore in Labrador. He called it Markland or Woodland. "This country was flat and wooded with white sandy beaches wherever they went; and the land sloped gently down to the sea," recorded the Greenland saga. At a point on the Labrador coast just south of Hamilton Inlet at Cape Porcupine, there are healthy stands of some of the best black spruce in the world. More than fifty kilometres of white sandy beaches stretch before a dark forest. This is it: the Wonderstrand.

Leif continued south and spent the winter at a place he named Vinland. In 1914 W. A. Munn, a Newfoundlander, identified L'Anse aux Meadows as that place, and Helge Ingstad and his wife, Anne Stine Ingstad, confirmed it in 1960.

The Viking record tells us that Thorvald Eiriksson later sailed north from Vinland to Markland. Magnus Magnusson's translation of the sagas recounts for us the tragic visit of Thorvald. His burial site is believed to be somewhere near the mouth of English River in Lake Melville.

Magnus Magnusson and Hermann Palsson

EXCERPT FROM
The Vinland Sagas: The Norse Discovery of America, 1965

Leif explores Vinland

Some time later, Bjarni Herjolfsson sailed from Greenland to Norway and visited Earl Eirik,[1] who received him well. Bjarni told the earl about his voyage and the lands he had sighted. People thought he had shown great lack of curiosity, since he could tell them nothing about these countries, and he was criticized for this. Bjarni was made a retainer at the earl's court, and went back to Greenland the following summer.

There was now great talk of discovering new countries. Leif, the son of Eirik the Red of Brattahlid, went to see Bjarni Herjolfsson and bought his ship from him, and engaged a crew of thirty-five.

Leif asked his father Eirik to lead this expedition too, but Eirik was rather reluctant: he said he was getting old, and could endure hardships less easily than he used to. Leif replied that Eirik would still command more luck[2] than any of his kinsmen. And in the end, Eirik let Leif have his way.

---

1   Earl Eirik Hakonarson ruled over Norway from 1000 to 1014.

2   "Luck" had a greater significance in pagan Iceland than the word implies now. Good luck or ill luck were innate qualities, part of the complex pattern of Fate. Leif inherited the good luck associated with his father.

As soon as they were ready, Eirik rode off to the ship which was only a short distance away. But the horse he was riding stumbled and he was thrown, injuring his leg.

"I am not meant to discover more countries than this one we now live in," said Eirik. "This is as far as we go together."[3]

Eirik returned to Brattahlid, but Leif went aboard the ship with his crew of thirty-five. Among them was a Southerner called Tyrkir.[4]

They made their ship ready and put out to sea. The first landfall they made was the country that Bjarni had sighted last. They sailed right up to the shore and cast anchor, then lowered a boat and landed. There was no grass to be seen, and the hinterland was covered with great glaciers, and between glaciers and shore the land was like one great slab of rock. It seemed to them a worthless country.

Then Leif said, "Now we have done better than Bjarni where this country is concerned—we at least have set foot on it. I shall give this country a name and call it *Helluland*."[5] They returned to their ship and put to sea, and sighted a second land. Once again they sailed right up to it and cast anchor, lowered a boat and went ashore. This country was flat and wooded, with white sandy beaches wherever they went; and the land sloped gently down to the sea. Leif said, "This country shall be named after its natural resources: it shall be called *Markland*."[6] They hurried back to their ship as quickly as possible and sailed away to sea in a north-east wind for two days until they sighted land again. They sailed towards it and came to an island which lay to the north of it.

They went ashore and looked about them. The weather was fine. There was dew on the grass, and the first thing they did was to get some of it on their hands and put it to their lips, and to them it seemed the sweetest thing they had ever tasted. Then they went back to their ship and sailed into the sound that lay between the island and the headland jutting out to the north.

---

3 A fall from a horse was considered a very bad omen for a journey. Such a fall clinched Gunnar of Hlidarend's decision not to leave Iceland when he was outlawed.

4 Southerner refers to someone from central or southern Europe; Tyrkir appears to have been a German.

5 Literally, "Slab-land"; probably Baffin Island.

6 Literally, "Forest-land"; probably Labrador.

They steered a westerly course round the headland. There were extensive shallows there and at low tide their ship was left high and dry, with the sea almost out of sight. But they were so impatient to land that they could not bear to wait for the rising tide to float the ship; they ran ashore to a place where a river flowed out of a lake. As soon as the tide had refloated the ship they took a boat and rowed out to it and brought it up the river into the lake, where they anchored it. They carried their hammocks ashore and put up booths.[7] Then they decided to winter there, and built some large houses.

There was no lack of salmon in the river or the lake, bigger salmon than they had ever seen.[8] The country seemed to them so kind that no winter fodder would be needed for livestock: there was never any frost all winter and the grass hardly withered at all.

In this country, night and day were of more even length than in either Greenland or Iceland: on the shortest day of the year, the sun was already up by 9 a.m., and did not set until after 3 p.m.[9]

When they had finished building their houses, Leif said to his companions, "Now I want to divide our company into two parties and have the country explored; half of the company are to remain here at the houses while the other half go exploring—but they must not go so far that they cannot return the same evening, and they are not to become separated."

They carried out these instructions for a time. Leif himself took turns at going out with the exploring party and staying behind at the base.

Leif was tall and strong and very impressive in appearance. He was a shrewd man and always moderate in his behaviour.

Thorvald explores Vinland

Thorvald prepared his expedition with his brother Leif's guidance and engaged

---

7   Booths were stone-and-turf enclosures which could be temporarily roofed with awnings for occupation.

8   On the east coast of the North American continent, salmon are not usually found any farther south than the Hudson River.

9   This statement indicates that the location of Vinland must have been south of latitude fifty and north of latitude forty anywhere between the Gulf of St. Lawrence and New Jersey.

Magnus Magnusson and Hermann Palsson

a crew of thirty. When the ship was ready, they put out to sea and there are no reports of their voyage until they reached Leif's Houses in Vinland. There they laid up the ship and settled down for the winter, catching fish for their food.

In the spring Thorvald said they should get the ship ready, and that meanwhile a small party of men should take the ship's boat and sail west along the coast and explore that region during the summer.

They found the country there very attractive, with woods stretching almost down to the shore and white sandy beaches.

There were numerous islands there, and extensive shallows. They found no traces of human habitation or animals except on one westerly island, where they found a wooden stackcover. That was the only man-made thing they found; and in the autumn they returned to Leif's Houses.

Next summer Thorvald sailed east with his ship and then north along the coast. They ran into a fierce gale off a headland and were driven ashore; the keel was shattered and they had to stay there for a long time while they repaired the ship.

Thorvald said to his companions, "I want to erect the old keel here on the headland, and call the place Kjalarness."

They did this and then sailed away eastward along the coast. Soon they found themselves at the mouth of two fjords, and sailed up to the promontory that jutted out between them; it was heavily wooded. They moored the ship alongside and put out the gangway, and Thorvald went ashore with all his men.

"It is beautiful here," he said. "Here I should like to make my home."

On their way back to the ship they noticed three humps on the sandy beach just in from the headland. When they went closer they found that these were three skin-boats,[10] with three men under each of them. Thorvald and his men divided forces and captured all of them except one, who escaped in his boat. They killed the other eight and returned to the headland, from which they scanned the surrounding country. They could make out a number of humps farther up the fjord and concluded that these were settlements.

---

10 Certain Red Indian tribes of the New England area used canoes made of moose-hide instead of the more usual birch-bark.

Then they were overwhelmed by such a heavy drowsiness that they could not stay awake, and they all fell asleep—until they were awakened by a voice that shouted, "Wake up, Thorvald, and all your men, if you want to stay alive! Get to your ship with all your company and get away as fast as you can!"

A great swarm of skin-boats was then heading towards them down the fjord.

Thorvald said, "We shall set up breastworks on the gunwales and defend ourselves as best we can, but fight back as little as possible."

They did this. The Skraelings shot at them for a while, and then turned and fled as fast as they could.

Thorvald asked his men if any of them were wounded; they all replied that they were unhurt.

"I have a wound in the armpit" said Thorvald. "An arrow flew up between the gunwale and my shield, under my arm—here it is. This will lead to my death.

"I advise you now to go back as soon as you can. But first I want you to take me to the headland I thought so suitable for a home. I seem to have hit on the truth when I said that I would settle there for a while. Bury me there and put crosses at my head and feet, and let the place be called Krossaness for ever afterwards."

(Greenland had been converted to Christianity by this time, but Eirik the Red had died before the conversion.)

With that Thorvald died, and his men did exactly as he had asked of them. Afterwards they sailed back and joined the rest of the expedition and exchanged all the news they had to tell.

They spent the winter there and gathered grapes and vines as cargo for the ship. In the spring they set off on the voyage to Greenland; they made land at Eiriksfjord, and had plenty of news to tell Leif.

Karlsefni in Vinland

That same summer a ship arrived in Greenland from Norway. Her captain was a man called Thorfinn Karlsefni.[11] He was man of considerable wealth. He spent the winter with Leif Eiriksson at Brattahlid.

---

11 The son of Thord Horse-Head, the son of Snorri, the son Thord of Hofdi.

Magnus Magnusson and Hermann Palsson

Karlsefni quickly fell in love with Gudrid and proposed to her, but she asked Leif to answer on her behalf. She was betrothed to Karlsefni, and the wedding took place that same winter.

There was still the same talk about Vinland voyages as before, and everyone, including Gudrid, kept urging Karlsefni to make the voyage. In the end he decided to sail and gathered a company of sixty men and five women. He made an agreement with his crew that everyone should share equally in whatever profits the expedition might yield. They took livestock of all kinds, for they intended to make a permanent settlement there if possible.

Karlsefni asked Leif if he could have the houses in Vinland; Leif said that he was willing to lend them, but not to give them away.

They put to sea and arrived safe and sound at Leif's Houses and carried their hammocks ashore. Soon they had plenty of good supplies, for a fine big rorqual was driven ashore; they went down and cut it up, and so there was no shortage of food.

The livestock were put out to grass, and soon the male beasts became very frisky and difficult to manage. They had brought a bull with them.

Karlsefni ordered timber to be felled and cut into lengths for a cargo for the ship, and it was left out on a rock to season. They made use of all the natural resources of the country that were available, grapes and game of all kinds and other produce.

The first winter passed into summer, and then they had their first encounter with Skraelings, when a great number of them came out of the wood one day. The cattle were grazing near by and the bull began to bellow and roar with great vehemence. This terrified the Skraelings and they fled, carrying their packs which contained furs and sables and pelts of all kinds. They made for Karlsefni's houses and tried to get inside, but Karlsefni had the doors barred against them. Neither side could understand the other's language.

Then the Skraelings put down their packs and opened them up and offered their contents, preferably in exchange for weapons; but Karlsefni forbade his men to sell arms. Then he hit on the idea of telling the women to carry milk out to the Skraelings, and when the Skraelings saw the milk they wanted to buy nothing else. And so the outcome of their trading expedition was that the Skraelings carried their purchases away in their bellies, and left their packs and furs with Karlsefni and his men.

After that, Karlsefni ordered a strong wooden palisade to be erected round the houses, and they settled in.

About this time Karlsefni's wife, Gudrid, gave birth to a son, and he was named Snorri.

Early next winter the Skraelings returned, in much greater numbers this time, bringing with them the same kind of wares as before. Karlsefni told the women, "You must carry out to them the same produce that was most in demand last time, and nothing else."

As soon as the Skraelings saw it they threw their packs in over the palisade.

Gudrid was sitting in the doorway beside the cradle of her son Snorri when a shadow fell across the door and a woman entered wearing a black, close-fitting tunic; she was rather short and had a band round her chestnut-coloured hair. She was pale, and had the largest eyes that have ever been seen in any human head. She walked up to Gudrid and said, "What is your name ?"

"My name is Gudrid. What is yours?"

"My name is Gudrid," the woman replied.

Then Gudrid, Karlsefni's wife, motioned to the woman to come and sit beside her; but at that very moment she heard a great crash and the woman vanished, and in the same instant a Skraeling was killed by one of Karlsefni's men for trying to steal some weapons. The Skraelings fled as fast as they could, leaving their clothing and wares behind. No one had seen the woman except Gudrid.

"Now we must devise a plan," said Karlsefni, "for I expect they will pay us a third visit, and this time with hostility and in greater numbers. This is what we must do: ten men are to go out on the headland here and make themselves conspicuous, and the rest of us are to go into the wood and make a clearing there, where we can keep our cattle when the Skraelings come out of the forest. We shall take our bull and keep him to the fore."

The place where they intended to have their encounter with the Skraelings had the lake on one side and the woods on the other.

Magnus Magnusson and Hermann Palsson

Karlsefni's plan was put into effect, and the Skraelings came right to the place that Karlsefni had chosen for the battle. The fighting began, and many of the Skraelings were killed. There was one tall and handsome man among the Skraelings and Karlsefni reckoned that he must be their leader. One of the Skraelings had picked up an axe, and after examining it for a moment he swung it at a man standing beside him, who fell dead at once. The tall man then took hold of the axe, looked at it for a moment, and then threw it as far as he could out into the water. Then the Skraelings fled into the forest as fast as they could, and that was the end of the encounter.

Karlsefni and his men spent the whole winter there, but in the spring he announced that he had no wish to stay there any longer and wanted to return to Greenland. They made ready for the voyage and took with them much valuable produce, vines and grapes and pelts. They put to sea and reached Eiriksfjord safely and spent the winter there.

MIKAK

About 4,000 years ago, Paleo-Eskimos, or Pre-Dorsets, made their appearance on the Labrador coast where they lived year round, taking advantage of the bounty of both the sea and the land. We know little about their dress or their art, but they resembled today's Inuit in appearance.

About 2,500 years ago, the Paleo-Eskimos were replaced by the Dorsets. Until about 1,200 years ago, they too lived mainly on the coast hunting seals and walruses, collecting berries, and catching fish in the ponds and char at the river mouths.

By the time of Christ, the Dorsets had spread onto the Island of Newfoundland, where they survived for the next thousand years. We know that within a century or two of their arrival in Labrador, the Thule Inuit had completely replaced them and spread as far south as Hamilton Inlet.

The Thule Eskimos, ancestors of today's Inuit, arrived in northern Labrador about seven hundred years ago. They arrived with dog-drawn sleds, large skin boats (umiaks), and kayaks. They were well prepared for the harvest of the sea and land with their toggling harpoons, bows and arrows, and spears. In winter, they lived in partly submerged structures of sod, wood, stone, and whalebone, while in summer they built rock-walled houses of hide.

The coming of the Europeans, especially those in the fifteenth and sixteenth centuries, changed their lives. Over time, the influence of the Europeans grew. The Inuit continued to hunt marine mammals; their houses did not change, nor did their treatment of the dead, but the cumulative impact was great. European goods became objects of great prestige, and some Inuit went to great lengths to acquire them. Outstanding hunters and leaders in the communities became traders for European wares, and Inuit middlemen established their own trading networks.

J. Garth Taylor

Gradually the Inuit moved farther and farther south along the coast, drawn either by a greater supply of wood and food and the milder climate or by easier access to European goods. By the seventeenth century there were Inuit settlements all along the Labrador coast from Killinek to Hamilton Inlet.

Now the Inuit were in regular contact with the Europeans. Slate and soapstone were replaced by iron, and skin boats by whalers. By the eighteenth century, they had abandoned the outer islands for settlements on shore. At this time, Inuit settlements were reported all the way from the Button Islands to Cape Charles in the south.

Baleen, oil, ivory, and sealskins were traded farther and farther south, and European goods were traded farther and farther north. Of course, the Inuit practised communal sharing, for they were a people unfamiliar with the ownership practices of the Europeans and the procedures of Western trade. They are reported to have "stolen" what they could not obtain by trade, though it is a matter of interpretation whether taking what they needed from what they perceived to be a common stock was stealing. Nevertheless, the Europeans retaliated, and relations between the two became characterized by hostility and treachery.

In 1763 the Treaty of Paris ended the Seven Years War, and Labrador was ceded to the British. This was the beginning of British hegemony on the Labrador coast. Governor Palliser realized that he had to put a stop to the raiding and bloodshed that had come to characterize British trading with the Inuit. He signed a legal agreement with the Inuit, and the Moravians paid the Inuit for the land they occupied. Palliser built Fort York in Chateau Bay and garrisoned it with an officer and twenty men. In 1767 Francis Lucas, a midshipman, was second in command. It was here that he brought Mikak and the remains of her party after a bloody skirmish that took the life of her husband and other Inuit men.

Garth Taylor, a well-known and well-respected Canadian anthropologist, describes how Lucas took Mikak to Britain and her encounter with the highest reaches of English society that was to give her such prominence in Labrador after her return. At that time, she named her son Palliser, and there are still Pallisers living in Labrador today.

J. Garth Taylor

"THE TWO WORLDS OF MIKAK," FROM *The Beaver*, 1983

Part I

"There is so much to be said in relation to the Esquimaux lady that I shan't be able to go through it." So wrote the Earl of Bathurst when, in 1769, he tried to tell a friend about the woman who had twice dined with him at his London residence. The woman must have faced similar problems when, back home in Labrador later that same year, she tried to tell her Inuit relatives and friends about the people she had seen in the strange world of the kablunat.

The "Esquimaux lady" was Mikak, and the events which had led to her presence in London were both violent and tragic. In November of 1767, she and eight other Inuit, including her seven-year-old son Tutauk, had been captured by British marines near Chateau Bay in southern Labrador. During the struggle which preceded their capture, some Inuit men had been killed. One of them was Mikak's husband.

The attack on Mikak's people was apparently a punitive action. An armed sloop had been sent after a group of Inuit who had stolen some wooden boats and killed three Englishmen at a British whaling post just north of Chateau Bay. When the sloop ran into a harbour to pass the night, the crew found themselves suddenly and unexpectedly in the midst of thirteen Inuit boats. At once a battle broke out, but the bows and arrows of the Inuit were little match for the "great guns, blunderbusses and muskets" of the English. As many as twenty Inuit were killed in the fray and the remainder took refuge in the woods at the head of the harbour.

According to one of the English sailors who was there, it would have been easy at that moment to retrieve the stolen boats without any further loss of life. However, the commander of the vessel, an Irish-born midshipman by the name of Francis Lucas, was apparently afraid to do so. Instead, he chose to withdraw and wait for reinforcements to help him "attack and kill" the remaining survivors.

That night the Inuit escaped under cover of darkness and the following day Lucas, now accompanied by two more boats, could not catch up with them. It may have relieved his frustration when, returning from the chase, he met with a small party of Inuit travelling in two boats. From this group, which included Mikak and her family, four men were killed and nine women and children were captured.

The Inuit prisoners were taken to York Fort, a fortified blockhouse which had been built in Chateau Bay one year earlier "for the protection of British fisheries." That winter Lucas, who was second in command of the crowded little garrison, took a special interest in Mikak who, like himself, was then in her late twenties. Through his association with her, he began to pick up some words in the Inuktitut language while she, in turn, began to learn some basic English.

When summer came Lucas took his Inuit prisoners to St. John's which, then boasting between 200 and 300 houses, had just been described by a visitor from London as "the Most Disagreeable Town I Ever Met With." There the Inuit were brought before the Governor of Newfoundland and Labrador, Commodore Hugh Palliser, whose flagship lay at anchor in the harbour. Mikak had probably seen Palliser in Chateau Bay where, three years earlier, he had negotiated a "peace treaty" with the Labrador Inuit. The treaty, which was made with the assistance of some Moravian missionaries who had learned the Inuktitut language in Greenland, was one of Palliser's many efforts to end the European-Inuit conflict which plagued his administration of Labrador. Palliser blamed the sudden failure of his peace initiative on vessels from New England which, contrary to his orders, "went to the northward, robbed, plundered and murdered some of their old men and women and children" whom the Inuit had left at home for the summer.

After speaking with Mikak, who impressed him as being very intelligent, Palliser wrote that "from her I have obtained more satisfactory accounts than any that have yet been got of those People respecting their numbers, their places of abode, etc." With such encouragement and similar enthusiasm, the Governor planned on using the prisoners to help him achieve his goal of "establishing communication and trade with the Esquimaux savages." They could be sent home as messengers who would assure their people that the British wanted to trade in a fair way but would be swift to punish either theft or murder.

Meanwhile, by treating the prisoners with kindness, Palliser hoped they would "impress a Respect and regard for the English amongst their Countrymen and their Posterity." Although the Inuit expressed great astonishment at being so kindly treated, they must have been disappointed to learn they would have to spend another winter away from home. Lacking an opportunity to send them back to Labrador in the autumn of 1768, Palliser was "obliged to provide for their subsistance" until the following year. It was finally decided that six of the Inuit would winter in St. John's, while three would sail with the Newfoundland Squadron on its annual return to England. Those who would experience the "power, splendor and generosity of the English nation" in this first-hand manner were Mikak, Tutauk and a twelve-year-old orphan boy named Karpik.

Mikak and Tutauk were accompanied on their trans-Atlantic voyage of discovery by Lucas, who took them to live with him in London. Shortly after they had settled into their strange new surroundings, Mikak must have been surprised to receive a visitor who could speak her own language. The caller looked familiar; he was one of the missionaries who had gone to Labrador in 1765, when he interpreted for Palliser during the ill-fated "peace treaty."

The visitor's name was Jens Haven, but Mikak's people had called him Johannesingoak—little Jens—because of his small stature. While in Labrador, he and his colleague, a fellow Dane by the name of Christen Larsen Drachard, had been forced by a sudden storm to stay overnight in one of the Inuit tents. Mikak had been there and she could remember a prayer that she had learned from the two strangers.

Mikak showed joy at seeing Haven again. Lucas, who had also seen Haven in Labrador, apparently demonstrated different sentiments. He first refused to let Haven into the house and only backed down after the missionary showed written orders from Governor Palliser, who had asked him to call on Mikak.

According to Haven's account of the reunion, Mikak listened with enthusiasm when he told her why he was in London. He had come to petition the British government to give the Moravians permission to establish a mission among the Inuit and to grant them land upon which they could build. He must have been delighted when Mikak "urgently" pleaded with him to return with her "to help her poor soon-to-be-ruined countrymen."

Mikak's comprehension of the Moravian plan would have been hampered by her knowledge of Christianity, which was still very limited. This was demonstrated when, somewhat later, Mikak and Lucas were invited to the residence of Governor Palliser. On that occasion, the Governor asked Haven, who was also present, to tell Mikak that "she should get to know about the Lord." Haven tried to put off the request until a later time, suggesting that for the moment such a discussion could only lead to problems. He probably anticipated interference from Lucas, who had tried to tell Mikak that there was a God, but had done so amid "much lightheartedness" and apparently, with little success.

Fully aware that Mikak "did not understand Lucas at all in this matter," Palliser was curious whether or not Haven would be more successful and urged him to try. Haven finally gave in and was encouraged when Mikak not only understood him quite well but promised, "I shall certainly get to know the Lord because I want to get to the eternal joy." Then Mikak asked whether this was the message that Lucas had been trying to tell her. After Lucas owned that it was, she turned on him with this sharp and spirited attack: "Oh, you miserable person! You know God and you live worse than the Inuit. I do not believe that you know God."

Mikak's reply was not understood by Palliser, who asked Haven to interpret what she had said. The missionary refused, saying that Lucas could do so if he wished, but by that time Lucas was starting to show his rash temper and was accusing Haven of turning Mikak against him. Palliser, now very serious, ordered the irate Lucas to be quiet and insisted that Haven should interpret for him. When he finally learned what Mikak had said, the Governor added to Lucas's discomfiture by saying:

"There you have it. A heathen woman can judge well who is a child of God and who is not. From the fruit you recognize the tree."

Mikak continued to live with Lucas, who had come to be regarded by the missionaries as a "fleshly" man, but she was often visited by Haven. On one occasion the Moravians managed, probably with Palliser's assistance, to have her brought to visit their headquarters at Lindsay House in Chelsea. While visiting with the Moravians, Mikak enjoyed a meal of salmon. It was one of the very few English foods she knew from home, which may explain the partiality she displayed for this familiar fish on other such social occasions. After her second dinner with the Earl of Bathurst, whose reference to "the Esquimaux lady" has already been noted, Mikak's host remarked that she would eat nothing but salmon though, as he was quick to point out, "I had very good dinners."

Mikak continued to support the Moravians and promoted their cause among the "many of standing" with whom she had frequent contact. One of those who were said to be "fond" of Mikak was Augusta, Dowager Princess of Wales and mother of King George II. The dowager princess once ordered that Mikak be brought to Carlton House, so that "she could have something handsome made up for her in her own country fashion." Lucas was recruited to help select the materials: red and white leather for boots, black velvet for under breeches, white shag for upper, white cloth with blue backing for a jacket, and gold lace for trim. Mikak insisted that she make up the material herself, "not suffering any man to touch her." When all was finished, fine embroidery was added to the breast and tail of the hooded jacket.

Though she professed to be "much pleased" with the colourful new costume, Mikak was not anxious to display it, much less model it in public. When taken to show it to the dowager princess at Carlton House, she asked to travel in a sedan chair so that she could draw the curtains and not be seen. After the princess had admired her new clothes, Mikak asked Lucas if she could be taken home so that she could change before going out to a dinner invitation. She seemed uneasy and, when questioned, admitted through Lucas that she could not dine in that costume with company and be seen by servants. All the English women wore petticoats and Mikak, in her Inuit woman's trousers, "could not bear to be laughed at". On hearing this, the princess took her into another room and fitted her out in a head-dress, a damask petticoat and a mantle, in which she went to dinner "very well satisfied."

Some of the curious Londoners who failed to catch a glimpse of the real Mikak were at least able to view a portrait of her, which was exhibited at the Royal Academy of Arts. The oil painting, executed by well-known society portraitist John Russell, must have appealed to anyone with dreams of imperial expansion. A tattooed mother, representing what was recently billed as "the most savage people in the world," appears benign and contented as she proudly holds the coronation medal of her new sovereign, King George II, on her left breast. On her wrist rests a bracelet given to her by the Duke of Gloucester, showing more acceptance of British friendship and generosity. Her cherubic son, Tutauk, peers out in wide-eyed (almost too wide for an Inuk) wonder, perhaps contemplating the grandeur of the Empire to which he now belongs. Unfortunately, nothing is known of Mikak's feelings about her portrait, though one of her patrons once observed, "She loves pictures and music extremely, but thinks it indecent to see the pictures of naked men and women."

Mikak's immersion in the sights, sounds and stench of old London finally ended in late spring, when she and her son were shipped home on the warship *Nautilus*. Shortly before they sailed, she learned that the government had just granted their long-awaited permission for the Moravians to establish a mission in "Esquimaux Bay." She promised to inform her countrymen that the missionaries would come to them the following summer in order to choose a place where they could build their house. She would urge them to be friendly.

On the long homeward voyage Mikak was escorted, as usual, by Lucas. In spite of a recent promotion to the rank of Lieutenant, Lucas had decided to leave the navy and start a trading company in Labrador. He instructed Mikak to pass on a number of messages to her people, commandments which she had heard him repeat many times. She was to tell them, among other things, that their land belonged to the good King whom she had seen in England. The Inuit were to obey the King, who was their overlord. The Inuit should no longer travel as far south as Newfoundland, where they formerly stole wooden boats. Next summer, however, they could and should come as far south as "a certain latitude" where they could trade peacefully with their good friend, Lieutenant Lucas.

Finally back in Labrador, Mikak was put ashore in the neighbourhood of Byron Bay, just north of Hamilton Inlet. Her family, with whom she was reunited after an absence of almost two years, saw such a change in her that her father started calling her "Nutarak"—the newborn. She, in turn, began referring to her son Tutauk as "Pallisea," after Governor Palliser.

Within a short time Mikak remarried. Her new husband, a man named Tuglavina, had been married to Mikak's younger sister. Since the girl—who was described as very young—had not yet borne him any children, Tuglavina was quick to leave her in favour of the older Mikak. Ambitious as he was, Tuglavina cannot have failed to appreciate the prestige and material wealth which Mikak had acquired through her visit to London.

Throughout the long winter, Mikak tried often to tell of the marvels she had witnessed on the far side of the ocean. Her eager listeners also heard of things to come of the trader Lucas who would meet them in the south and of the missionaries who would soon come and settle in their midst. Mikak escaped the special scorn her people reserved for liars when, early the following summer, at least one of her prophecies came true.

Mikak and Tuglavina were on their way to trade in the south when word came that a European ship lay near by. Four Inuit men had been aboard and had seen some of the missionaries of whom Mikak had spoken so often. It was 16 July 1770, and they were near Byron Bay, the place where Mikak had been landed the previous summer. It was also the place where she had hidden most of the treasures she had brought from London.

Mikak's father, wearing an English officer's breastplate and fine wash-leather gloves, went ahead in his kayak to tell the missionaries that his daughter longed to see them. Not far behind came the wooden boat of Mikak and Tuglavina. Mikak was "shining" in the goldtrimmed jacket which she had received from the dowager princess. As she approached the ship, the missionaries were astonished to see how well her costume, now more than a year old, had been preserved.

As she came aboard the little Jersey packet, which was not even three kayaks in length, Mikak received many compliments from the crew. She must have understood them because her own responses, though couched in simple English phrases such as "How do you do sir; Very good sir; Thank you sir," were all used at the appropriate moments. Everything went smoothly even though Tuglavina, who feared the Europeans might come too near Mikak if he let her "out of his hand," was visibly upset when the Captain gave her a kiss. To prevent any misunderstanding, Jens Haven spoke to the Captain and easily persuaded that "honest, simple, sensible man" not to do it again.

Mikak and Tuglavina, together with Tutauk, were invited into the cabin. There they were offered some pieces of meat that the ship's crew had cut from a whale carcass they had come across during the voyage. After the guests had accepted gratefully, eaten heartily and "assured us it was good," Haven addressed them in their own language. Mikak listened with pleasure while he told her how glad he was that she was now married to a good man whom the missionaries knew from their earlier visits and who, even then, "liked to hear of the great Lord." She was less pleased when Haven gave a stern warning that, if the Inuit should try to kill the missionaries, they would defend themselves with guns, go back to their own country and never come again.

Mikak responded by first of all affirming that her husband was indeed a good man and that they loved one another. Then she said that she was happy that Haven had kept his word by returning to the Inuit, who all wanted the missionaries to live among them and would never give them reason to leave. However it made her unhappy to learn that Haven thought her people could harm the missionaries, and she bluntly told him not to think so badly of them.

The conversation warmed up when Haven told Mikak she should not talk to him like that since he knew that "there are great thieves and murderers among you." He may have been thinking about the Moravians' first attempt to settle in Labrador, eighteen years earlier, which had failed after seven people had been killed by the Inuit. In any case, Mikak hit back with spirit by answering that "In England there are also thieves and murderers." Haven replied that in England such people were hanged, but that the missionaries refused to do such a thing and would simply go home if they could not live in peace with the Inuit. Mikak, who had recently lived in the strange kablunat world, where public hangings were a common form of recreation, decided to close their heated exchange on a conciliatory note. She repeated her invitation for the missionaries to come and stay, adding "You will see, we shall make it nice for you."

Quickly changing topic, Mikak asked about Karpik—the orphan boy whom she had left with Governor Palliser. It was a question Haven must have been dreading, and to which he gave only the incomplete answer that Karpik stayed in England. He did not go into the sad details, which were that Karpik, after being placed in the custody of the Moravians by Governor Palliser and making great progress in reading and writing, had suddenly died of smallpox on 4 October 1769. He had been baptized by the Moravians and lay buried in their cemetery at Fulneck in Yorkshire, where he had gone to stay with Drachard after Mikak and Tutauk returned to Labrador.

Mikak's next question raised emotions of a different kind. She wanted to know where Mr. Lucas was, and whether he also wanted to come. Haven, who was worried that Lucas would try to influence Mikak against the Moravians, said that he could not answer either question. Then he told her not to ask him any more about Lucas, saying "You know him yourself." It must have given him some satisfaction when Mikak turned to her new husband and said that she knew Lucas to be a liar.

After waiting out a sudden storm, which forced several Inuit to stay overnight aboard the ship, Mikak invited Drachard to come ashore with her early the next morning. As the old missionary stepped out of her boat, Mikak gripped him under the arm and led him to her tent, a large one she had received from Governor Palliser. In the eyes of Drachard, who was happy to get Mikak's permission to call all the people there for a sermon, it appeared that his benefactress "commanded not only all the Eskimos here, but her own husband also."

When Drachard had finished preaching in her tent, Mikak offered to take him back to the ship. She had learned that one of the men on the Jersey packet would trade with the Inuit and was curious to see what he had to offer. Back aboard the ship, the Captain continued to allow Mikak, Tuglavina and Tutauk to enter the cabin.

It was a privilege no longer extended to the other Inuit, who were now trading on the crowded decks.

Mikak and her husband remained in the cabin until about noon, first trading and then eating with the missionaries. She showed interest when Drachard, confessing that the missionaries were not sure how to find "Esquimaux Bay," asked whether she and Tuglavina might be willing to stay aboard and guide them there. The Inuit couple went ashore to talk it over. They stayed a few hours and, when they came back, Mikak offered to pilot the ship northward to "her land" for payment. The Captain approved and the missionaries were delighted.

Mikak was also pleased with the arrangement. She and her husband and son were to share a berth, which was promptly vacated by the ship's mate and one of the missionaries. Small as their berth must have been, they were better off than the seamen in the steerage, and were thankful for the "beautiful sleeping places." Mikak said that she would have her own boat taken on ahead by "her servant." In a moment of overwhelming enthusiasm, she is said to have exclaimed, "I have no words to thank you and to show my joy for having found you here."

Because of fog and unfavourable wind conditions, the trip north to Nain Bay, though less than 300 kilometres, lasted two weeks. Mikak and Tuglavina were exposed to what amounted to a crash course in contemporary Moravian religious beliefs, with daily conversations and sermons from both Haven and Drachard. They "listened gladly" and at one point asked whether the King of England also knew the Lord. When Haven answered in the affirmative, Mikak immediately asked "Why then have I in England not heard of the good Lord in heaven?" Haven felt that he "almost owed her an answer."

The Inuit couple continued to express their gratitude to the missionaries for taking them along. They were especially thankful for the whale flipper, an Inuit delicacy which, not surprisingly, they preferred "by far" over the ship's provisions. Mikak must have given Haven great cause for jubilation when she uttered the following words: "I have always heard you say that you are our friends and love us...but now I start understanding what this means. I feel something which I did not feel before."

A few days later Haven reached the conclusion that "both have never been so happy in their lives as now with us" and declared that Mikak had become "a totally different person" than in London. The relationship between Mikak and the Moravians continued on this euphoric level for most of the trip. There were a few minor setbacks, such as when the ship once ran aground and the Inuit were heard to complain in an "overly loud" manner. To console them the Captain, using Haven as interpreter, assured them that he would rescue them before any of the others. This "sounded good to them" but they nevertheless remained sceptical until the ship had come off and was safely afloat.

Further tension was evident two days later, when Tuglavina was asked to accompany Haven ashore so they could seek out a good passage from a higher vantage point. The suspicious husband refused, saying that he did not want to leave his wife alone on the ship. In order to relieve Tuglavina's fears, Drachard asked Mikak whether she and her son wanted to go to their berth and rest until her husband returned. Only when she had done so and Drachard had given his assurance that nobody would come to Mikak while the boat was ashore, did Tuglavina consent to go.

Mikak's entourage increased in size when, shortly before reaching their destination, she was allowed to bring another passenger aboard the ship. It was Mikak's stepson, who had apparently asked to be with his younger "brother" Tutauk. He had the same name as Mikak's father—Nerkingoak—and his father had been Mikak's first husband. Finding the boy to be "shabby, lousy and dirty," Mikak gave him fresh clothes and took great pains to clean him and remove his lice, of which she had "a good meal." She was very grateful when Haven helped her out by rubbing something into the boy's scalp.

On 1 August the Jersey packet reached its destination and anchored by Amitok (now Barth) Island in the mouth of Nain Bay. The ship had been expected and Inuit had converged on the island, which was a traditional summer gathering place, from settlements that were spread out for more than 300 kilometres of coastline. The missionaries counted 48 tents and estimated that there were about 500 people.

Mikak marked the occasion by dressing "like an English lady." She wore the silken gown which the dowager princess had given her, and which she had just recovered from its hiding place in Byron Bay a few weeks earlier. It was the first time she had dared to wear the gown in Labrador and she was so anxious about the reaction of her countrymen that she begged Haven to protect her.

While the Jersey packet lay at anchor off Amitok Island during the next three days Mikak, who had moved ashore the morning after their arrival, continued to see the missionaries often. As soon as she had finished pitching her tent, she asked Drachard if he would like to come and use it for an Inuit assembly. Her large tent was soon filled with listeners, so she had the ends lifted up "that 200 might hear."

After Drachard had finished his own sermon, Mikak and Tuglavina started to display their new knowledge by preaching about "the five holy wounds of Jesus." Then, when Drachard was pleading with the Inuit not to kill any more Europeans, Mikak supported him by passing on a message from King George II. As far as she had understood from Lieutenant Lucas, the "great Lord in London" had said that when the Inuit wanted peace with the English and would trade in an orderly manner without stealing or murdering, then no more Inuit would be shot, much less killed. This announcement prompted one old man, suspected of past murders, to pay her the compliment, "We believe your words."

When Haven offered to hire Tuglavina and his boat, in order to search for a good building site, Mikak said she also wanted to come along. They set out at 5 o'clock on the morning of 3 August, and Mikak "helped diligently" with the rowing. Though the missionaries failed to find a suitable building site, they returned in the afternoon to pay the Inuit for the land they would be needing. Tuglavina was the first of 67 Inuit men whose names appear on the "deed," which was signed with the help of a "guiding hand" from the missionaries.

Early the next morning Mikak had a visit from Drachard. The ship would weigh anchor that evening and he had come to pose some last-minute questions. Among other things, he asked whether she would help the missionaries when they came back and whether she would meanwhile tell her countrymen why they would return, which was "to tell daily of Jesus' love." After agreeing to these and similar requests, Mikak paid one farewell visit aboard the ship, where she frequently repeated how anxious she would be to see the missionaries again. Then she asked them to deliver some presents to her friends in England: two white fox skins for the dowager princess, a black one for the Duke of Gloucester, and two red ones for Governor Palliser. Then, according to Haven, she went away and wept.

Although Mikak saw the missionaries no more that summer, Tuglavina paddled in his kayak to their new anchorage, about five miles away, the next day. He had been asked to come and help them in one last effort to select their future building site and, after conferring with Mikak, had agreed. He repeated that his wife was ashamed about the way the Inuit had behaved, perhaps referring to the theft of some rope from the ship a few days earlier.

Haven asked Tuglavina to greet Mikak and tell her to "love her countrymen and not despise them." Tuglavina seemed "very well satisfied with this" even though he might not have agreed totally with the content. All that day he had been so worried that somebody else might take his wife while he was away, that the missionaries decided they should not pressure him to stay longer, even though they had still not found their site. At a time when wife stealing was a common occurrence among the Labrador Inuit, Tuglavina's worries over his wealthy and prestigious wife were obviously not restricted to the Captain's kisses or the antics of a half score of British sailors.

It is not known how or where Mikak spent the rest of that summer. It seems unlikely however, that she resumed the southern trip on which she had earlier embarked and which she had willingly interrupted upon meeting the Moravians. Had she gone south after the departure of the Jersey packet, as did several of her countrymen, she would most probably have encountered Lieutenant Lucas, who came to Labrador a few weeks later and searched in vain for her until early October.

In his quest for Mikak, Lucas only made it as far north as the Inuit settlement of Arvertok, near present-day Hopedale. There he persuaded a whole family of nine to return with him to his newly-opened post at Cape Charles. Several of these people were later taken to England by Lucas's business partner, Captain George Cartwright, where all but one suffered a fate that Mikak and Tutauk had mercifully escaped—death by smallpox. As for Lucas, about whom Haven had predicted "he will scarce know how to spend the winter without Mikak," he went down when his schooner carrying a cargo of fish disappeared a few months later somewhere in the North Atlantic.

CARTWRIGHT

A second visit by Labrador Inuit to England was conducted by George Cartwright, a business partner of Lt. Francis Lucas, who had earlier taken Mikak thither.

Cartwright was perhaps the most prominent British trader to set up on the Labrador coast, largely because of the journal that he kept and published. A captain in the British Army, he was drawn to Labrador after his visits to the island of Newfoundland with his brother John, the first Lieutenant of HMS *Guernsey*, which brought Governor Sir Hugh Palliser to Newfoundland.

Hearing that Labrador was practically virgin country, he was irresistibly drawn to the wild and free life of a settler on the coast. He entered into a partnership with Francis Lucas, along with two others, to trap, hunt, fish, and trade with the Inuit. The following excerpt is from his Labrador journal, which was first published in 1792.

Cartwright had good relations with the Inuit. Because Francis Lucas had learned Inuktitut from Mikak, Cartwright was able to persuade the large family of Attuiock to settle near his company of a dozen or so men at Charles River. Some of Cartwright's employees took Inuit women for their wives, and Cartwright treated all with courtesy and respect. He was fair and yet firm. He said of them: "They are the best-tempered people I ever met with, and the most docile; nor is there a nation under the sun, with which I would sooner trust my person and property."

However, when he took the Inuit to England with him, the trip resulted in tragedy. While the Inuit caused quite a stir in London, one of the women, Caubvick, came down with smallpox, and eventually the others were stricken as well. All of the Inuit died except for Caubvick, who recovered only to spread the disease to other natives once she returned home.

This is Cartwright's account of the visit to London by Attuiock, Tuglavina, and their wives.

George Cartwright

EXCERPT FROM
George Cartwright and his Labrador Journal
ED. CHARLES WENDELL TOWNSEND, 1911

Monday, December 14, 1772. I went down the river this morning, met the vessel in the Pool, and brought the women on shore. They were greatly astonished at the number of shipping which they saw in the river; for they did not suppose that there were so many in the whole world: but I was exceedingly disappointed to observe them pass through London Bridge without taking much notice of it. I soon discovered that they took it for a natural rock which extended across the river. They laughed at me when I told them it was the work of men; nor could I make them believe it, till we came to Blackfriars Bridge, which I caused them to examine with more attention; shewing them the joints, and pointing out the marks of the chizzels upon the stones. They no sooner comprehended by what means such a structure could be erected, than they expressed their wonder with astonishing significancy of countenance.

On landing at Westminster Bridge, we were immediately surrounded by a great concourse of people; attracted not only by the uncommon appearance of the Indians who were in their sealskin dresses, but also by a beautiful eagle, and an Esquimau dog; which had much the resemblance of a wolf, and a remarkable wildness of look.[12] I put them all into coaches, with as much expedition as possible, and drove off to the lodgings which I had prepared in Leicester Street.

---

12 The Eskimo dog of Labrador of the present day resembles very closely the northern wolf, except that it usually carries the tail curled over the back instead of partially extended behind.

In a few days time, I had so many applications for admittance to see the new visitors, that my time was wholly taken up in gratifying the curiosity of my friends and their acquaintance; and the numbers who came made my lodgings very inconvenient to the landlord as well as to myself. I therefore resolved to look out for a house. I soon hired a small one, ready furnished, for ten guineas a month, in Little Castle Street, Oxford Market, and removed thither.

Being willing, as far as lay in my power, to comply with the incessant applications of my friends for a sight of the Indians; and finding it impossible either to have any rest, or time to transact business, I appropriated two days a week to that purpose, viz., Tuesdays and Fridays. On those days, not only my house was filled, even to an inconvenience, but the street was so much crowded with carriages and people, that my residence was a great nuisance to the neighbourhood.

As their skin dresses had a dirty appearance and an offensive smell, I provided a quantity of broad-cloth, flannel, and beads, together with whatever else was necessary; and the women now having leisure to work, and being excellent taylors, soon clothed them all anew; preserving their own fashion in the cut of their garments.

I once took the men to the opera when their Majesties were there, and we chanced to sit near Mr. Coleman, the manager of Covent Garden Theatre, who politely invited all the Indians and myself to a play at his house. He fixed on *Cymbeline*, and they were greatly delighted with the representation. But their pride was most highly gratified, at being received with a thundering applause by the audience on entering the box. The men soon observed to their wives, that they were placed in the King's box, and received in the same manner as their Majesties were at the opera; which added considerably to the pleasure which they felt from the *tout ensemble*. Never did I observe so young a child pay such unremitting attention to the whole representation, as little Ickeuna; no sooner did the swords begin to clash, in the fighting scene between Posthumus and Iachimo, but she set up a most feeling scream.

About a fortnight after our arrival in town, having provided great-coats, boots, and hats for the men, in order that they might pass through the streets unobserved, I took Attuiock with me and walked beyond the Tower. We there took boat, rowed up the river, and landed at Westminster Bridge; from whence we walked to Hyde Park Corner, and then home again. I was in great expectation, that he would begin to relate the wonders which he had seen, the instant he entered the room; but I found myself greatly disappointed.

He immediately sat down by the fire side, placed both his hands on his knees, leaned his head forward, fixed his eyes on the ground in a stupid stare; and continued in that posture for a considerable time. At length, tossing up his head, and fixing his eyes on the ceiling, he broke out in the following soliloquy: "Oh! I am tired; here are too many houses; too much smoke; too many people; Labrador is very good; seals are plentiful there; I wish I was back again." By which I could plainly perceive, that the multiplicity, and variety of objects had confounded his ideas; which were too much confined to comprehend any thing but the inconveniences that he had met with. And indeed, the longer they continued in England, the more was I convinced of the truth of that opinion; for their admiration increased in proportion, as their ideas expanded; till at length they began more clearly to comprehend the use, beauty, and mechanism of what they saw; though the greater part of these were as totally lost upon them, as they would have been upon one of the brute creation.

Although they had often passed St. Paul's without betraying any great astonishment, or at least not so much as all Europeans do at the first sight of one of those stupendous islands of ice, which are daily to be seen near the east coast of their own country, yet when I took them to the top of it, and convinced them that it was built by the hands of men (a circumstance which had not entered their heads before, for they had supposed it a natural production) they were quite lost in amazement. The people below, they compared to mice; and insisted, that it must at least be as high as Cape Charles, which is a mountain of considerable altitude. Upon my asking them how they should describe it to their countrymen on their return, they replied, with a look of the utmost expression, they should neither mention it, nor many other things which they had seen, lest they should be called liars, from the seeming impossibility of such astonishing facts.

Walking along Piccadilly one day with the two men, I took them into a shop to shew them a collection of animals. We had no sooner entered than I observed their attention riveted on a small monkey; and I could perceive horror most strongly depicted in their countenances. At length the old man turned to me and faltered out, "Is that an Esquimau?" I must confess, that both the colour and contour of the countenance had considerable resemblance to the people of their nation; but how they could conceive it possible for an Esquimau to be reduced to that diminutive size, I am wholly at a loss to account for; unless they had fixed their attention on the countenance only, and had not adverted to any other particulars. On pointing out several other monkeys of different kinds, they were greatly diverted at the mistake which they had made; but were not well pleased to observe, that monkeys resembled their race much more than ours.

The parrots, and other talkative birds, next attracted their notice. And it was a great treat to me, both then and at all other times, to observe their different emotions, much more forcibly expressed in their countenances, than is possible to be done by those, whose feelings are not equally genuine. Civilized nations imperceptibly contract an artificial expression of countenance, to help out their languid feelings; for knowledge, by a communication with the world and books, enlightens our ideas so much, that they are not so liable to be taken by surprise, as the uninformed mind of the savage, who never had the least hint given him, that certain things are in existence; consequently, they break upon him as unexpectedly, and forcibly, as the sun would do upon a man who was born deaf and blind, in case he should suddenly be brought to sight on a clear day.

Being on a dining visit, with that excellent surgeon and anatomist, the ingenious John Hunter,[13] in the afternoon Attuiock walked out of the room by himself, but presently returned with such evident marks of terror, that we were all greatly alarmed, fearing some accident had happened to him; or, that he had met with an insult from one of the servants. He seized hold of my hand, and eagerly pressed me to go along with him. I asked the cause of his emotion, but could get nothing more from him than "Come along, come along with me," and he hastily led me into a room in the yard, in which stood a glass case containing

---

13 Noted surgeon, anatomist and physiologist; author of "Trestise on the Blood, Inflammation, and Gunshot Wounds," etc. 1728 to 1793.

many human bones. "Look there," says he, with more horror and consternation in his countenance, than I ever beheld in that of man before, "are those the bones of Esquimaux whom Mr. Hunter has killed and eaten? Are we to be killed? Will he eat us, and put our bones there?" As the whole company followed us, the other Indians had also taken the alarm before the old priest had finished his interrogatories; nor did any of them seem more at ease, by the rest of us breaking out into a sudden and hearty laugh, till I explained to them that those were the bones of our own people, who had been executed for certain crimes committed by them, and were preserved there, that Mr. Hunter might better know how to set those of the living, in case any of them should chance to be broken; which often happened in so populous a country. They were then perfectly satisfied, and approved of the practice; but Attuiock's nerves had received too great a shock to enable him to resume his usual tranquility, till he found himself safe in my house again.

Passing through Hyde Park, in our way to Holland House, and observing his Majesty looking at the regiment of Old Buffs, which were then going to Plymouth, we got out of the coach and went up to the front; where I explained to them the use of that body of men, and of the evolutions which they were performing. After his Majesty had reviewed the regiment collectively, the recruits were drawn out at a few paces distant from the left flank, that he might examine them separately. So great a crowd had gathered round us, as incommoded our view of the troops, and attracted the notice of the King, who then sent General Harvey to order me with the Indians, into the vacant space between the regiment and the recruits. Here his Majesty rode slowly past them, and condescended to salute them by taking off his hat, accompanied with a gracious smile; honours which they were highly pleased with, and often mentioned afterwards with great exultation. Nor were they in the least displeased that his Majesty did not speak to them; since I had previously told them not to expect it; and they observed that he spoke to none but the commanding officer, and one or two of those who were in attendance.

They were afterwards greatly diverted at the expence of the Hon. Stephen Fox. That gentleman came to Holland House on purpose to see the Indians there; but when he arrived, they were at the end of a long gallery: Stephen being rather out of wind with walking up stairs, sat down at the door to wait their return, where he unfortunately fell fast asleep. Although we continued a long time in the house with Lord[14] and Lady Holland, he did not awake from his slumber till we had got into the coach to go away; when he mounted his poney and gallopped off. His manner of retreat made them express great compassion for the poor beast, whose unfortunate lot it was to carry so great a weight at such a rate; nor could I help censuring him myself for cruelty, till I was informed that he would have fallen asleep on horse-back had he gone slower. Then, indeed, I pitied both horse and rider.

I continued in London till the month of February; at which time I took the Indians with me to my father's house at Marnham in Nottinghamshire, where we stayed six weeks. While we were there I amused them with all kinds of field diversions: we also made several visits in the neighborhood; particularly one to Kelham, where Lord George Button politely invited our whole family, and entertained my friends with a fox-chase. Fortunately we had an excellent run of twelve miles, and it was very singular, that, although the Indians had been on horse-back only three times before, they were both in at the death; which happened in an open field, with three couple and a half of hounds, out of twenty-five couples; a proof how hard they must have driven him.

I soon found the country agreed much better with their inclinations, as well as their health, than London. Here they could enjoy fresh air and exercise, without being distressed by crowds of people gathering round them whenever they stirred out; which was always the case in town.

The women, according to the universal disposition of the fair sex, enjoyed visiting and dancing; and I must say, that Caubvick attained to great perfection in that graceful accomplishment, during her short stay. The men were best pleased with sporting; the exquisite nose of the hound, which could follow an

14 Henry Fox, first Lord Holland, was the father of the above mentioned Stephen Fox, afterward second Lord Holland, and of Charles James Fox. Henry died in 1774, the year following Cartwright's visit, and the death of Stephen soon followed, as might be expected from the description of this gentleman as given by our author. Holland House, which became a great social centre during the life of the third Lord Holland, Henry Richard Vassall Fox, is still standing in Kensington.

animal by the scent, over an open country or through a thick wood, almost as swiftly as he could have done had the creature been in view, the sagacity and steadiness of the pointer, and the speed of the greyhound, were matters of great astonishment to them. But above all, they were most struck with the strength, beauty, and utility of that piece of perfection in the brute creation, that noble animal, the horse.

The face of the country did not pass unobserved by them, and their expression was "The land is all made;" for they supposed that we had cut down the woods, and levelled the hills. In the former supposition they were certainly right; and I do not wonder at the latter, since they would naturally suppose that all the world was like the small part of it which they had formerly seen; and which is almost an entire collection of hills covered with thick woods. As they had never before seen any cultivated land (except a few small gardens, which they observed were dug with a spade) they formed an idea of our immense numbers, by being able to till so much land and consume the produce of it in a year; exclusive of the animal food with which they saw our tables and markets abounded. How the inhabitants of London were supplied with food, I could never make them fully comprehend, any more than I could the number of people by which the metropolis was inhabited. Their arithmetic goes no higher than the number twenty-one; therefore, the best I could do, was to tell them, that a certain number of large whales would serve them for one meal only. Nothing surprised them more, than to meet with a man who assured them he could not shoot, had never killed an animal, nor seen the sea in his life.

After my return to town, by his Majesty's permission, I took them to Court; where their dresses and behaviour made them greatly taken notice of. They were also at the houses of several of the nobility and people of fashion; and I omitted nothing, which came within the compass of my pocket, to make their stay in England agreeable, or to impress them with ideas of our riches and strength. The latter I thought highly necessary, as they had often, when in Labrador, spoken of our numbers with great contempt, and told me they were so numerous, that they could cut off all the English with great ease, if they thought proper to collect themselves together; an opinion which could not fail to produce in me very unpleasant reflections. But they had not been long in London before they confessed to me, that the Esquimaux were but as one, compared to that of the English.

At the same time, I did not neglect to provide everything that was necessary for my return. I represented to the Earl of Dartmouth (who was then at the head of the board of trade and plantations) the unjust proceedings of Noble and Pinson, in dispossessing me of my fishing-posts, and obtained an order for my salmon-fishery in Charles River to be restored; but I could not succeed with respect to my sealing-post near Cape Charles. I also presented to his lordship a plan for the encouragement of the trade in Labrador, and was examined by the board upon that head. Their report was laid before his Majesty in council, and my plan was partially adopted.

The term of my partnership with Perkins and Coghlan being expired, I dissolved it, and made preparation for returning to Labrador on my own bottom; which the liberality of my father enabled me to do, by assisting me with two thousand pounds.

The End of the First Voyage

The Second Voyage

May, 1773. Having purchased a brig of eighty tons, and named her the *Lady Tyrconnel*,[15] I shipped on board her all such goods as had been provided in London; and having ordered others at Lymmington, Weymouth, and Waterford, I quitted my house on the fifth of May, and embarked on board my vessel in the river Thames; together with Mrs. Selby, the Indians, Mr. John Williams, a surgeon, whom I had engaged to serve me in the capacity of clerk also, his wife, a maidservant, a cooper named William Mather, and two apprentice boys. The command of the vessel I gave to Mr. George Monday, late Master of the *Mary*, in which I returned from Labrador; and I brought along with me a brace of greyhounds, a terrier, and some tame rabbits. A party of friends dined on board with me, and we had a merry leave-taking.

---

15 The name of Cartwright's aunt.

Saturday, May 8, 1773. Having now completed all my business in town, and the wind being fair, at two o'clock this afternoon we made sail down the river; the Esquimaux well pleased in the expectation of soon seeing their native country, their relations and friends again; and I very happy in the prospect of carrying them back, apparently in perfect health.

Tuesday, May 11, 1773. We passed through the Downs this evening, when I discharged the pilot, and went to sea.

Thursday, May 13, 1773. The pleasing prospects which I so lately had before me were of very short duration; for this evening as Caubvick was going to bed, she complained of great sickness at her stomach, had a very bad night, and daily grew worse. On my arrival at Lymmington on the thirteenth, and consulting a surgeon there, (for my own, I found, was utterly ignorant of her complaint) he declared her malady to be the small-pox: which had nearly the same effect on me, as if he had pronounced my sentence of death. As it was vain to expect that the rest should escape the infection, medicines were immediately given to prepare them for it; and I thought it a fortunate circumstance, that an opportunity offered for doing it.[16]

Having taken on board forty tons of salt, and some other goods, I sailed from thence on the eighteenth, and arrived in Weymouth Roads a few hours after. There I received on board some nets and other goods from Bridport, and had the pleasure to find Caubvick go on as well as possible; her disorder being of the mild kind. I took the others out in the boat every day, and we went to the Bill of Portland to shoot murrs.[17]

On the twenty-second Caubvick turned the height, and did not appear to be in the least danger. At the same time Ickongoque began to complain. We sailed for Ireland on the twenty-eighth, but the wind taking us ahead when we got off the Bill of Portland, we put back and anchored in Portland Road. Tooklavinia now was taken ill.

---

16 Vaccination was first practised by Jenner in 1796.

17 Murre or common guillemot, *Uria troille*.

At two o'clock in the morning of the twenty-ninth, we weighed again, and proceeded down the channel with a fair wind and pleasant weather; still in hopes of arriving in sufficient time for my business; but at ten o'clock, so dreadful a stench pervaded the whole vessel, all the Indians being now ill, that three of the ship's crew now were seized with a fever, and we had reason to expect, that a pestilential disorder would soon attack us all. I therefore ordered captain Monday to carry the vessel into Plymouth, although I foresaw that measure would prove an immense loss to me, by the ruin of my voyage, and we came to an anchor in Catwater the next afternoon at two o'clock. I went on shore immediately, and made a personal application to Earl Cornwallis, Admiral Spry, and the Mayor of Plymouth, for an house to put the Indians in, but could not succeed.

Monday, May 31, 1773. Ickeuna died this morning, Caubvick had a violent fever on her, and the rest were extremely ill. In the evening I bargained for a house at Stonehouse, for two guineas and a half per week. At four o'clock the next morning we weighed and removed the vessel to Stonehouse Pool. I got the Indians on shore immediately, and Ickcongoque died that night.

Wednes., June 2, 1773. On the second I engaged Dr. Farr, the physician to the Naval Hospital, and Mr. Monier, an apothecary of Plymouth, to attend the Indians; and, by the doctor's directions, I removed the two men into separate tents, which I had pitched in an adjoining close. In the evening I went to Plymouth, in order to set off for London, which I did the next morning at six o'clock, and arrived there at two in the afternoon of the fifth.

On the morning of the sixth I waited on the Earl of Dartmouth, his Majesty's Principal Secretary of State for America, and acquainted his lordship with what had happened. And I must take this opportunity of gratefully acknowledging the many obligations which I had the honor to receive from his lordship upon this, as well as upon several other occasions.

Thursday, June 10, 1773. I left London on my return to Plymouth at six o'clock this morning, and arrived at Stonehouse on Saturday evening. I was now informed that both the men died in the night of the third Instant, and that Caubvick had been given over, but was at length in a fair way of recovery, though reduced to a skeleton, and troubled with a great many large boils. She recovered so very slowly, that it was not until the fourth of July that I durst venture to remove her, when I once more embarked with her and all the rest of my family (except my maid whom I had discharged for bad behaviour) to proceed on my intended voyage.

We sailed from Plymouth early in the morning of the fifth, but meeting with contrary winds we had a tedious passage to Waterford, for we did not arrive there till the afternoon of the tenth. It was some consolation, however, to be favoured with fine weather, and to catch great plenty of mackarel every day.

My time was taken up till the sixteenth, in purchasing and getting on board such provisions as I had occasion for; I also hired another womanservant, and on that day I sailed for Labrador.

As voyages across the Atlantic at this time of the year are generally tedious, by reason of the prevalency of the westerly wind, I was not surprised, that this proved longer than was convenient to me. The weather, in general, was exceedingly fine, and we caught plenty of fish of different kinds; such as mackerel,[18] a small shark, a few fish greatly resembling tench, (which I killed with an Esquimau birding-dart under the stern) a porpoise and a dolphin. It is not usual for dolphins[19] to come so far north, but we saw two, three bonetas[20] and a few flying-fish[21] in the latitude of 49° 15', on the twelfth of August.

Caubvick's hair falling off, and being matted with the small-pox, I had much difficulty to prevail on her to permit me to cut it off, and shave her head. Notwithstanding I assured her that the smell of the hair would communicate the infection to the rest of her country folks on her return, yet I was not able to prevail on her to consent to its being thrown overboard. She angrily snatched it from me, locked it up in one of her trunks, and never would permit me to get sight of it afterwards; flying into a violent passion of anger and grief whenever I mentioned the subject, which I did almost every day, in hopes of succeeding at last.

---

18 *Scomber scombeus.*

19 *Coryphama hippurus.*

20 Probably tuna or horse-mackerel *Thunnus thynnus.*

21 *Exocoetus volitans.*

Friday, August 27, 1773. This evening at sunset we got sight of the land, and judged ourselves to be nine or ten leagues from it; the next morning at daylight we found ourselves about three leagues from Cape St. Francis, and at eight o'clock at night came to an anchor in Charles Harbour.

Sunday, August 29, 1773. Early in the morning I went on shore at Stage Cove, and found the house locked up. I sent the boat to the Lodge, and walked across the Barrens to Bare Point, where I met her again, with two of my people on board. From them I learned that they had killed in the winter as many seals as produced twelve tuns of oil; and caught fifty tierces of salmon this summer. I shot six curlews, and a grey plover[22] in my way thither, and returned to the boat.

Tuesday, August 31, 1773. About noon almost the whole of the three southernmost tribes of Esquimaux, amounting to five hundred souls or thereabouts, arrived from Chateau in twenty-two old English and French boats (having heard of my arrival from some boats belonging to that port, which returned from this neighborhood in the night of Saturday last) but the wind did not suit them to come hither till this morning.

I placed myself upon a rock near the water-side, and Caubvick sat down a few paces behind me. We waited for the landing of the Indians with feelings very different from theirs; who were hurrying along with tumultuous joy at the thoughts of immediately meeting their relations and friends again. As the shore would not permit them to land out of their boats, they brought them to their anchors at a distance off, and the men came in their kayacks, each bringing two other persons, lying flat on their faces; one behind and the other before, on the top of the skin covering. On drawing near the shore, and perceiving only Caubvick and myself, their joy abated, and their countenances assumed a different aspect. Being landed, they fixed their eyes on Caubvick and me, in profound, gloomy silence. At length, with great perturbation and in faltering accents, they enquired, separately, what was become of the rest; and were no sooner given to understand, by a silent, sorrowful shake of my head, that they were no more, than they instantly

---

22 The bird known in England as the grey plover is called by American ornithologists the black-bellied plover, *Squatarola squatarola*.

set up such a yell, as I had never before heard. Many of them, but particularly the women, snatched up stones, and beat themselves on the head and face till they became shocking spectacles; one pretty young girl (a sister to the late two men) gave herself so severe a blow upon the cheek-bone, that she bruised and cut the flesh shockingly, and almost beat an eye out. In short, the violent, frantic expressions of grief were such, as far exceeded my imagination; and I could not help participating with them so far, as to shed tears most plentifully. They no sooner observed my emotion, than, mistaking it for the apprehensions which I was under for fear of their resentment, they instantly seemed to forget their own feelings, to relieve those of mine. They pressed round me, clasped my hands, and said and did all in their power to convince me, that they did not entertain any suspicion of my conduct towards their departed friends. As soon as the first violent transports of grief began to subside, I related the melancholy tale, and explained to them, as well as I could, the disorder by which they were carried off; and pointed to Caubvick, who bore very strong, as well as recent, marks of it. They often looked very attentively at her, but, during the whole time, they never spoke one word to her, nor she to them. As soon as I had brought the afflicting story to a conclusion, they assured me of their belief of every particular, and renewed their declarations of friendship. Their stay afterwards was but short; they presently reimbarked, weighed their anchors, and ran across the harbour to Raft Tickle, where they landed and encamped: the rest of the afternoon and the whole of the night was spent in horrid yellings, which were considerably augmented by the variety of echoes, produced from the multiplicity of hills surrounding the harbour, till the whole rung again with sounds that almost petrified the blood of the brig's crew and my new servants.

HAVEN

During Sir Hugh Palliser's years as governor of Newfoundland 1764–68, a decision was made that profoundly affected the lives of the Labrador Inuit. Relations between the seasonal British fish merchants and the Inuit had been characterized by conflict and bloodshed. Palliser believed the fishermen were responsible for most of the trouble. Partly to protect them, and partly to protect the Inuit from them, he took steps to confine the Inuit to northern Labrador. He made an agreement with the Moravian Church whereby, for his support of their conversion of the Inuit to Christianity, they would contain the aboriginal people north of Hamilton Inlet.

As a result of Palliser's agreement, a group led by Jens Haven received a charter to establish a mission among the Labrador Inuit. Perhaps the oldest Protestant denomination, the Moravian Church had originated in what is now the Czech Republic in the middle of the fifteenth century. Before coming to Labrador, the Unitas Fratrum, as they were known, had established more missions around the world than all other Protestant denominations had during the two preceding centuries.

An earlier attempt to establish a mission by Johann Christian Erhardt had failed. Nevertheless, Haven, a Dane and a carpenter by trade who had served in the Moravian Mission in Greenland, where he learned to speak Inuktitut, set sail with his wife, Mary Butterworth, and a small company, arriving in northern Newfoundland in August of 1764. Haven's leadership was crucial to the establishment of the missions in northern Labrador. He was a man of courage and conviction who also had a great asset that not many of his contemporaries possessed: he spoke the local language. What follows is from Haven's *vita*, which appeared in *Periodical accounts relating to the missions of the Church of the United Brethren, established among the heathen* (1798), and which has recently been carefully and expertly presented by Dr. Hans Rollman of Memorial University on his website.

Br. Jens Haven

Memoir of the Life of Br. Jens Haven,
the First Missionary of the Brethren's Church
to the Esquimaux, on the Coast of Labrador, 1798

Our late Brother was born June 23rd, 1724, at Wust, a village in Jutland, where his father possessed a farm. In his early years, he shewed a great capacity for learning, made considerable progress at school, became well versed in the Holy Scriptures, and was instructed with great care by the Rev. Mr. Langgaard, minister of the parish, previous to his confirmation. Being, according to the usual custom, called upon to answer several questions, in presence of the congregation, he endeavoured to make a shew of his knowledge of the doctrines of Christianity; when he received this wholesome reproof from the minister: "My child, your head is full enough, but THAT, I fear, is all, and your heart is empty." When he partook of the Lord's Supper for the first time, he was greatly affected, and surrendered himself to God, as His sole property; but afterwards, forgetting his pious resolutions, followed the impulse of his natural disposition, which was rough and ungovernable; though, in the opinion of the world, he maintained the character of a sober and religious man. About this time, a great awakening took place in his neighbourhood, by the blessing of God, on the labours of the Rev. Mr. Langgaard, and many souls brought earnestly to obtain salvation. These he opposed with violence, thinking himself good enough, and calling all those hypocrites, who would know of no righteousness and salvation but in the death and merits of Jesus. But, being once out in the fields, a storm of thunder arose, and a flash of lightning suddenly penetrated the earth just before his feet, which threw him senseless to the ground. When he recovered, he prayed fervently to God, that his life might be spared, and time allowed him for conversion; for he now saw, that his own righteousness, upon which he had hitherto depended, would not save him in the hour of death, and that he was a lost and condemned sinner in the sight of God. He had no rest, day nor night, but wept and cried incessantly to God, to have mercy upon him, till he felt a divine assurance, that, if he relied in faith upon the merits of Jesus Christ, and turned to Him for help, he should be saved. He now joined the awakened people, and frequently visited the Rev. Mr. Langgaard, whose testimonies of the Gospel were attended with great blessing to his soul. He grew more and more in the knowledge of the Saviour, and being persuaded that he was accepted and owned by Him as His blood-bought property, the whole world began to appear trifling to him, and he wished to become an inhabitant of one of the Brethren's settlements, of which he had received some intelligence. But, before he made application for it, he resolved to go apprentice to a joiner at Copenhagen, the better to qualify himself to earn his own bread. On the road thither, he reflected, that in the midst of the world he might again lose the blessings he had become possessed of, and that it would be better for him at once to join the Brethren. This he did; and having served a regular apprenticeship to a Brother at Copenhagen, he visited Herrnhut in the year 1748, obtained leave to live there, and was soon admitted to the Lord's Supper with the congregation. While he was thus enjoying the privilege of living in communion with the people of God, and growing in grace, he felt a strong desire to serve the Lord among heathen nations, and took occasion to mention it to Bishop Johannes de Watteville, during his visitation at Herrnhut. Here his own narrative commences, as follows:

"In the year 1752, hearing, at Herrnhut, that Br. Erhardt, a Missionary, sent to the coast of Labrador, had been murdered by the Esquimaux,[23] I felt for the first time a strong impulse to go and preach the Gospel to this very nation, and became certain, in my own mind, that I should go to Labrador. I agreed with a Brother of the name of Jeppe Nielsen, that, as soon as there appeared the least

---

23 See Periodical Accounts, vol. XVI, p. 5.

probability of our going, we would offer ourselves for that purpose. Meanwhile, in the year 1758, I received a call to go to Greenland, which I cheerfully accepted, in reliance upon our Saviour. Before my departure, I had a confidential conversation with the late Count Zinzendorf, in which I told him, that though I never felt a call to go to Greenland, but for these seven years past had earnestly desired to go to Labrador, yet I could consider this appointment as coming from the Lord, and would therefore go in His name, with a willing heart. I travelled in company of Br. Matthew Stach, and my own brother, Peter Haven, by way of Copenhagen, and arrived safe at Lichtenfels. In the year following, I was remarkably happy in my situation, learnt the Greenland language, felt great love for the people, and began to believe that it was my destination to spend my days in this country. But I had scarcely formed the resolution to make myself easy and happy in this land, than I was alarmed by a remarkable dream: I thought I heard somebody say to me, 'This is not the place where you are to stay, for you shall preach the Gospel to a nation that has heard nothing of their Saviour.' I awoke, and being unwilling to quit this country, considered it as fancy and fell asleep again. But, to my surprise, I heard the same words repeated a second and a third time. On awakening, I wept exceedingly, and cried, 'Ah, Lord! What am I? I am unfit for Thy work; but if this be Thy will, Thou must Thyself prepare the way.' I was again assured of my call to Labrador, but felt quite resigned to the will of God as to time and circumstances. In the year 1762, I obtained leave to pay a visit in Europe, and arrived, in January, 1763, in company of Br. David Crantz,[24] at Herrnhut, where I staid till 1764, and where my return to Greenland was again proposed to me. But, as I answered, that I did not wish to return without a direction by lot, having prayed the Lord to signify to me His will by this means, I received a negative, and on stating my objections in writing to my Brethren, they were satisfied that I acted uprightly before God. I then proposed, that I would first go to England, and enter into the service of the Hudson's Bay Company as a sailor or ship's carpenter, and thus watch for an opportunity to begin a Mission on the coast of Labrador, or at least to discover whether they were a part of the Greenland nation, and had the same

---

24 The well-known author of the History of Greenland.

language or not. On further consideration, this project appeared to me liable to great difficulties, and I began to feel much timidity as to the execution, on which I turned in prayer to the Lord, and opening the Scriptures, found immediately that text: 'Do all that is in thine heart; behold, I am with thee according to thine heart.' I Sam. xiv. 7. This strengthened my drooping faith, and I devoted myself anew to God, entreating Him to grant me wisdom, grace, and power to execute my purpose. On considering my proposal, the Brethren advised me not to go to Hudson's Bay, but rather to seek to get to Labrador by way of Newfoundland.

"February 2nd, 1764, I was dismissed, with prayer and supplication, by the Bishops and Elders of the Church, and set out on foot for Holland, whence I arrived with much difficulty in London, not understanding the English language. After many fruitless attempts to attain the object proposed, I was at last recommended to the Governor of Newfoundland, Sir Hugh Palliser, who received me with great kindness, and even offered to carry me out on board his ship. This I declined, but begged for a recommendatory note to the Governor of St. John's, which he willingly provided for me; and I now went with the first ship to St. John's, where I lodged at the house of a merchant who shewed me all possible civility. I worked here at my trade, and expected patiently the arrival of the Governor. Meanwhile, many people, having heard of my intentions, came to see me, and several proposals were made to me, to establish myself and make my fortune in Newfoundland. As soon as the Governor arrived, he issued a proclamation concerning my voyage to the coast of Labrador, stating my views, and commanding that every assistance should be given me. In this proclamation it is said: 'Hitherto the Esquimaux have been considered in no other light than as thieves and murderers, but as Mr. Haven had formed the laudable plan, not only of uniting these people with the English nation, but of instructing them in the Christian religion, I require, by virtue of the powers delegated to me, that all men, whomsoever it may concern, lend him all the assistance in their power,' etc. This proclamation was the foundation of all that liberty and protection which the Brethren have enjoyed ever since, under the British Government. Having soon found a ship bound to the north, I went on board, and proceeded with her to the north-coast, where, after many fruitless attempts to continue my voyage, I went on board an Irish fishing shallop, which was bound to the coast of Labrador. When we arrived on that coast, I saw the Esquimaux for the first time, rowing about in their KAYAKS, but none were permitted to approach us, being fired upon by our boat's crew. Having once landed, I found their huts, utensils, etc., made exactly in the Greenland fashion. But all my attempts to meet and converse with them were in vain; for it happened, that when I landed, not one Esquimaux appeared, and scarcely had I left the coast, when many arrived. The boat's crew, therefore, laughed at me, and the few who expressed sorrow at my disappointment advised me to return, refusing to lend me any further assistance: I was even told that a resolution was formed to kill all the Esquimaux. All this gave me the most pungent sorrow, and made me cry unto the Lord for help in this distressing situation, so heavy both for my mind and body. As I was once writing down my thoughts in my journal, the master entered my cabin, and seeing me in tears, asked me whether I was going to make a complaint to his owners. I answered, 'No; but I mean to complain of you to God, that He may notice your wicked conduct on the present occasion, for you have taken His name in vain, and mocked his work,' etc. He was terrified, begged I would not do it, for he had offended God too much already, asked my pardon, and promised, that from henceforth he would do everything to promote my design. This he punctually performed, and brought me the next day to Quirpont. Here some people had arrived, who intended to destroy the Esquimaux, and were holding a council for that purpose. I went boldly to them, shewed them the Governor's proclamation, found it difficult to divert them from their evil designs, but succeeded at last.

"SEPTEMBER 4th, 1764, was the joyful day when I saw an Esquimaux arrive in the harbour. I ran to meet him, and called to him in the most friendly manner, addressing him in the Greenland language, which, to my inexpressible joy, he understood. I desired he would return and bring four of the chiefs of his tribe, which he willingly complied with. Meanwhile I dressed in my Greenland habit, and met them on their arrival on the beach, inviting them to come on shore. They cried, 'Here is an INNUIT (or countryman of ours).' I answered, 'I am your countryman and friend.' They were surprised at my address, behaved very quietly, and I continued my conversation with them for a long time. At last they desired me to accompany them to an island, about an hour's row from the shore, adding, that there I should find their wives and children, who would receive me as a friend. This seemed at first a most hazardous undertaking, but conceiving it to be of essential service to our Saviour's cause, that I should venture my life amongst them, and endeavour to become better acquainted with their nation, I turned simply to Him, and said, 'I will go with them in Thy name. If they kill me, my work on earth is done, and I shall live with Thee; but if they spare my life, I will firmly believe that it is Thy will that they should hear and believe Thy Gospel.' I went accordingly, and as soon as we arrived, there was a general shout, 'Our friend is come!' They carried me ashore, and I was immediately so closely beset on all sides, that I could neither stir nor turn about. I endeavoured to make them place themselves in rows before me, which being done, I told them my view in coming to visit them—to make them acquainted with their God and Saviour; and promised, that, if they were willing to be taught, I would return next year with more of my brethren, build a house on their land, and speak to them every day of the way to life and happiness.

"Having entered into much agreeable conversation with them, I returned in the same boat, and staid about a fortnight longer at Quirpont, where I had several opportunities of preaching to the boat's crew, being filled with joy and gratitude to God, who had thus mercifully heard my prayers and helped me.

"After our return to St. John's, which was attended with many hardships, I waited upon Sir Hugh Palliser, who received me with great kindness, and expressed his entire approbation of my proceedings. I returned to England in a frigate, and arrived, November 5th, with my brethren in London. Here, I entered into a negotiation with several gentlemen in office, relating to the proposed Mission on the coast of Labrador, and had several conferences with them, as also with Lord Hillsborough, who made several advantageous offers for the promotion of that cause.

"Having made another voyage to Newfoundland, I returned to Germany and spent four weeks at Herrnhut, where I gave a verbal account of my proceedings to the Brethren, to whom the direction of the affairs of our Missions was then committed. But hearing that an order of council was soon expected by our

Brethren in London, to begin a Mission in Labrador, I hastened to England, where I found things not so far advanced as was expected. In 1767 I went to Zeist, in Holland, where I spent some time with much profit to my soul. But the Mission in Labrador remained the constant subject of my prayers and meditations, nor could I find freedom to accept of any appointment to other places, several of which were proposed to me, believing that God had not caused me to see such wonders of His mercy and preservation among the Esquimaux in vain.

"As the Brethren appointed to manage the affairs of the Unity were going to England this year, I asked and obtained leave to accompany them. On our arrival in London, several circumstances seemed to point out to me that the time was now come when the negotiations concerning Labrador might be renewed, and I therefore delivered a memorial to the Brethren, stating my reasons for thinking that an application to the English government would now be attended with success. I received for answer, that I had their permission to do what should appear most advisable to me in this business; and, having maturely considered my plan, and with prayer and supplication commended myself and the cause I was to serve unto the Lord, I waited upon Mr. Pownall, a gentleman in office, and delivered a petition, praying that a piece of land on the coast of Labrador might be given us, on which we might build a dwelling-house and church, and make a garden. This was well received, but the answer was somewhat delayed. Meanwhile the well-known Esquimaux woman, Mikak, was brought from Labrador to London. She rejoiced exceedingly to find in me one who could speak her language, and earnestly begged that I would return with her and help her poor countrymen, who were almost ruined, many of them having been shot in an affray which happened between them and the English. Her repeated applications were of great use in putting forward the business of the projected Mission, for she was noticed by many persons of rank and influence, and her request attended to. We now received the long-wished for grant from the Privy Council, by which the Brethren's Society for the Furtherance of the Gospel obtained permission from the king and his ministers, to make settlements on the coast of Labrador, and preach the Gospel to the Esquimaux.

"In the year 1769, I obtained leave to attend the general Synod of the Brethren's Church, held at Marienborn in Wetteravia. Here I experienced rich spiritual blessings, and was particularly led by the Holy Spirit to examine, whether my mind and temper were made conformable to the mind and will of my Saviour. I confessed my deficiency in this respect, and prayed him to deliver me from everything, that might either retard the completion of His work within me, or prove injurious to his cause, especially from the natural impetuosity and roughness of my disposition, which, as I was well aware, must give pain to those about me. The Synod resolved, that I should make another voyage to Labrador to examine the coast, and that in the year following a Mission should be established there. My heart and lips overflowed with praise and thanksgiving, that our Saviour had thus far helped us. In the year 1770, some brethren in London, who felt much interested in the Mission, purchased a vessel, with which they resolved to send us to the coast of Labrador, and to supply us annually with the necessaries of life, and, that they might be better able to support the undertaking, they agreed to commence some kind of traffic with the natives. With this vessel, Br. Drachart, (formerly a Missionary in Greenland), Br. Stephen Jensen, and I, set sail, to explore the coast and find a place fit to build on. We made the land at a place called Arnitok, an island about six miles from the spot where Nain now stands. Here we found twenty-nine boats full of Esquimaux, who began to behave with great insolence, and would not be quiet, till the report of our great guns frightened them into order. Having waited two days, we went on shore, met them in a friendly way, and preached the Gospel to them. After this, Br. Stephen Jensen and I went up and down the coast unmolested, seeking a proper spot for building, but in vain. We therefore set sail again, and ran into an harbour, upon the most eastern point of the main land near Nain. From hence, we passed by and between a number of islands and sunken rocks, and were mercifully protected from harm, though obliged to venture along this unknown coast, without charts, or pilots, or any guide whatever. I cannot describe the joy and gratitude we all felt, both for the temporal mercies and protecting care of God, which was every morning new, and particularly that He gave us favour in the sight of the Esquimaux, who willingly sold us their land, and earnestly begged us to return the next year and settle amongst them; as likewise that we had found a spot fit for a settlement, and hitherto met with everything according to our wishes. I had the best hopes, that His thoughts were thoughts of peace concerning this poor benighted nation, and that in His own time, He would glorify His saving name amongst them. We returned to London in autumn, and were employed during winter with building a house of framework, which now stands at Nain.

"April 11th, 1771. I was married at Chelsea to Mary Butterworth, of Fulneck, and in May, we again set sail for the coast of Labrador. I will not enumerate the many hardships and alarms necessarily experienced on a voyage along a rocky, unfrequented, and inhospitable coast, but only observe, that God sent his angels and brought us safe to land on the 9th of August, without the least accident, when we immediately found the spot pitched upon for the erection of our house at Nain. We had great trouble in putting it up, but the Esquimaux who visited us were so obedient and quiet, that we were not in the least disturbed by them. Many were the remarkable occurrences during the years 1771, 1772, and 1773, some of which gave me pain and trouble, but I cannot name them at all: the Lord maintained His work amidst all my mistakes, and in the last-mentioned year, the visit of Br. Layritz to this Mission, by commission of the Elders' Conference of the Unity, proved a great comfort to me and all my fellow-labourers.

"In the year 1774, I received a commission to go with the Brethren Brasen, Lister, and Lehman, to explore the coast to the north of Nain. Just as we were setting out, an uncommon horror and trembling seized me, so that, contrary to my former experience, I was exceedingly intimidated, and wished rather to stay at home.

"We had the misfortune to suffer shipwreck on our return. It had snowed the whole night, and was very cold. A brisk gale sprung up from the north-east, which inspired us with the hope that we should soon reach Nain. September 14th, towards four p.m., we all at once found ourselves in shoal water, which surprised us exceedingly, as we were in the usual channel between Nain and Navon, and more than a league from the nearest island. We tacked about immediately. Scarcely had we done this, when the vessel struck on a rocky bottom, which, as we afterwards learned, is dry at spring-tide. The boat was lowered immediately, in order to take the soundings round the ship, and, as we found deep water at the bows, we proposed casting an anchor forwards. There was too much sea, however, to allow us to row out with it; we therefore let down a small anchor to steady the boat during this operation. But no sooner was the large anchor on board the boat, than the sails got loose, and drove it before the wind; so that it took the men half an hour's hard rowing to get back to the sloop, and reach the rope which we threw out to them. After the anchor was cast, we endeavoured to wear the ship off, but finding that the anchor drove, and that we had now only four feet of water, we were obliged to desist, till the tide should turn, and commend ourselves meanwhile to the mercy of God. We had, however, but slender hope that the ship would hold out so long, as the waves broke over us incessantly, and we expected every moment to see her go to pieces. We secured the boat as well as we could, by means of three strong ropes two inches thick, and, in full resignation to the Lord's will, determined to stay in the sloop till morning, if possible. The wind roared furiously; every wave washed over us; and the foaming of the deep was rendered yet more terrible by the thick darkness of the night. Towards ten o'clock, the ship began to roll most violently, and to drive upon the cliffs in such a manner, that everything on board was turned upside down, and we could not but fear that the timbers would soon part. Shortly after ten, the rudder was carried away by a huge wave, which broke over the whole vessel, and covered us as with a winding-sheet. Our two sailors entreated us to take the boat, if we wished to save our lives. We represented to them the danger of braving so rough a sea in so small a boat; and that, supposing it could outlive that, it must inevitably perish in the breakers on the coast, which we could not avoid in the darkness. We begged them to stay by the ship as long as possible; perhaps we might maintain the post till daybreak, and, at all events, should it come to the worst, we had the boat to fly to. They appeared to give in to our arguments; but we were obliged to watch their motions, lest they should slip off with the boat. We waited in stillness what our dear Lord should appoint for us. "By two o'clock in the morning of the 15th, the sloop had shipped so much water, that the chests on which we sat began to float, and we were obliged to leave the cabin and go on to the upper deck, where a fearful scene presented itself. The middle deck was entirely under water, and the waves were rolling mountains high. All were now convinced that it was time to leave the vessel. But here we were met by a new difficulty. The sea was so rough, that, had we brought the boat alongside, it would inevitably have been stove in. We therefore drew it astern, and, climbing one by one down the anchor-shaft, jumped into it, and through the mercy of God, we all, nine in number, succeeded in reaching it. We now found that we had taken this step only just in time, for two of the three ropes by which the boat was moored had already given way, and the third held only by one strand, the others having parted, so that we should very soon have lost our boat. Our first business was to bale out the water which the boat had shipped in no small quantity. Our oars being useless in such a sea, we let the boat run before the wind, which it did with incredible celerity. We attempted in vain to get under the lee of different islands, as the breakers drove us off from the coast whenever we approached it. At length we thought we saw a prospect of finding harbourage between two is-lands, but we were interrupted again by rocks and breakers. The boat filled with water, which kept us constantly at work, and as there appeared to be no other resource left, we resolved in God's name to run the boat on shore, which was about twenty yards distant, but begirt with cliffs on which the waves were dash-ing furiously. We darted rapidly through them, when the boat struck on a sunk-en rock with such violence, that we were all thrown from our seats, and the boat instantly filled with water. The captain, John Hill, and the two sailors, threw themselves into the sea, and swam to land, which they gained in safety, and from whence they reached out an oar to assist the rest in landing. Br. Lister was the first who neared the shore, but he was driven back into the sea by the violence of the waves. On approaching the rocks a second time, he found a small ledge, by which he held on, till the oar was extended to him by his companions on the strand. I had been thrown out of the boat by the first shock, and resigned myself to the Lord's gracious hands to do with me what He pleased. After swallowing a large quantity of water, I was hurled back into the boat, and, as it drifted to the shore, I succeeded in grasping the friendly oar. At the same time, the Esquimaux pilot clung to my legs, and thus we were both drawn up the rocks together. Br. Brasen thrice gained the rocks, and twice caught hold of the oar, but he was so exhausted, and encumbered besides by his heavy garments, that he could make no effort to save himself, and finally sank. Br. Lehman was heard exclaiming, as the boat struck, 'Dear Saviour, I commend my spirit into Thy hands!' We all thought that he had got on shore, but it pleased the Lord thus to take him to Himself. The rest of us who had reached dry land were rescued for the present from a watery grave, but we found ourselves on a bare rock, half dead with cold, in so dark a night, that we could not see a hand before us, without shelter, without food, without boat, in short, without the smallest gleam of hope that we should ever leave this fearful spot alive. We knew that no Esquimaux were likely to come this way, as they had all resolved to winter to the south of Nain. The cold was intense, so that we were obliged to keep ourselves warm by constant motion. When morning came, we sought for our boat, but in vain: a few fragments of it which had been washed on shore, was all that we could find, and we concluded that it had gone to pieces. We also met with a few blankets, some broken biscuits, and other articles, which we collected very carefully. At low water, we discovered the bodies of our two Brethren lying close together on the strand, but they were quite dead. They were safe from all trouble, and had Brethren surviving to bury their remains, while we had no other prospect than to pine away with hunger, and then leave our bodies to be entombed by birds and beasts of prey. About seven o'clock in the morning, we had the joy to see, first the prow and then the stern of our boat emerging from the water. But our joy was damped on dragging it to land, for the planks were torn off from both sides of the keel, and the few ribs left were in splinters. Happily, however, the prow, stern, and keel, were yet entire. We now set ourselves to repair the boat, impracticable as it seemed with such a lack of materials for the purpose. Yet we contrived to lash the blankets over the open spaces, sewing to them, in addition, all the seal-skins we could muster from our upper and nether garments, including even our boots. We spent three days in these miserable repairs, and, on the 18th, we launched our boat for Nain, which, by the help of an Esquimaux party that we met not far from the settlement, we succeeded in reaching the same evening.

"After our return to Nain, I was overwhelmed with sorrow, spent days and nights in sighs and tears, thought much of my past life, cried to the Lord for help, and forgiveness of all my many failings, and renewed my vows to devote myself entirely to His service. In spring, 1775, I went with the Brethren Lister and Beck to explore the south coast, when we penetrated beyond Old Hopedale, and, after some research, found a spot near Arvertok better suited for the purpose of a Mission settlement than any hitherto discovered. When Br. Liebisch arrived this summer at Nain, he brought me a commission to begin the new settlement at Okkak, north of Nain. I felt not a little anxiety on this occasion, knowing the difficulties attending such a commission, but accepted of it in reliance upon our Saviour's help. Br. Stephen Jensen accompanied me, and we purchased the land from the Esquimaux, placed stones to mark the boundaries, and made a plan for the building. In 1776, the timber was cut and prepared at Nain, and the ship having arrived from England, it was put on board, and we sailed with it to the place of our destination. My wife had lain in but eight weeks, but she and our little infant son bore the voyage very well. We immediately went to work, and set up the house. I had the grace in all trying circumstances to cleave to my Saviour, of whose gracious assistance I had manifold experience. He was with us, and gave us success in our present enterprise.

"Having finished the building of our house, we moved into it, and at our first conference were so united, by the power of Jesus' grace, in brotherly love and harmony, that we made a covenant with each other, to offer soul and body to the Lord, to serve Him without fear, and bear each other's burdens with a cheerful heart: nor did we meet with the least interruption during this whole year, so that I justly count it the happiest of my whole life. I could preach the Gospel to the Esquimaux with a cheerful heart, and the Lord blessed my weak testimony of His death and love to sinners, so that several of them became concerned to obtain deliverance from sin and everlasting life, and most were sober and attentive hearers.

"In autumn, 1777, I was invited to visit Europe, which proved both to me and my wife a great refreshment. Though my wife was so ill at sea, that she never could leave her cabin, and we had three small children with us, two of our own and a son of our late Br. Brasen, whom I was obliged constantly to attend to, yet I remained cheerful, and the Lord helped me through in many remarkable instances. We arrived at Niesky, in Upper Lusatia, in January, 1778, and, both

there and at Herrnhut, were received and treated with the most affectionate regard and love by the congregations. March 10th, our youngest son, Samuel Peter,
departed this life by occasion of the small-pox, and soon after, having received
the needful instructions from the Elders' Conference of the Unity, by whom we
were earnestly commended in fervent prayer to the grace and protection of the
Lord, we returned to Labrador by way of England. The American war raged at
that time, and the seas swarmed with privateers; but we ventured upon God's
help, and sailed without convoy. We saw no enemy, and met with no kind of
disaster; but, when we came near the coast of Labrador, we discovered an ice-
mountain of prodigious extent and height before us, and had scarce passed it in
safety, before it fell to pieces with a tremendous crash, putting the surrounding
sea into the most dreadful agitation and foam. Had this happened but a few
minutes before, we must have perished in the immense ruin. Filled with thanks
to God for our deliverance, we arrived safe at Nain, August 30th, and proceeded
thence to Okkak, where we found twelve baptized, and candidates for baptism.
I was much concerned, how to take proper care of these souls committed to
our trust. During the following three years, which I spent at Okkak, our labour
among the Esquimaux was attended with many vicissitudes; yet the preaching
of the Gospel proved its power in the hearts of many, and in 1781, the number
of baptized Esquimaux amounted to thirty-eight souls, which, with those who
were considered as candidates for baptism, made a congregation of nearly fifty
persons. In autumn, I was called to Nain to assist in the erection of the Mission-
house destined for Arvertok, (now Hopedale), which was conveyed thither and
set up in the year following. My heart rejoiced at the increase of the work of God
in this country; and, when we began to proclaim the Gospel of Jesus in these
parts, it produced blessed fruits in the hearts of several Esquimaux. Some, indeed, opposed the truth with violence, but others came to ask, what they should
do to be saved. During the winter, the awakening spread still further among the
Esquimaux, which made all our trials and troubles appear easy to us, because we
perceived that the Lord was with us and blessed us.

"But now both I and my wife began to feel the effects of age and hardships, and
our strength seemed exhausted. The year 1783 was, amidst all bodily weakness, a

period of blessing for our souls; and though we were quite resigned to the will of our Lord as to our future stay in this land, yet we thought it incumbent upon us to represent to our Brethren in Europe, that, in our present state of infirmity, we were not able to do the work committed unto us in the manner we wished, and therefore proposed to them to take our return into consideration. Meanwhile the Gospel was heard with uncommon attention by the people at Hopedale and its neighbourhood, and we were anxious lest the proper attention should not be paid to the awakened souls. They were exceedingly desirous to know more of their God and Saviour, and we prayed the Lord, that we might have grace to treat them with wisdom and profit. In 1784 we had seventeen candidates for baptism."

Thus far the written narrative of our late Brother is continued in his own handwriting:

He obtained his dismission in the same year, and arrived safe at Herrnhut, as his future place of rest. Though he possessed an extraordinary degree of activity, and his zeal for the service of our Saviour, in which he had experienced many trials and sufferings, was very great, yet he felt no uneasiness in his present situation, but seemed to enjoy true rest and peace in soul and body. He highly valued the privilege of living in a place, where he could daily converse with children of God, and frequently declared his gratitude in the most lively terms, for the love, regard, and active benevolence of the Brethren and Sisters. It was the delight of his heart to attend the daily meetings of the congregation, nor would he ever miss one of them as long as he was able. He also worked at his trade, and endeavoured to earn his own bread as long as his sight would permit.

In the year 1786 he had a stroke, which greatly weakened his nerves, and particularly his sight; yet he consented, in reliance upon the help of the Lord, to accompany some Sisters who were going in the year 1788 to Sarepta, in Asia, as far as Petersburg, from whence he returned safe in September. For the last six years of his life, he was quite blind. Trying as this situation was to a man of his vivacity of spirit, he never murmured, or ascribed it to the hardships he had suffered, but took it patiently, as out of the hand of the Lord, and, by His grace, shewed exemplary resignation and cheerfulness, to the great edification of all who visited him. His conversation was profitable even to persons of rank, who never failed to call upon him when they visited Herrnhut, and none who came hither with a view to profit for their souls neglected to converse with him; for it was plain that what he said proceeded from the experience of a heart living in constant communion with God, and rejoicing in his salvation. His manner was always undisguised, plain, and without any fear of man; but, whenever he was conscious of having given away in expression to the natural impetuosity of his temper, he acknowledged his fault with great concern and begged pardon for it. He grew at length quite helpless, and was the more thankful for the faithful care and nursing of his wife. His son was a continual object of his prayers, and he never failed daily to offer up prayer and supplication for all children of God everywhere, the church of the Brethren, and in particular for the Missions among the heathen, and especially that on the coast of Labrador. Last autumn, he grew considerably weaker, and was subject to frequent fits of faintings, oppression in the breast, and headaches; yet the Lord blessed the medical assistance he received so as frequently to remove the pain attending these maladies. He thought and spoke much of departing to the Lord, and his joy was great indeed, when he meditated on the promise given by our Saviour in His word, concerning the bliss of His redeemed ones, when, delivered from all the sorrows and vicissitudes of this earth, they shall flee him face to face. When the Sacrament was administered to him last Maundy Thursday, he said: "This will be my last on earth." On the 12th of April, he fully expected that he would be permitted to depart that day, but though disappointed as to the day, he was remarkably cheerful, and even in the night of the 15th rose out of bed to help himself to some refreshment. But early in the morning of the 16th, he began to shew symptoms of fast approaching dissolution, which was hastened by a fit of apoplexy about half after five o'clock, when his soul went over into everlasting bliss, having spent little short of twenty-two years in this vale of tears. Upon a slip of paper, found after his decease, were these words. "I wish the following were added to the narrative of my life: on such a day Jens Haven, a poor sinner, who in his own judgment deserved eternal condemnation, fell happily asleep, relying upon the death and merits of Jesus."

NEWMAN

After the Moravians, the next non-governmental organization to exert control over Labrador society was the Hudson's Bay Company. While it was by no means the first fur-trading company in Lake Melville and along the coast, it became the most influential. By the time the Bay came to Hamilton Inlet, the island of Newfoundland had representative government, but little was known of it in Labrador. In the absence of government, elected or appointed, the Company, with all of its self interest, filled the role of patron.

It was the coming of Donald Smith that brought the Bay in Lake Melville its golden age. He was not only factor but also judge and doctor. He grew turnips, cucumbers, and peas and built a three-kilometre track, Labrador's first road, for his ox-drawn sulky. When fur revenues declined, he exported red berries and salmon packed in ice as well as canned salmon. He noted the presence of minerals that would later be developed. Shrewd and imaginative, he went on to head the Hudson's Bay Company, as Peter C. Newman records here in this authoritative and witty excerpt from his history of the Bay.

One of the greatest popularizers of Canadian historical fiction, Newman paints Smith, warts and all, in both suspenders and top hat, in the store as well as in the drawing room. Later Smith would be an eminent Canadian financier, his money-raising for the CPR warranting the historical picture of him driving the last spike. As well, he was a member of Parliament and a prime ministerial envoy in the Red River Rebellion. But as Lord Strathcona, he never lost interest in Labrador; for years the MV *Strathcona* plied the stormy water off the Labrador coast, bringing medical succour to the descendants of those whose furs he had bought in North West River and Rigolet.

Peter C. Newman

"GROWING UP COLD," FROM *Merchant Princes*, 1991

Donald Smith's peremptory arrogance was particularly galling to those aware of his inconspicuous beginnings. He was born on August 6, 1820, at Forres, a storied Scottish trading town in that brooding countryside where Shakespeare's Macbeth and Banquo encountered the prophetic trio of witches. One of three sons and three daughters, he was much less influenced by his father, a shopkeeper clinging to solvency with alcoholic indecision, than by his mother, Barbara Stuart, the feisty and admirable Highland dame who brought up the family.[25] "Her voice was low, and she disliked loud noises," her son remembered. "She set great store by courtesy and good manners, and our bonnets were always off in her presence. She insisted on scrupulous cleanliness in house, person, and apparel, and herself set an example of perfect neatness in dress." Among other things, she taught young Donald to recite metrical versions of the Psalms then popular in Scotland, one of which he repeated "without error, pause or confusion" on his deathbed.

While his elder brother attended the University of Aberdeen and studied medicine at Edinburgh (he became a doctor on the northwest frontier with the East India Company and a major in the Army Medical Corps), young Donald was articled to Robert Watson, Town Clerk of Forres. He spent most of his time hand-copying documents, but apprenticing to succeed Watson was far

---

25 Alexander Smith, the father, was a brother of George Stephen's mother; Barbara Stuart was a Grant on her mother's side, distantly related to Cuthbert Grant, the Métis leader who staged the massacre at Seven Oaks. (See *Caesars of the Wilderness*, Chapter 7.)

too humdrum a prospect to enlist his energies or talents. He was much more excited by the arrival on retirement leave of his mother's brother John Stuart, a doughty former Nor'Wester who had been second-in-command during Simon Fraser's daring exploration of the Fraser River in 1808 and later served as a Chief Factor with the HBC. Stuart promised to recommend the youngster to George Simpson, the HBC'S all-powerful overseas Governor, and Donald set out on foot from Forres to Aberdeen, where he caught a London-bound schooner. Armed with his uncle's letters of introduction to Simpson and other influential Montrealers, Smith sailed for North America on May 16, 1838, aboard the *Royal William*, a 500-ton timber-trade windjammer. Just before leaving, Smith wrote to his mother, breathlessly enumerating the wonders of the British capital: "I have already visited the West End of town, walking all the way from the Mansion House, where the Lord Mayor resides, to Hyde Park, where the aristocracy are to be seen riding and driving.... Here the trees and flowers are a good month in advance of ours in Scotland, or at least in Forres. Had I been in the Park an hour later or earlier, I should have been rewarded by the spectacle of Her Majesty. The Queen and the Duchess of Kent, her mother, drive every day, I am told; so I shall hope to enjoy the privilege."

Much of Smith's fifty-day voyage was spent studying the only reference book aboard, Francis Evans's *The Emigrant's Directory and Guide*, which stuffily advised: "Canada is a country where immigrants should not expect to eat the bread of idleness, but where they may expect what is more worthy to be demonstrated as happiness—the comfortable fruits of industry." Smith landed in Montreal at a time when nationalist stirrings had reached their culmination in the Papineau rebellion, and his vessel passed the steamer *Canada*, carrying the last of the *Patriotes* of the 1837 uprising to Bermudan exile. British North America then had a population of 1. 2 million, with most of the lands north and west of what is now Ontario belonging to "The Governor and Company of Adventurers of England Tradeing into Hudsons Bay." Montreal was a crude bush settlement numbering scarcely 30,000 inhabitants, its only patch of sidewalk being in front of the Cathedral of Notre Dame. On dry days, blinding limestone-powdered wind eddies made walking difficult, while rain turned the streets of the hilly town into mudslides that made getting about all but impossible. McGill College consisted of a medical faculty staffed by only two part-time professors.

Smith walked upriver to Lachine, where Simpson administered the Hudson's Bay Company's 170 trading posts, scattered not only across the Prairies to the Pacific but also down to the Oregon Country, through half a dozen future American states, south to San Francisco, and as far west as Hawaii. The young Scot was hired at "£20 and found" a year and assigned to counting muskrat skins in the Company warehouse.[26]

The initial drudgery in the Lachine warehouse was a useful lesson for Smith in learning how to differentiate the various qualities of pelts, and he soon graduated from muskrat to grading beaver, marten, mink and otter, learning to judge the value of a silver fox by the number of white hairs in its glossy patina. Buoyed by his uncle's introductions, he spent a memorable evening mingling with some of Montreal's leading citizens, including his host, the international financier Edward Ellice, HBC Arctic explorer Peter Warren Dease, Duncan Finlayson, then about to leave for his new assignment as Governor of Assiniboia at Fort Garry, and Peter McGill, chairman of the Champlain and St. Lawrence Railroad and president of the Bank of Montreal. The Forres apprentice would leave Lachine soon afterwards and not return to Montreal permanently for another thirty years, but the memory of the sweet adrenalin of social acceptance he had experienced that brief, magic evening never left him.

The circumstances of Smith's departure remain mysterious. One version involves Frances Simpson, the Governor's vivacious wife, twenty-six years younger

---

26 At the time, apprentice-clerks worked five-year terms at a gradually increasing salary that culminated at £50 in the final twelve months. If their records were acceptable, they could then sign up for another five years at £75. A third contract with a £100 maximum was offered to the best of them, followed, after a total of at least fifteen years of loyal and efficient service, by a chance to be promoted to a Chief Trader's and, eventually, Chief Factor's commission. These two ranks were eligible for shares in the Company's annual profits that ranged as high as £2,000. Retired commissioned officers received half-pay for seven years. All HBC personnel were granted free board but had to buy such basic goods as soap and boots from Company stores, at a one-third discount. They were responsible for providing their own bedding and room furniture. Typical yearly food rations consisted of 240 pounds of flour, 20 pounds of tea, 120 pounds of sugar, 10 pounds of raisins, and 5 pounds of coffee or cocoa per person. Their annual liquor allowance was two gallons each of sherry, port, brandy, rum, Scotch whisky, and all the lime juice they could drink.

than a husband who spent most of his time away on inspection tours. According to a fellow apprentice, the lonely Mrs. Simpson, who "took a friendly interest in the 'indentured young gentlemen'...was attracted by the simplicity and gentle address of the new-comer's manners." They seem to have enjoyed an innocent flirtation, the odd boating excursion on Lake St. Louis and several cups of tea. Harmless it may have been, but the Governor was not amused. He called Smith into his office soon after his return and was heard shouting that he was not about to endure "any upstart, quill-driving apprentices dangling about a parlour reserved to the nobility and gentry." Smith was abruptly banished to the Company's career purgatory, the King's Posts district at Tadoussac.

Owned by the French Crown before 1760 and mainly by British monarchs thereafter, the seven tiny trading locations had been leased in 1830 by the HBC, which also rented the more easterly Seigniory of Mingan. Trade was slow because most of the territory had been beavered out and the Company did not enjoy the monopoly there it had elsewhere. Assignment to the region was regarded as an unwelcome alternative to being fired.

Tadoussac itself was one of the oldest trading points in North America; this was where Jacques Cartier had obtained his furs in 1535. Summers were cool and damp, the winters bitterly windy; nothing disturbed the rugged, sterile geography—certainly not the huddle of huts in the hollow of a mountain without even the presumption of a stockade, near the confluence of the broad St Lawrence and the deep Saguenay. That was the Tadoussac of Smith's initial assignment. He spent seven of his most unhappy and unproductive years in the area, trading principally for fox, marten and sable pelts with the Montagnais Indians, who paddled down annually from the Quebec Labrador plateau. "You would have to travel the whole world over to find a greater contrast to the Scotch than these same Indians;" the young trader wrote home. "If civilisation consists in frugality and foresight, then the Montagnais are far worse than dogs, who at least have sense enough to bury a bone against an evil day. In some of their lodges even before winter has properly begun their rations have come to an end. Everything about the place has been swallowed that can be swallowed, and starvation stares them in the face. They stalk in the tracks of a solitary caribou, and in their excitement forget their own hunger, but this does not make their families forget theirs. The caribou eludes them. They wander farther afield and at length bring down a bear. They cut him up and return to find their families dying or dead, which is what happened last month near Manwan Lake."

Smith tried to keep his spirits up by reading such classics as Plutarch's *Lives* and Benjamin Franklin's *Correspondence*, but often he found himself scanning every line of outdated copies of the Montreal *Gazette* and Quebec *Mercury* left behind by travellers. At this point he also suffered a strange "second sight" experience, dreaming that Margaret, his favourite sister, on a sickbed in Forres, was muttering "Donald! Oh, Donald" with her dying breath. Letters that reached him later revealed she had indeed died, of smallpox, on January 12, 1841, at the very hour, allowing for difference in longitude, of Smith's nightmare.

Eventually placed in charge of Mingan, the most remote of the King's Posts (opposite North Point on Anticosti Island) and an even more dreary locale than Tadoussac, Smith incurred the wrath of Simpson, who arrived for a surprise inspection in the summer of 1845. The post's account books, which to Simpson were the Company's secular bibles, were far from satisfactory. Following his visit, the Governor sent the young clerk this devastating assessment: "Your counting house department appeared to me, in a very slovenly condition, so much so that I could make very little of any document that came under my notice. Your schemes of outfits were really curiously perplexing, and such as I trust I may never see again, while letters, invoices and accounts were to be found tossing about as wastepaper in almost every room in the house...if you were but to give a few hours a week to the arrangement of your papers your business would be in a very different state to that in which I found it."[27]

Smith hoped to redeem himself by submitting a neater set of accounts the following season, but on September 29, 1846, his house burned down. He had

---

27 Smith's successors at the various King's Posts where he had kept the books had similar complaints, and the originals in the HBC Archives are scrawled with frustrated notations such as "Hang Donald S.!" or "Damn Donald Smith, I cannot make head or tail of this!" But there is evidence that Smith, rather than being careless, was beginning to exercise his penchant for secrecy and that the accounts were kept in a code to which he alone had the key.

been briefly away on an errand, and one of his assistants had salvaged most of his belongings. With the Company records destroyed, Smith turned so despondent that he descended into a highly uncharacteristic public display of anger and frustration. According to eyewitnesses, he danced around the still-burning pyre of the tiny post, feeding the flames with his clothes and private papers, cackling incoherently: "Let them go, too, if the Company's goods have gone!"

The following winter he suffered from snow blindness and feared he might become permanently sightless without medical attention. Not bothering to wait for official permission, he boarded the HBC's Montreal-bound supply ship *Marten* and reported his condition to Simpson. The Governor immediately ordered an eye examination. When the attending physician found no clinical problem, Simpson accused his clerk of malingering, then interrupted his catalogue of Smith's perfidies in mid-flight to offer him another chance.

It was not a typical Simpson gambit. Smith had now been with the Company most of a decade. He was twenty-eight and had done little to distinguish himself. Yet Simpson must have sensed a potential in the intense but sensitive young Scot that Smith himself probably didn't recognize. At the time, the HBC was busy trying to revive its Labrador district, partly to counter competing freebooters moving in from Newfoundland and also to prevent nomadic Indians from evading their Company debts as they migrated from one post to the next.

Simpson's business acumen was attracted by that mammoth, frigid Labrador peninsula for precisely the reason no sane man wanted to go there. For its latitude, it was the coldest place on earth. Mercury froze in thermometers. Snow fell early and deep; it stayed so long that winter stretched over nine months. To survive in that harsh climate, animals had to grow extra thick, tight pelts that fetched premium prices at the HBC's London auction house. As early as 1828, a Company trader named William Hendry had sailed up the Ungava coast from Moose Factory in James Bay as far as Richmond Gulf and explored an overland route into Ungava Bay. Two years later, Nicol Finlayson established Fort Chimo about thirty miles above where the Koksoak River flows into Ungava Bay. There he waited twenty months for the local Naskapi to appear. When they finally did, Finlayson described them as "the most suspicious and faithless set of Indians I ever had to deal with...they must be sharply dealt with before they are properly domesticated." The primitive tribe, then numbering less than three hundred, suffered from having no internal political structure—no chiefs, no social organization larger than the family, no ritual ceremonies to facilitate trade, no formal alliances with any other groups. They were subsistence hunters, living off migrating caribou, and it was mainly their addiction to the HBC's rum and tobacco that prompted them to become trappers. As trade expanded, Simpson opened Fort Nascopie on the northwest arm of Lake Petitsikapau (near present-day Schefferville) and purchased from some Quebec merchants their post at North West River on Esquimaux Bay (now known as Lake Melville) about halfway up the eastern Labrador coast.

Just before Smith came to Lachine with his eye problem, word had reached Simpson that Chief Trader William Nourse, then in charge of that faraway region, had been incapacitated and badly needed medical attention. The Governor directed the "malingering" Smith to leave immediately at the head of an emergency winter relief party to North West River. Although he had come out of the bush seeking solace for bruised eyes and for an even more seriously damaged ego, Smith now found himself with a challenging option. The bristle of his Scottish nature had been touched: if Simpson was mean enough to issue such an order, Donald Smith was too proud not to obey it. Accompanied by a young HBC clerk named James Grant and three Iroquois boatmen, Smith accomplished the thousand-mile journey in record time, almost starving to death along the way and being lost for extended periods in snowstorms. It was the toughest physical ordeal of his life. Years later he refused to dwell on the details, though it is known that two additional Indian guides hired along the way starved to death.

Once in Labrador, Smith found Nourse paralysed, the victim of a serious stroke. While Grant stationed himself at North West River, Smith took temporary charge of the smaller but more strategically located post at nearby Rigolet. The North West River station (near modern-day Goose Bay airport) was tucked into a clearing on the shore of a 110-mile-deep salt-water gash in the frowning eminence of the unexplored Labrador coast, with mountain ranges rolling out of both horizons. Rigolet sat nearer the Atlantic, at the mouth of the rocky gorge that joined Hamilton Inlet to Esquimaux Bay. The unpredictable riptides of those treacherous narrows had already claimed many an over-confident vessel, including the British man-of-war Cleopatra. Smith placed the gravely ill Nourse aboard the annual supply ship, and by September his successor, Chief Trader Richard Hardisty, had arrived from Montreal. Smith was promptly relegated to his earlier rank of clerk, though he was delighted to welcome his new superior and especially his accompanying family. Hardisty, who had served in Wellington's army as an ordnance officer in the Peninsular campaign and the Battle of Waterloo, came to Labrador accompanied by his Mixed Blood wife (Margaret Sutherland) and their lively daughters, Isabella, Mary and Charlotte.[28]

While the Hardisty family moved inland to live at North West River, Smith remained at Rigolet. Under his direction, the little station became more than the mother post's maritime outlet. He met head-on the marauding free traders who were attempting to lure the Naskapi to their shore trading posts, ranging far back into the fur country to finalize his trades and claim *de facto* exclusivity over a territory outside the HBC's Charter.

Though he could move fast on snowshoes, Smith acquired few of the proficiencies of frontier life. He was a terrible shot, attempting to down birds by firing without first taking the trouble to aim, and there is a record of his bagging a lone wolf, which he noted proudly in a letter to his mother. He never learned to ride, though he introduced the first horses to Labrador, and could not properly handle a canoe. He very nearly drowned when a kayak he was attempting to paddle overturned after only a few yards. "I went straight home and took a glass of wine," he later recalled, confessing, "the only time, by the way, I ever tasted liquor by myself." Yet he could be brave, too, and when the *Marten*, sailing out of Rigolet, ran aground, he personally commanded the rescue boats that saved

---

28 Each of Richard Hardisty's six sons joined the HBC, with varying degrees of career success. The best known of the sextet was his namesake Richard, who rose to the rank of Inspecting Chief Factor and in 1888 was appointed the first senator for the old Northwest Territories, representing the district of Alberta. Richard's granddaughter Isabella, known as Belle, married James Lougheed, himself named to the Senate for the Northwest Territories in 1889 and knighted in 1916. One of Senator Lougheed's grandsons, Peter Lougheed, was the longtime premier of Alberta.

Peter C. Newman

cargo and passengers though not the captain, who committed suicide rather than face the wrath of the HBC Governor.

By the autumn of 1850, Smith was writing letters directly to Simpson, not exactly disparaging Hardisty's efforts but clearly implying that the Company might expect better returns from the district if a younger Chief Trader from, say, Forres, were in charge. For his part, Hardisty seemed genuinely impressed with Smith, recommending him to Simpson at every turn. These exchanges produced results in 1851, when Hardisty requested permission to leave Labrador on furlough the following year. As soon as it was agreed that Smith would temporarily replace the older man (though still in his rank of clerk), he grew bolder in his criticisms. He wrote to Simpson that Hardisty was much more suited to a great inland post than to the actively competitive Labrador situation and criticized the Chief Trader for not seizing the local commerce more energetically. He openly attacked Hardisty's slackness in the face of increasingly vicious competition and criticized his plans for diverting staff and funds to improve some of the local Company posts. None of this backbiting seemed to disturb Hardisty. "He is all fire, and indefatigable in his endeavours to promote the interests of the Company," he wrote to Simpson about Smith, "and having a thorough knowledge of the business carried on in this district, I consider him in every respect competent to succeed me...."

On July 8, 1852, only four years after arriving in Labrador, Smith was formally promoted to commissioned rank and placed in charge of the Esquimaux Bay District. "I have much confidence in your energy and desire to turn the business to good account," Simpson wrote, adding an important codicil, "but trust you will adopt a greater degree of regularity and system than characterized your management at Mingan. You no doubt remember that on my visit to that place while you were in charge, I had occasion to note what appeared to me a want of method and punctuality in your household arrangements, as well as in the shipping office business. I now revert to this matter in the most friendly spirit with a view to putting you on your guard against a repetition of such a ground of complaint which in your present more important charge might be productive of greater injury...." Smith took the admonition under advisement and moved out of the barren clapboard hut at Rigolet to the much grander Chief Trader's residence at North West River, which boasted a winter fireplace and a summer veranda.

The senior Hardistys departed alone. Their youngest daughter, Charlotte, had recently died, while Mary had wed an HBC clerk named Joseph McPherson and moved away to Kibokok, a small post northwest of Rigolet. Isabella, who was twenty-three when she first arrived in Labrador, had shortly afterwards married James Grant, Smith's companion on the long overland trek from Montreal. Because there were no clergy in that empty place, the ceremony was performed by the bride's father. He had no official authority to do so since he was neither a clergyman nor sanctioned to perform marriages by his HBC commission because Labrador lay outside the Company's Charter territory. Such country marriages were routinely performed by anyone or no one, requiring only the consent of the couple involved. James and Isabella had a son named James Hardisty Grant in 1850 but shortly afterwards separated when, as Donald Smith explained, Isabella's husband exercised "no command of his passions." Just before Richard Hardisty left Labrador, Isabella and Smith decided to marry and went through an informal ceremony on March 9, 1853. The presiding official at that wedding was none other than the groom himself. Smith later claimed that he had been appointed a lay preacher by the Governor of Newfoundland and thereby had properly sanctioned Isabella's first real wedding (to himself), making an ostentatious fuss about the illegitimacy of her previous match.

The following year saw the arrival of Margaret Charlotte, Isabella and Donald's only child. To everyone's embarrassment, including his own, James Grant remained at the post another two years. Smith did his best to undermine his rival's career, complaining to Simpson that young Grant "has [very] much to learn before becoming an experienced trader, his long residence at North West River having been anything but advantageous to him, as while there he had little or nothing to do with the trade, and literally got no insight into the manner of keeping accounts which beyond a blotter or an invoice, he was rarely, if ever, permitted to see." In the same letter he lied to the Governor about his own romantic involvement: "It is just possible these remarks might lead to the supposition that I myself have been an unsuccessful suitor, but the case is so far otherwise that up to the present time I have not been so presumptious [sic] as to aspire to the hand of any fair lady."[29]

It took Smith seven years to acknowledge his marriage in correspondence with Simpson. Even then he referred to having wed a "Miss Hardisty" rather than any "Mrs. Grant." Although it was a routine event in the bush ethic of the time, the episode was magnified and made infinitely more wicked by the rub of Donald Smith's Presbyterian conscience—a flexible instrument that failed to censor some of his far more questionable pecuniary ploys.

During his twenty years in Labrador, Smith developed the cold insensibility that allowed him to betray political and business associates at will. The pressures that made him one of the most frigid, class-conscious aristocrats of his era had their origins here in Smith's lonely treks through the boreal wilds of Labrador, apparently forgotten by the glittering world he had barely glimpsed before his exile. He never admitted that there might have been a dramatic event to blame for his bitter turn of spirit. All he would say was that Labrador had toughened him. ("A man who has been frozen and roasted by turns every year must be the tougher for it, if he survive it at all.")

The Naskapi who traded in Smith's territory experienced grave difficulty adapting their lives and seasonal cycles to the white man's requirements. Their main source of food was the enormous herds of caribou migrating semi-annually across their turf. The Naskapi had to stalk the animals through deep snow, which required infinite patience and great skill—until, of course, the local HBC posts supplied them with guns and powder. These made the hunt relatively simple: so simple, in fact, that the old skills were quickly lost, and the hunters soon could not survive without weapons. Their independence had been broken. "Because

---

29 James Grant left Labrador and the HBC in 1855, moved to New York, remarried, and became a successful stockbroker. His son with Isabella used Smith's name and was mentioned in Smith's will, but when the family left Labrador, he lived apart from their household.

the HBC controlled the supply of ammunition," the late Dr. Alan Cooke of the Hochelaga Institute pointed out, "the Naskapis were obliged to spend part of their time trapping furs, mainly marten, whether or not they preferred to hunt caribou. When they abandoned their traditional techniques of hunting caribou for the new technology of guns and ammunition, they gave themselves into the traders' hands. There was no return."

The Naskapi were further endangered because the marten trapping and caribou-hunting seasons coincided. The marten is one of the few woods animals that carries almost no edible meat, so the Indians were caught in a vicious circle: they could hunt caribou—their sustaining food supply—with guns and ammunition that the traders would provide only if they turned in good marten skins. But they couldn't keep themselves alive long enough to trap the pelts because that diverted them from pursuing the caribou. This dilemma could be avoided if the local HBC trader was understanding and advanced them the necessary ammunition, assuming that over several seasons he would come out ahead. (One such Company clerk, Henry Connolly, himself part Indian, did just that and found himself reprimanded for having been too generous in his allotments.)

During the winter of 1843, three families of Naskapi numbering twenty souls starved to death within sight of the HBC's Fort Nascopie, then managed by Donald Henderson. Three winters later, three dozen more Naskapi died, and in the winter of 1848 there was mass starvation in the area. Most of this was caused by Henderson's denial of enough ammunition to the local hunters. Henderson eventually left the service; but word of the disaster had spread, and Simpson demanded an explanation. As Alan Cooke observed: "Indians starving to death was, of course, regrettable, but the loss of hunters in a sparsely populated region that produced valuable furs was a serious matter.... During the space of six years, a 'proud' and 'independent' population of 276 persons had been reduced to about 166, with what hardship, misery and sorrow, and with what effects on family and social life no one today can imagine or understand."

These tragic events at Fort Nascopie had taken place before Smith's arrival, but there is evidence that he was directly involved in the subsequent famines of the mid-1850s, the worst of them all. For one thing, it was well-documented knowledge within the service that "no matter how poor the post might be, Donald Smith always showed a balance on the right side of the ledger." At this time he was trying to make the best possible impression on Sir George Simpson and his principals in London by maximizing fur returns at any cost. During the 1857 deliberations of a British Parliamentary Select Committee studying the HBC, a letter was tabled that former Chief Trader William Kennedy had received from a Company clerk at Mingan. "Starvation has, I learn, committed great havoc among your old friends, the Nascopies, numbers of whom met their death from want last winter; whole camps of them were found dead, without one survivor to tell the tale of their sufferings; others sustained life in a way most revolting, as [sic] using as food the dead bodies of their companions; some even bled their children to death, and sustained life with their bodies!" In another undated note, Kennedy's correspondent stated that "a great number of Indians starved to death last winter, and _____ says it was _____'s fault in not giving them enough ammunition." Since these blanks appeared in the Committee's final report, Smith's name was not officially linked with this harrowing episode, but he was in charge of the region at the time, and because of the very tight control he maintained over trade expenditures, it is not unreasonable to assume that the famine, which wiped out so many lives, was his direct responsibility.

Smith's own reminiscences of Labrador mention few specific Indians; the natives were simply there, like trees or the wind. As the HBC's Chief Trader, he was North West River's community leader and that often meant medical duties as well. He achieved modest success treating wounds with a pulp made from the boiled inner bark of juniper trees, a method authenticated by Lord Lister, who introduced the principles of antiseptics to surgery in 1865.[30]

At night, the vast Labrador stillness was interrupted only by the hoot of a hungry owl, the subdued yelp of a dreaming dog or, during spring breakup, the thud and groan of heaving ice. Smith stayed up late, writing to his mother, reporting on each day's events even though his letters could be sent out only once a year

---

30 Fifty years later, Smith, now Lord Strathcona, delivered a lecture on his primitive but effective techniques to medical students at Middlesex Hospital in London.

via the HBC's supply ship. That vessel also brought Smith annually from London issues of *The Times*, which he carefully perused over breakfast—each newspaper exactly one year after publication. On Sundays he held religious services with his household, HBC staff, and a dozen or two Indians as the congregation. "To-day we all assembled for prayers in Mrs. Smith's parlour—every mother's son scrubbed and brushed up to the nth—even old Sam, who looked positively saint-like with a far-away expression, although he was probably only counting the flies which were buzzing on the window pane," one of Smith's clerks later recalled. "We sang three hymns, I coming out particularly strong in the Doxology."

To provide his family with a proper diet, Smith sent to the Orkney Islands for hardy seed grains, poultry, and cattle and to Quebec for horses, sheep, goats, and an ox. On seven painstakingly cleared acres, fertilized by fish offal, he grew cucumbers, pumpkins, potatoes, and peas, ripening more fragile fruits and vegetables in a large greenhouse. Charles Hallock, afterwards head of the Smithsonian Institution in Washington, was exploring "bleak and barren Labrador" when he happened on Smith's farm. "Then the astonished ear is greeted with the lowing of cattle and the bleating of sheep…," he wrote of his visit in *Harper's New Monthly Magazine*. "In the rear of the agent's house are veritable barns, from whose open windows hangs fragrant new-mown hay; and a noisy cackle within is ominous of fresh-laid eggs.…Donald Alexander Smith, the intelligent agent of the post, is a practical farmer, and, by continued care and the employment of proper fertilizing agents, succeeds in forcing to maturity, within the short summer season, most of the vegetables and grains produced in warmer latitudes." To complete the tableau, Smith built a two-mile track from his house to the farm—Labrador's first road. In summer he would take Isabella for sundown outings aboard his ox-drawn carriage.

North West River hosted another distinguished visitor in 1860, Captain (later Admiral) Sir Leopold McClintock, then in command of HMS *Bulldog*, a Royal Navy survey ship, who had gained prominence during the search for the Franklin Expedition. His log provides one of the few physical descriptions of the Labrador Chief Trader at this point in his life: "Smith…was about forty years old, some five feet ten inches high, with long sandy hair, a bushy red beard, and very thick, red eyebrows. He was dressed in a black, swallow-tail coat, not at all according to the fashion of the country, and wore a white linen shirt....His talk showed him to be a man of superior intelligence." McClintock in later years told Smith that he had foreseen at the time of the visit "Labrador won't hold this man...."

To prove his worth to Simpson, Smith not only reported unprecedented fur-trade returns but began diversifying the district's sources of revenue, expanding into a salmon fishery (and eventually cannery), exporting barrels of seal oil, and even sending out rock samples for geological tests. "I believe," he predicted, "that there are minerals here which will one day astonish the world."[31] The most beneficial consequence to Smith of these activities was that the fishery, which involved shipping the iced or canned salmon to England, gave him an excuse for corresponding directly with HBC headquarters in London, bypassing his aging benefactor, Sir George Simpson. The Company eventually formalized this arrangement by separating Labrador from its Lachine administration, so that Smith now reported to London on all his activities. In one of his last letters, Simpson warned his ambitious protégé against being heavy-handed trying to impress his British superiors: "When you want to bring any point strongly under notice, it will have a better chance by putting it in a few clear and appropriate words than by spinning out the theme so as to make it look important by the space it occupies on paper."

Smith ignored that advice and his letters grew embarrassingly verbose. As soon as he felt a promotion might be in the works, Smith did what he would always do in later life: he remarried Isabella. This particular wedding, performed either by an itinerant missionary or a visiting sea captain, must have been staged so that Smith could not only salve his conscience but also specifically refer to the sanctioned ceremony in his London correspondence.

He was appointed Chief Factor shortly afterwards at the age of forty-four, and in 1864 decided to take his first home furlough in twenty-six years. After visiting

---

31 Simpson ignored the rocks, but Smith proved to be correct. The area he pinpointed as having valuable mineralization later proved to contain a huge iron-ore body, as well as lesser quantities of titanium, lead, zinc, nickel, asbestos, columbium and uranium.

his mother, who was now almost blind, he hurried to London and spent the balance of his leave trying to ingratiate himself with the bigwigs at the HBC's Fenchurch Street head office. He met the Governor, Sir Edmund Walker Head, his deputy, Curtis Miranda Lampson, Eden Colvile, a future Governor, and most of the other important Committeemen. "Smith, the officer in charge of our Esquimaux Bay District," Colvile reported to Lampson, "...gives a good account of our affairs in that region, where he has been stationed for many years. As he is just the sort of man you would like to meet, shrewd and well-informed upon every topic relating to that *terra incognita* of the British Empire, I have asked him to dine with us on the 14th." Lampson, in turn, had been predictably charmed by the visitor who from now on was a marked man in the Company's future planning. There was one small hitch. As was their custom, on the eve of the departure of the supply ship (which would carry Smith home), the Company directors proposed hearty toasts to the well-being of its Commissioned Officers. But when he was called on to reply, Smith had vanished. Overcome by a fit of shyness, the Labrador trader (who had known he would be requested to speak and had prepared his notes) could not face the distinguished gathering, afraid that he might somehow blot his copybook. It was the first public evidence of Smith's well-deserved reputation as a clamshell.

Smith was back in North West River by August 1865, but the visit had transformed him. He now knew there was still a chance for him to participate in the great events of his time. Despite his geographical isolation, Smith's reading of the Company's prospects was amazingly accurate. Perhaps because he had never been there and had no vested interest in the HBC's main fields of operation in the West, he could clearly see that the future would not run with the buffalo hunters or fur-trade canoes but with the oxcarts and ploughs of settlers come to claim new lives in the new land. "I myself am becoming convinced that before many decades are past," he wrote to a friend at the time, "the world will see a great change in the country north of Lake Superior and in the Red River country when the Company's licence expires or its Charter is modified.... You will understand that I, as a Labrador man, cannot be expected to sympathize altogether with the prejudice against settlers and railways entertained by many of the western commissioned officers. At all

Peter C. Newman

events, it is probable that settlement of the country from Fort William Westward to the Red River, and even a considerable distance beyond, will eventually take place and with damaging effect to the fur trade generally."

Within a year, the newly self-confident Smith had decided to visit Boston, New York and Montreal. Ostensibly, his trip was to view the sights of the city he had left twenty-seven years earlier. "The object I most wanted to see…," he explained, "was the Victoria Bridge, which is truly one of the wonders of the world, and gives Montreal an unbroken railway communication of 1100 miles…." In reality, he was seeking belated acceptance in the milieu he felt had suddenly become accessible to him.

The most important part of his trip, at least in retrospect, was a call on his cousin George Stephen. The son of a Banffshire carpenter, Stephen had emigrated from Scotland at twenty-one to become a clerk in his cousin's Montreal drapery business, in which he eventually purchased a controlling interest. He studied banking and had become associated with some of Montreal's leading entrepreneurs. The cousins' initial meeting was hardly propitious. The Smith family had gone shopping, and Donald had purchased a gaudy crimson carpetbag for his Labrador journeys. Later, he wouldn't discuss his encounter with Stephen, but when Isabella was asked whether his cousin had been happy to see Smith, she burst out: "Really, why should Mr. Stephen be glad to see country cousins like us—all the way from Labrador? I wish… [my husband] had waited until he had met Mr. Stephen before buying that red carpet-bag. But he wouldn't let me carry it and the rest of us waited outside." Still, Stephen did condescend to introduce his country cousin to friends at the Bank of Montreal and leading members of the city's shipping circles. All the talk was about domestic electricity, still considered a risky innovation, William Gladstone's surprising eloquence in the British House of Commons, Alfred Tennyson's latest verses and the prospects for Canada under Confederation, then only a year away.

Smith reluctantly returned to North West River, but mentally he had already left Labrador behind. Simpson had died in 1860, and his successor, Alexander Grant Dallas, had transferred the Company's North American headquarters to Red River, closer to its main field operations. Since Smith was already in charge of the Labrador District, all that remained in Lachine was direction of the relatively minor Montreal District, which included the King's Posts along the St Lawrence as well as trading forts up the Ottawa and Mattawa rivers. After the retirement on June 1, 1869, of the Montreal District's Chief Factor, E.M. Hopkins, "Labrador Smith," as he had become known in the Company's service, was appointed to the job.

And so Donald Alexander Smith came out of the wilderness at last. He was forty-nine years old, his skin permanently blackened by two decades of snow tans, his nerves as taut as those of a sprinter about to start his championship turn.

Montreal by then had a population of about 100,000, its streets had been paved and its harbour dredged, and the city (North America's tenth largest) was becoming an important rail and steamship terminus. Smith fitted in as if he had never left. "I called to-day to pay my respects...," reported a startled HBC Factor shortly after Smith's arrival, "and was surprised to find him so affable and assuming, with no trace of the ruggedness you would associate with the wilderness. You'd think he had spent all his life at the Court of St James instead of Labrador...." One reason Smith was treated as an equal by members of the city's financial elite was that in a modest way he was already one of them. During most of his time in Labrador he had put away virtually his entire HBC earnings (arriving in Montreal with a grubstake of $50,000), but starting in 1853 with the purchase of two shares, he had also quietly been accumulating stock in the Bank of Montreal. Coincidentally, George Stephen had been doing the same thing, and within the next four years the two cousins would become the Bank of Montreal's second-largest shareholders.

Overnight, Smith seemed to be launched on the urban business career that had been his long-postponed dream. Then a confluence of circumstances intervened and hurled him into the vortex of a strange rebellion gathering momentum halfway across the continent.

CAMPBELL

In the 1770s, English traders had begun moving into Hamilton Inlet. The first two white English settlers were William Phippard and John Newhook, but Ambrose Brooks, the father of Lydia Campbell, soon followed. From him and others like him sprang a trapping and fishing culture unique in its time and place. It is perhaps best described in its maturity by Elliott Merrick:

> *Our friends the scattered families that inhabit the bay are a unique race with oddly combined cultures: Scotch Presbyterian in religion, old English in speech and custom, Indian in their ways of hunting and their skill with canoes ascending the big rivers bound for the trapping grounds far in the country. Sometimes it seems as though they had taken for their own the best qualities of the three races, the Eskimo laughter-loving happiness, the Indian endurance and uncanny instinct for living off the country, the Scotchman's strength of character and will.*

Lydia Campbell was part of this culture in its early years. Many in Lake Melville still trace their ancestry to her, including Doris Saunders, the originator and guide of *Them Days* magazine, a fine Labrador publication now celebrating 25 years of capturing, as has no other, the history of Labrador and its people in their own words and stories. Courage, humour, love, endurance, and good common sense allowed this outstanding woman to live to a ripe old age and to set down for us in her charming prose the story of her life.

Lydia Campbell

EXCERPT FROM *Sketches of Labrador Life*, 1894

Introduction

By Rev. Arthur C. Waghorne

(The Evening Telegram, Dec. 3, 1894)

I sent an old woman of Groswater Bay an exercise book and begged her to write me some account of Labrador life and ways. I venture to transcribe this account for your readers. It is the production of an old woman of seventy-five years of age, born and bred on the Labrador, never having been off that coast; of one who has never been to school, has led and still lives a hard laborious life. Yet trying as such a life must be, her own account will manifest clearly and therein lies much of its pathetic beauty and interest...that her life has had its absorbing and varied interests and pleasures; in fact, has yielded to her, as in the case of hundreds of others who inhabit the weird and lonesome coast, as much comfort and peace and happiness as fall to the lot of most of us. I have a special regard for the Labrador people, who in many cases, in spite of the inevitable hardnesses and trials, show so much contentment and undoubtedly find life as much worth living as other people do; who in the face of many disadvantages under which they live will bear favourable comparison with the labouring classes, probably the world over, certainly with those of England. True they fall short in educational matters but the wonder is not that they have so little but that they have so much. The census of 1891 tells that of the 2,719 people who live between Hamilton Inlet and Blanc Sablon, 1,750 can read and 906 can write; northward, owing to the Moravians work, things are better. It is not uncommon for Newfoundlanders to get some of the Labrador people to conduct their correspondence for them in the summer; and at present there are Labrador folk in St. John's who have never been to school who do the same for their less educated neighbours.

I have given this account as it was written by my friend, omitting only a sentence or two of no particular interest and gave a little punctuation to render the narrative clearer.

Sketches of Labrador Life
By Lydia Campbell

You must please excuse my writing and spelling for I have never been to school, neither had I a spelling book in my young days, me, a native of this country, Labrador's Hamilton's Inlet, Eskimaux Bay. If you wish to know who I am, I am old Lydia Campbell, formerly Lydia Brooks, then Blake, after Blake, now Campbell. So you see ups and downs has been my life all through and now I am what I am, Praise the Lord.

Mulligan River, Dec. 25, 1893

Christmas Day, as this is a holy day for us, the Campbells and Blakes, my family, I think that it is a nice time to write a few loins a beginning of this winter. I have been busy all this fall in particular for I has a lot to do with three little motherless granddaughters to work for, besides their poor father and a big son, going off hunting and wood chopping, and the weather so cold as to need all the warm clothing possible to warm them. The weather 30 below zero and myself off to my rabbit snares, about four miles going and coming over ice and snow, with snowshoes, axe and game bag. Some days I has three rabbits in one day caught in snares, for I has about twenty-four snares, made myself to set them up, and I gets pretty tired some days. Often the snow is deep and soft; just now about three feet deep in the woods. But it can't be expected otherwise with me to get tired, for I am now the last birthday seventy-five years old, last month, first November. I have seen many ups and downs, but the good Lord has safely brought me through. I have been bereaved of my first husband and four of his children. One is left me, Thomas Blake. It is his little children that I has to look to now. The present husband that I has now is nearly as old as me. We has three children left by him out of eight, two boys and a girl. They all has a family to look to. We have been meeting some times and when our large rivers freezes over hard enough to go on, then comes the time for trouting, as we call it, then most of our granddaughters and grandsons gather together here to trout. Our family, John Campbell's children comes along shore, about four miles he lives. My oldest son Thos. Blake, my first husband's son, and his motherless children is near us next door, none near us but them and our dear childrens' graves. We can see their headstones at a distance over on the cranberry banks, so pretty it looks in the fall when we come home from our summer quarters, above 70 miles from here. When we are sailing up in our large boat, to see the ducks in our bay when we are nearing the river, and when we get ashore to the pretty river banks and walking up the path under our large trees, some 50 feet and some 60 feet high, we often meet with a flock of partridges flying up to the trees. Before we get to the house, so pretty, then is the scramble among the young ones who will see the first turnips and potatoes, and sure enough all around the house is green with turnip tops, and between them and the wall of the house is hanging red with moss berries, some falls.

Then we're home to our winter house for ten months or more, but we are home among ducks, partridges, trout, rabbits, berries, traps for snaring foxes, martens, wolverines, mountain cats, muskrats, minks; and most of all them kind of things that I have caught in my lifetime. Sometimes we has a visit from black bears and wolves, which the former we often gets, but seldom the wolf. Some winters we have the luck what we calls about here, to get a deer or two. Sometimes formerly we have had as many as ten or more in one winter. I myself have been deer hunting and shot two, but my sister, Hannah Michelin have killed 3 in one spring, that was while I was still afraid to shoot. I shut up my little children in the house, took my gun, went down to the river and waited for 2 deer and shot one of them and my eldest daughter came to me with a paddle to strike it on its head, and the dogs heard the report of the gun and came running down so we had work to drive them away. When it was dead, Susan [Blake] and me took it on a komatik, took it to the house, skind it and jointed it and put it away in the store, and hear comes the joke. When Mr. Daniel Campbell and Thos. Blake, my eldest son, came home with two deers hearts, I give them some dinner. While they were eating I went out to the door slyly, and took in my deer's heart and put it with the other two, and when I asked them how many deer they had killed they said only two. I said, What three hearts is this? They looked foolish like. They said some Mountaineers must have brought it hear. I said no Indians has been hear. They asked each other who killed it. I said I killed it today. Then we all had a laugh over it. That was our happy days, with all our little children round us. That was about 30 years ago now. Ah, well, all works together for good we are told, (such is life).

Now when I look back it seems not very long yet. When I look for my Susan, she has been married, left our home, went away with her husband, a Hudson Bay Company clerk, and they had three children. She died up to Seven Islands. Now it is only him and his son left. He is a young man now and a clerk up in Montreal in Canada.

Mulligan River, Jan. 1, 1894

While I was writing the above, all our young people went off to the Hudson Bay Company's post to keep New Year's Festival, that is, Elizabeth Campbell, our daughter-in-law, Esther Blake, our girl and our boy Henry R., out of our house. Thomas Blake and his son out of their house, they lives next door to ours, and James Baikie and his two sisters, Annie and Ellen, went from their house and left their mother and two little boys with her. She is our only daughter now, our Margaret, and out of my old sister Hannah's and her husband's house her two granddaughters, Alice and Elizabeth Meshlins and two boys, Meshlins. So there was a lot of people, about 50 in all, one gentleman with Mr. Cotter, the Hudson Bay clerk, and our mountainmen and four Canadians who come hear to this country. While they was gone our daughter-in-law, Martha Campbell, came hear. She lives about four miles from hear, it was snowing and blowing, she staid one night and went off in very bad weather on her snowshoes.

Her husband, John Campbell, tracked a large bear this fall after a little snow fall and came up to it while it was eating blueberries around the stump of an old tree. He shot and wounded it, it moved itself and reared and bellowed frightful, stood on its head and he shot it again, it came down then. He had hard work to get it out from the country, far in the wood. We found it nice, the piece we had, for it lived on blueberries. It was very fat.

Now this is the 13 or 14 of January—14—Monday. We are all scattered today, my husband Dan Campbell is not home yet from Labacatto, he went there to see our brother-in-law, Mensie Michelin [Mercier Michelin from Trois Rivieres], a Canadian about 70 years old, not able to work now, but his wife Hannah, my old sister, she is over eighty years old, yet she takes her gun and axe and game bag and shoots a white partridge or two now and then. I have known the old woman fighting with a wolverine, a strong animal the size of a good size dog, she had neither gun nor axe, but a little stout stick, yet she killed it after a long battle. It was very wicked. I wish there were more Hannahs in the world for braveness. She brought up her first family of little children when their father died, teached all to read and write in the long winter nights, and hunt with them in the day, got about a dozen foxes and as many martens. She would take the little ones on the sled, haul them over snow and ice to a large river, chop ice about 3 feet thick, catch about two or three hundred trout, large ones, and haul them and the children home perhaps in the night; catch salmon and seal in the summer the same way. And then the men of the Hudson Bay Company's servants used to get her to make a lot of things, that is, clothing, such as pants, shirts, flannel slips, draws, sealskin boots, deerskin shoes, caps, washing, starching, ironing and whatnot. She had all the care of the children when a widow. In that way a Canadian got married to her, for she had every thing to his hand such as we used in this country. My husband is come home from Labacatto, and he found them not well in health. My poor sister have not been able to go to her rabbit snares for 2 weeks, she is failing fast now, she tried to sing hymns, morning and evening, with prayers, and she can't go on now. Poor old Saint, may the good God be with her to the end. Dear friend, I have been a widow like her, brought up children while a widow, but had a brother-in-law and a mother-in-law, and 3 sister-in-law, but I still worked pretty hard to bring them up. I would have been content if they let me have the money that he left me and the children but that was denied us. Ah well, I am alive and well and able to work yet with some few little motherless granddaughters and grandsons, the Lord be praised—and when I feel lonely I goes and sees the graves, altho under the ground and deep snow, I oft sing an hymn or a prayer—comes home light-hearted, and think it won't be long now my journey home thank God, then to a better country, a better home for us to journey to, although I am only old Aunt Lydia Campbell now.

Mulligan River, Jan. 1894

My dear friend you want to know more things about the country ways and fashions. It has been my home ever since I was born, and seen many ups and downs.

When I first remember to see things and to understand, I thought there was no place as good as this in the world, and that my father and mother and my two sisters was the best in the world; but our good father used to take me on his knee and tell me his home was a better country, only it was hard to live there after his good old father died and his mother could not keep him so he stayed with a good old minister, that was living in the parish, until he died, and then he came out to this country to try his fortune in this place, for the wars was raging between England and France and all over the world and the pressgangs were pressing the young men, so he and a lot more English people came out up the shore for woodcutters, seal fishing and cod fishery, which was the highest in those days. Then of course they had to take wives of the natives of this country. There were very few white men here, much less women, but if it was not for the cursed drink what the agents and the few merchants had hear, the men would have been happy together with their wives. We lived up in the river head at a long bay and no one nearer to us than about 70 miles. I think we lived happy together until our dear Elizabeth got married to a young half-breed as we was. That was my first grief, to leave her behind. She got married down to Cuffingham, near our summer houses, cod fishery place. Well, that is about 60 years or above, that break-up in our family circle. Our dear father had no school book to teach us in nothing but a family Bible and a Common Prayer Book to teach us in. So we learned a little that way. So if you see a lot of mistakes in the writing and spelling please excuse my scrall for I have never been to school nor any Church until lately. We has one to go to now when the weather permits in the summer. We has strong tides to go against sometimes for it is far from our summer house, the Methodist Church, there is a good many people gathers there.

Mulligan River, 1984

As I am writing these few lines before day-light, my use in the morning is rising to make a fire, say my prayers, wash lamps, get on breakfast, sweep the house, after then I am ready with our Bible and hymn books and prayer books on the table near while sitting. Then I say it is time to call up my husband and our big boy, Hugh R. Palliser and my girl Esther Slake and my daughter, Ella, our little pet, for her poor father is in the States, sick in the hospital up in Portland. So after breakfast, I, old Lydia Campbell, 75 years old, I puts on my outdoor clothes, takes my game bag and axe and matches, in case it is needed, and off I goes over across the bay, over ice and snow for about 2 miles and more, gets 3 rabbits some days out of 20 or more rabbit snares all my own chopping down. It looks pretty to see them hung up in what we calls hystys. And you say, well done old woman. But such is life in Eskimaux Bay among the few whites, some is naked and half-starving for want of exercise, and a little more. But I am not able to see to thread my needle in the night without the little ones to do it.

Well, as I said, I can't write much at a time now for I am getting blind and some mist rises up before me if I sew, read or write a little while. In that way I can't tell you as I could if it was a while back. I had my life wrote down and gave it to Rev. A. A. Hadams, but he lost it. So, good friend, if it goes wrong, correct it for me please. We are not in want so far, but we don't know how long. We are told that whoever trusts in the Lord shall want no manner of goods. We growd our own potatoes up hear, and turnips, and we gather berries, enough of 2 or 3 kinds for the winter, and we gets ducks in the fall and a scattered seal, and when the ice comes in on the rivers, for we has two, then is what we calls trouting. Our grandchildren comes from their homes to gather hear. Then the ice is alive with trout, fine large ones and little ones. What fun following the trout as the tide rises or the falling water, all chopping ice as hard as they can. I have been late and early at it with my children. Alas, where are they now? Still there is four left yet, but not with us…families of their own.

Lydia Campbell

1894

It was thought that if anyone had deers meat cooked and seal meat cooked at the same time and someone eat it at the same time they had to eat a little white moss between the two to keep the two kinda apart, it would keep them from quarreling inside the person. Well, I suppose that was the doctor's laws among them that made that law, if they had any, so we heard in my young days. And the children were kept from eating different kinds of berries according to their names. But those laws and customs are all done away with now…and they are so very few now. In that time the Eskimos was very plentiful all along the shore and islands, but now there is only about 6 or 7 families now, since I remember…but where are they now? The poor souls had no religion whatever, besides the rum bottle and biscuits and butter, more shame to the white people that sold them rum and tobacco, that wretched weed.

How tall and pretty that first race of Eskimo was, and so lively. When I first remember to have seen them but they have dwindled down so small with the cursed drink and tobacco smoking, and keepin and pressing down under the debts to the agents. Now they are few and small, half-starved and possibly naked, but one blessing is done for them, that the agents of the Hudson Bay Company doesn't bring rum or spirits for sale, such as they bring is drunk among the higher sort, I suppose no fear for them to be found fault with.

About forty years ago there was a gathering at our house on a Sunday. We saw two smart young men rowing or paddling along by the shore going home. They had been to the post and had brought a gallon or two in their kayaks, nice looking boats, skeeming along so pretty in the sunshine. We lookt at them for the last time, poor boys, William Meeks and John Palliser. As the evening was drawing near we heard them call out to each other. They was on the opposite side of the river from us. The river was about a mile across from where we were. While we was kneeling down to prayers we heard them fire 2 or 3 guns, then we heard them call out, but we thought after a while they must have been upsot and going to each others help both had found a watery grave. That bad rum had sunk both body and soul into…where? Oh, where? How many have lost their lives in this manner?

I knew one large family, a nice lot. They was thought a good deal of by the white people and they seemed happy together, the old woman so proud of her big grown-up sons, 4 in number, her boys, a daughter and her husband. Ill luck befell them. The youngest, a young man, fell through the ice and got drowned. One shot himself, so I heard, accidentally. Another got some rum, and started to go down outside with his wife, both got drunk. The wife lay down in the boat and her husband got knocked overboard while steering with an oar and was never found. When the other boats came up to them, no one was in the boat but the wife…asleep. She never woke up until the others awoke her. She was friendless, and at the end of summer or a month or 2, there was another young man, which was a English half-breed, wanted a wife so he bethought himself, why not go get that young widow. So he and his brother, Andrew, took a boat and went off to the island where the tents was. He went into one tent with his brother, found the widow and got down by her side. No sooner then when he asked her to be his wife, they heard someone walking very heavy, so they lookt to the door and sure enough, in came her husband in size and shape with a dicky on his body…hood up over his head, and he came up to where they was sitting and put his hands out towards her. She leaned back trembling with fear and trembling. When she lookt up he was gone. The people in the tent never saw him go out but vanished out of sight. Strange to say, about a month after he went and got married to her, but after few years they parted again.

When his poor old mother heard what had be fallen her third son, she nearly went out of her mind. When her last child died she did not live long after, to the sorrow of most of the white people, for she was a mid-wife for their wives. Well, one day when the men and women and children were all out of the tent, she hung herself up to one of the poles of the house or tent down at Indian Stanhan. We the Blake family went down that way fishing it a while. The day she was buried, Captain Norman and his planters buried her, that same day we got there. What lamentation there was that day. It seems a long time ago to me but not a secon in our Maker's eyes. I was about 20 then, I think, I never kept an account of the time or how it went, but I was teaching the children of the large family that I got married into. I could not write then but I could read and teach them to read, sing hymns and to pray oft, as my dear old father teacht me.

There was no school teachers nor ministers, them times, hear in this country.

Jan. 1894

Well, I never seen a ghost in my life, and I hardly believe there is none that will hurt anybody providing they don't keep their minds on such things. The greatest ghost I ever saw was myself. When I do anything as a mistake I call myself a stupid ghost. But I know of different people living near our summer place that was drove out of their house different times by a middle aged woman which died under her husband's care about 30 years ago. Now she came to a strange death, not to speak of, and yet she dwindled away till she died, and she could not bear to see her husband and a girl that they was keeping, but what the reason was, I could not larn. But we know that he wanted the girl for a wife. Yes, he could often see the ghost of his wife troubling him often. He was an Englishman. Wherever he went he could see her, so we heard, and the people that lived in the house afterwards was troubled as well.

Mulligan River, April 7, 1894

My dear old friend;

Since I last wrote on this book I have been what the people calls cruising about hear. I have been visiting some of my friends all though scattered far apart, with my snowshoes and axe on my shoulders. The nearest house to this place is about 5 miles up a beautiful river, and then through woods, what the French calls a portage it is what I calls pretty. Many is the time that I have been going with dogs and komatik, 40 or 50 years ago with my husband and family, up to North West River, to the Hon. Donald A. Smith and family to keep New Year or Easter. But my children grew up, 10 in number, some got married, some died, young men and women, some in the bay, a daughter, Margaret Drake. I have visited last month, on my way up to Sebaskachu, a mountain near by, up to see my dear old sister, Hannah Meshlin [Michelin], who is going on for 80 years old now and she is smart yet. She hunts fresh meat, and chops holes in 3 foot ice this very winter and catches trout with her hook, enough for her household. Her husband is not able to work he has a bad complaint. My husband and me went up last month to see him, or them. Was not they glad to see the oldest couple in the bay besides themselves. We driving with two dogs and a komatik, that was ten miles from them. When Easter time was drawing near we came home, in that Blessed season to pray and read over our Blessed Saviour's death, and on Good Friday our minister Mr. Hollett came with his driver, John Graves [Groves], and had service on that Sunday evening…a beautiful sermon to that day. Easter Eve he stayed with us and Easter Sunday morning I was glad to see 2 of my young women, granddaughters, Maggie and Sarah Campbell, to help us cook and to hear him preach. Then in the evening the minister and driver and the 2 girls and me and our girl Esther Blake went down to John's house, and we had great times singing and praying. It was a good time, in one of my sons house with his numerous family, 4 miles from hear, the nearest house to us. Easter Monday evening Esther and me walkt home from John's on the pretty ice and Mr. Hollett and the driver came back after us.

1894

There were landed here some people looking for a place, I think. These 2 people were given provisions and were promised to get picked up the next year, but the people never came back for 3 years, so my father told us, for he saw them when he came from England, as a prentice boy, a few years after. Well, they went to a place to live in which there was a river and plenty wood, and that river was called English River to this day. The Indians Mountaineers, and Eskimaux was at war with each other then, but they was kind to the whites. As their clothing was worn, they went to the Eskimaux (for they was plentiful at that time) and got seal skin clothes from them and meat to eat. When the white people came back to see whether they was dead or alive, they found them drest like the natives about hear at that time. When they went on shore and these two, William Phipperd and John Knocks [Newhook], went to meet them, the sailors and whoever went ashore, they thought it was savages and they got afraid until they called out and told them it was friends instead of foes. They stayed a few days with them and bid farewell to them again. But they landed more white people to a place called Lister's [Lester's] Point to this day. About this time people began to settle, one after another, mostly French people, few English, for everything was plentiful at that time. People could stand on the rocks and hook fish ashore on the beach and spear the salmon that was swimming along shore. I heard Father say that people could not row up and down the river with any tide, they would have to wait until the tide would turn for to clear the fish and caplin away before they could row through them. Everything was so plentiful. The white whales was in the bay then, so was the walrusses and the white bears. I have seen but one of each kind since I remember. There is a lot of partridge and rabbits and foxes and martens, but they are far in the country. That is what most people depends on for their provisions, deer. Even I got one out in the landwash this winter I mean near the waterside in the woods. Well, as I was saying, the people has to go further into the country now for furs, and deers and otters and beavers. I have sat and shot deer myself, when I was young, and I have seen the deer in the country when me and my dear sister-in-law, Elizabeth Blake (poor girl, gone long ago), standing at our door and looked at 101 deer walking, so pretty on the beautiful ice; how pretty they looks. That is long, long ago, when I was living with my first husband and my father.

The Eskimaux's Notion about the Flood,
Handed Down From Generation to Generation
May 24, 1894

They had it to say that once upon a time the world was drowned and all the Eskimaux were drowned but one family, and he took his family and dogs and chattles and his sealskin boat and kiak and komatiks, and went on the highest hill that they could see, and stayed there till the rain was over, and when the waters dried up they descended down the river and got down to the plains. When they could not see any more people they took off the bottoms of their boats and took some little white pups and sent the poor little things off to sea, and they drifted to some islands far away and became white people. Then they done the same as the others did, and the people spread all over the world.

Such was my poor father's thought, the poor people can read it for themselves in the Bible what few there are in this bay. They say that the thunder came about after an old woman was replening a seal skin, and the skin did rattle so like all sorts of seal skin will after they are dry, and rubbing and tramping on them they will get apt. So they said that the seal skin blew away up to the clouds and began to rattle and that is has been thundering ever since betimes.

There is a big rock about a half a mile from our summer house with a large crack in it, and the natives hear about said every time that they passed that rock there would be a little woman looking out of the rock or standing by it, and that the rock goes by the name of Angnasiak, meaning pretty woman. We pass that rock every day in the summer, for our salmon nets is alonside of it. The only thing alive that is of any consequence was a deer standing by that rock about 60 years ago and my poor husband came out of the woods and shot it, and it howled past and lodged against the rock, and we saw it for years after it was done.

Mountaineer's Superstitions

There is up the main river, a large fall, the same that the American and Englishmen have been up to see. Well, there is a large hole, or whirlpool at the bottom of the fall. The Indians that frequent the place say there is three women...Indians... that lives under that place, or near it, so I am told, and at times they can hear them speaking to each other louder than the roar of the falls. There was a good old man came here from Canada, by the name of Lowe. He took an Indian wife, and they used to pass up and down that place, winter, spring and fall, and he said that he have heard for truth that he have heard them speaking. I think it must have been the different sounds of the water passing down in the everlasting rapid hole. Well, the poor man died 2 years ago. He had a dream and I will tell it to you as I heard it from him.

He told me that he was thinking that he was not going to live long, and that he did not feel happy at times. He thought that he was going on a journey, and was going to cross a large river in company with a lot of Indians, and they crossed on foot over the water, he thought, and he thought he was going to get into a boat which was left behind. As far as he lookt at the Indians, Mountaineers, they crosst in their canoes, and he began to cry and wisht that he could cross over to the pretty country. So something seem to tell him to come. When he put his feet into the water, he did not sink, but went across easy, but when he came to the bank at the side of the river, he could not get up for a long time, but when he got up over on the top of the hill he saw such a pretty country it made him wonder. He saw a large plain and it was shining bright and so pretty, he did not know how he felt. There was a point of pretty shining woods and he saw the Indians passing the point of woods. And when he saw them going on he wisht he was among them. While he lookt and lookt, he saw a woman with her son passing the Indians, coming towards him with a fine looking jug and large pitcher in her hand. She came to him and offered him a drink and her pretty little boy lookt at him so pityful and he made a motion for him to drink. When he drank he felt so light and so happy and before he could see where they went he turned to go back to his wife and people. He got home and told them, they said it must have been Jesus and his mother. He woke and behold it was a dream, but it seemed to make his life happier, poor old man. I was sorry that I could not see his end to read and pray with him.

My Silliness in My Younger Years
July 26, 1894

There has been many strange things happening to us in this world. I remember as having no better thought that when a little child died, that his or her soul would be lost (as many are thinking yet) unless they was christened. So one day as I was getting myself and children, 2 little uns, one 3 weeks old and the other 5 years old, to see my rabbit snares, I put my little baby, after putting on the hood to put my three weeks old baby in, on the bed. It rolled on to the floor and stund itself for a little while. I got a fright because she was not christened. So I took the book and baptized it with my dickie and out-door clothes on, and my Sarah, 5 years old, standing by. The father and grandfather, and Aunt Sarah and Uncle George was off hunting. I alone, reading to it. When she could suck I thought she was all right, and I took it on my back, and lead the other by the hand with my axe, through the snow, to my rabbit snares and got a few rabbits…not for want of hunger…but for custom. Such was life among the half-breeds in Eskimaux Bay. That same time that I have been writing about, 3 days before my little Susan was born, my husband, William, was out looking for a place to set traps. He went up along shore 3 or 4 miles distant from our new habitation and saw 3 fine large deer and shot them all. He came home and told us about the deer. His mother and sister and brother went off with him and left me and my little girl, Sarah, and brought home the deer after skinning and jointing them up. They had a little boat load. This was Saturday, I think, and little Susan was born on Sunday evening. I was nearly catcht alone in child bearing far away from other habitation. Well, that was the little girl I christened about 3 weeks after she was born, the one I thought I killed, when she rolled off the bed, when I was going to take her out to my rabbit snares. Well, you see ups and downs has been my life.

I have been cook for that great Sir D. D. Smith that is in Canada now, at that time he was at Rigolet post (HBC), a chief trader only. Now what is he so great? He was seen last winter by one of the women of this bay. She went up to Canada and came back this summer. He is grey-headed and bended, that is Sir. D. D. Smith.

Life among the Natives in Eskimaux Bay Long Ago
Dul de Sac, August 1, 1894

My dear friends:

You will please excuse my writing and spelling, for I has to look from the paper for what I am doing…it swims by me, my eyesight is dim now, and I has a lot to do besides.

When I was about 11 Years old, after my poor mother had died, and Father took me to live with an old Englishman by the name of John Whittle, and his wife was blind and lame. I lived with the poor little woman, and her old man never took her out at all, but when he was going to their summer house above 10 miles from there. I used to listen to her talking about her young days. She was a native of this country, and before John Whittle took her she was married to one of the first Englishmen that visited this country, but as the Eskimaux was not civilized at that time, her half-brothers killed him while crossing from Double Mer through the woods, going for two large nails to build a large boat to cross to this bay where we are living now. They was going to a port about 90 miles from Double Mer, and as the distance was so far for them, when they got half way across the neck, they killed him. And the other man was left with his wife and this poor man's wife and her little boy. The little half-breed boy died when he was playing out-doors.

Well, that was a long time ago. I was not thought about and I am 75 now and my present sister Hannah is older than me and our eldest sister was five years older than she, and that was about 10 or 12 years before Father married to my mother. Ah, my dear mother, ah my dear father, where are they now? Mother died saying the Lord's Prayer and my dear old father died singing a hymn, with, Oh Lord remember me, at the end of every verse. So died my poor parents, I hope to meet them in a better world. My good mother has been dead and buried so long ago that people that lives there in winter says that the large juniper and white spruce is now very large, growing on her grave and two old Englishmen by her side. No one can see the mounds now. I remember that time so well when Father met us at the door as we came home from seeing our rabbit snares, with a book in his hand, and told us she was dying. We all kneeled down near our good mother, breathing her last. By the time Father was done reading and praying, she was gone. Oh, what did I do? Where to go? Far from any other habitation, only 5 of us, but the Lord was with us.

I will tell you now how I past that winter, 3 or 4 years after my good old mother died, when Father took me to live with that poor blind and lame woman. We would often be left alone in the fall and winter. Old John Whittle and Father, Ambrose Brooks was his name, they said one day that they had a lot of socks and vests to make, and that little Lydia was too young to make them for the winter, that they would have to look for a woman somewhere to help me. I was glad to think that I was going to have a chum with me. Off they went and was gone for a day or two. I was left alone with that poor little blind woman for the first time in my life. I had never been parted from my sister Hannah before and I found it lonely. So they came home with a paralitic woman and when this poor thing tried to show me how to make things, and cut out things, that I had to make, she was worst than me, for she jumpt and trembled so, did poor native Betsy, that she would give up, and then the blind Sarah would slide along on the bench, for she could not walk, and put her fingers on it, she would run over it and tell me what way to do it. I was then about 11…no wonder I found it rather hard at that time. Well, I would laugh at them sometimes when they had rum. In that days they used to have booze, they called it. They would be jealous of each other, the blind woman and the paralitic woman while the licker lasted, one speaking in Eskimaux language, the other in broken english. Then they would laugh sometimes, and the old John Whittle would call out at them so rough that they had to be quiet. Well, that was strange to me.

About Winter Weather

So the time came for Betsy to go home and I was left alone again and I missed the poor Eskimaux woman. In the winter I was left alone with the lame woman, Sarah by name, and the weather was so cold that Father and John Whittle could not get home, for the cold and drifting for about a week and I was so afraid I would be stifflet in the drift geting water from a distant brook. Behold me, about 11 years old, with my little dickie on made out of kersy and my serge frock under. The little woman said to me, "Are you afraid to go?" "A little," I said. "Well, then," she said. "I will sit here and sing as loud as I can and that will keep you company." But when I got out as far as the porch, I lost the sound of her voice. Poor little woman with her native dress and a dickie and breeches on and little seal skin boots on her feet, on a little stool plaiting deer sinew for to sew on boot taps.

That night after the storm, I was sleeping with the old woman, and when it was daylight, she then woke me up and said, "Get up, Alakalouksvah, for it is day." It was a pet name she called me in Eskimaux, and when I woke I could not see any light. I told her it was dark yet and very dark. She told me the sun must be shining. To please her I got up and I told her, "I cannot see anything without a lamp." "Ah," she said, "We are snowed up. The house is buried up child." "What shall we do?" I said. She told me it is nothing strange in the winter after a snow storm. She told me to go in the porch and look up and see if I could not see some light green. Yes, I saw light green when I opened the porch door nothing but a hard wall of snow, no person near for miles and miles, I did not sit down and cry, but took a wooden shovel and got up on a high bench and tried to punch a hole through the snow. After a long while I made a hole big enough to go through, then I could breathe free. When I got a hole big enough to creep through, I took an axe and chopt a hole large enough to walk through. The two men came home and found us living, ever after that I was sorry to see Father going away.

Still she told me that her husband was hard to her, and he used to leave her alone, she was blind and lame. He used to leave her and her little boy with no provisions, but some little biscuits and a little flour, when that was gone they had nothing to eat but dog's feed. He an Englishman, she a poor native of this large lake, with her little half-breed boy. In that state my father found her one day when he went to visit to her house. Father said he was hungry. She said she had nothing to eat as well as Father and would he get something. As there was a lock on the door, he could not get in so he raised the roof and took some flour and pork, molasses and tea. Her husband told her not to unlock it or he would beat her. She said he would. So Father cooked it and told her and the little boy, Henry, to eat as much as they wanted, and he would pay for it some way or other, and if her husband spake to her about it or ill-used her, he would hammer him, then he would be beat so he could not beat her again.

The end about the blind woman. That same boy, when he grew up to be a man, took a wife or concubine and ran away from his father and mother and lived in the woods for a while. When his father hunted him like a wild beast with a gun to bring him back home, he got my first husband, a youth then, William Blake by name, to go with him. They found them sitting by a fire. He took hold of his son and made him go home with him, but he did not shoot him. He told his mother, she was blind then, that he could not live with his father. She told him to go and God bless him and her too. That was the last she heard him speak, for he took his wife and a boat, in the night, and ran away again, to a place called Back Bay, and killed a large black bear and salted meat for winter use, on the mainland to a friend's winter house. But alas, they never eat any of it, for they went off to an island far off from the land and the boat drifted away, and they lived twenty days by the work of his gun and they made a shelter out of sod and grass and died in each others arms, and were not found till the winter, poor people. It was sad news for the poor mother.

The times have changed now from them times that I have been writing about. The first time that my dear old father came from England what few whites was hear they was scattered about hear and there. It was lovely, he said often about hear, no one to see for miles but Eskimaux and Mountaineers and they was plentiful. He said that dozens of canoes of Mountaineers would come down out of the Big Bay as it was called then, what is now called Hamelits Inlet or the Large Lake. They used to come skimming along like a flock of ducks, going outside egg hunting on the island. Well, I know it is a pretty sight to see a lot of birch canoes shining red in the sunshine. I have seen them paddling along, I have, men steering, the women paddling and the children singing or chatting…where are they now? Hardly ever see a family now except in winter when we will, now and then, get a visit from a family or two. Oh our Indians have been killed with drink, the dirty tobacco and strong tea. How few they are now.

August 3, 1894

I have seen 15, as far as 20, Eskimos seal skin tents in my time scattered hear in little groups not far from each other, 5 or 6 tents together and such a bustle, women cleaning seal skins and covering kiaks. Their little boats. The men out on the water after a large scove of seals, throwing their darts at the end of their houliack harpoon strap. They use a bladder, mostly young seal skin skinned on the round and made tight, to float a seal after being harpooned. What work to kill them then. It was pretty to see them at that time. I do not know when I saw the last seal skin tent, the few that is left is living in wooden houses, and I seen one kiak this summer, only one now! There was only 3 or 4 small families before but the World's Fair people is come now. They are across on the By Island, we are just going over to see them. Mr. Campbell, and Betsy Campbell and me and Esther Blake and Fred and Mary came on. Well, off we goes, a pretty day, I would like for you to see it.

Well, we has been over on By Island and saw the most of them, how changed all can talk english and dress like the people of another country. They has the picture of the World Fair in different forms.

My dear friends, my time is too short to write much longer. We are now going to get our winter fish while we can. Men, women and children all does what they can to get something for the winter, for people that don't try to get something in the summer will not have much to carry off to their winter places. Our winter house and gardens is about 70 or 80 miles from here. We are never in want yet, although my old man and me are getting past 70 and no one to work for us but a poor crippled boy and a young girl, an orphan, and our daughter-in-law and her little girl, our own little Ella, our little pet. Her father has been gone for three years in the States. Well we grows our own potatoes and turnips for the winter and we gets plenty of trout for the winter, fresh trout caught thro the ice, and we gets plenty of partridges, white and spruce ones and rabbits and other provisions we get in the summer time. But we has no milk. We gets cranberries, as much as we wants for the winter. We gets a fox now and then and marten and others. Their skins is valuable. We gets seals in the spring on the ice. Oh, we never stops work unless we are eating or sleeping in the night or singing or reading prayers. On Sunday then we has a spell, on that happy day.

I remember one Christmas day that we in my father's house was wishing that we could see some lady to help eat our good Christmas fare. We thought that someone was coming since the dogs was barking but no one came at that time. No other house near to ours than about 30 miles distant, but we would enjoy ourselves pretty well for there was my sister Hannah to be talking and reading with me, Father and Mother and an old Englishman by the name of Robert Best, my best friends, I thought. That was all that was living together as our eldest sister was married and away. We had not many to speak to. Hannah and me, we would go and slide on the Mountaineers sleds, what Father would buy from them, and we were thought a good deal of by the Mountaineers. They would bring some pretty snowshoes to us two sisters, and some pretty deer skin shoes to wear in or out, they all painted so pretty. It was and is our custom to give anyone, dark or white, something to eat while they are at our house, and bedding, so the Indians was always kind to us. Poor despised Indians, the traders selling them rum and the foolish people buying all they could, and they getting lost, falling overboard, losing bodies and souls…but that has changed now.

MERRICK

During the era of the Hudson's Bay Company at Lake Melville, particularly around the turn of the century, a unique culture developed. Perhaps it was somewhat like that of similar areas of the North, where Europeans and aboriginals met and mated, but in this place, at this time, it was unique. These people of mixed ancestry became the dominant population in central Labrador and the primary trappers for the fur trade. More and more men, mostly from the Orkney Islands but some from other parts of Britain and from Quebec, settled in Lake Melville as "planters" and took wives and partners from among the Inuit women there. While initially the Bay had hoped that the Innu would be their main source of fur, they were bound to the caribou hunt with which they had strong spiritual and economic ties. They were reluctant trappers, furs being for them a source of emergency food supplies. So it was that the settler Labradorians became the chief suppliers of the Bay. Through the late nineteenth and early twentieth century, they built an extensive network of family trap lines and tilts, often many days' distance from their homes.

This life was perhaps best described by Elliott Merrick, an American writer who heard the call of the Grenfell Mission and stayed on in North West River to experience for himself the life of the trapper on the line. He and his wife, the Australian nurse, Kate Austen, both journeyed many miles on his remote trap line with John Michelin, a famous trapper and guide. Like Mina Hubbard, they met the Innu with the latter in their own habitat, not yet on the slippery slide into social disintegration. While John was descended from French Canadians, he did not speak French but he did speak some Innu-aimun. The Innu, on the other hand, spoke French fluently as a result of their early gathering in settlements on the Quebec north shore and their early contact with French priests.

When all else failed, they communicated through signs and body language. The Innu and the settlers both inhabited the same country. They came from different worlds and spoke different languages, and because they both drew their support from the land there were tensions between them. However, there was also caring, sharing, and mutual understanding.

Elliott Merrick

EXCERPT FROM *True North*, 1933

November 4

The frost was not melted from the long brown grass this morning when we heard women and children's voices on the river. For a second we were almost afraid. Then the others ran down to the water and I limped, and we all yelled, "Helloo."

Back across the water came "Bo jou" and children's laughter as pretty as thin broken ice washing in and out among the rocks. There were three canoes, all one big family of Indians. The prow of the foremost touched the pebbles and the man advanced, a tall man with little feet in minutely plaited sealskin moccasins. His long legs were wrapped around with rags and salmon twine. Worn, cloth breeches, a very dirty white coat, and a pair of knitted mittens covered the rest of him. The straight black hair under his mouse-colored, ancient felt hat was well down over his ears and collar. He leaned on his long-bladed Indian paddle, his straight, lean body bent and his wrinkled face laughing from embarrassment. Then, wiping his hand on his coat, he held it out to John, saying, "Bo jou, Puckutushand," for he had seen this one before. Then he shook hands with me, half looking at me from under his eyebrows, but with Kay he would not, for she was only a woman.

With him were a little girl and his woman, whom you would have thought to be fifty-five years old, had she not dug down among the bags amidships and unearthed a pair of sparkling shoe-button eyes belonging to a one-year-old baby.

As soon as the eldest son's canoe grounded, he advanced and shook hands, too, a good-looking fellow about twenty, with a round, Chinese-looking face.

With him were his French-Canadian wife, a little Indian hunting dog and Poone, a pert, plump little brother in a red cap.

The last canoe was paddled by three children. Two of them were boys about twelve and fourteen, and the third a pretty girl around fifteen. In the middle of their load sat a mongrel hauling dog, his nose tied up tight with a *babische* thong.

All three canoes were small. Indians never make them longer than seventeen feet, and generally fifteen or sixteen, to be more suitable on the portages. And they floated light. The whole family hadn't as much of a load as two white trappers would require for the hunt till January. The Indians were cold from sitting cramped in their canoes. John was dancing for joy on the stones. "I love Indians," he said to me. "Come up, come up, and have some tea," he repeated to them.

As we scrambled up the slippery bank, the old man pointed to the tilt and said, "Cheena meetchwop, your house, 'ee sez."

Whenever Indians try to talk English they always interlard the conversation with that curious "'ee sez." I think it comes from the use of interpreters. They have noticed that when an interpreter turns from an Indian to a white man, he always precedes his remarks with "'ee sez," and frequently repeats it as he goes along. They haven't any idea what the expression means. They think it is some strange but customary way of beginning an English conversation and filling up the pauses in that absurd tongue. And when they speak English there are many pauses to be filled.

The kettle was soon boiling and they wanted to run and get their grub bags, but we, in an enthusiasm of hospitality, wouldn't let them. We scraped together three cups, two deep dishes and two little kettles for them to drink their tea from; the baby sipped from its mother's cup. The family was ranged all round the walls, on the bunk, on the floor, on boxes and a lard pail. John was conversing with the men sixteen to the dozen. Occasionally he vouchsafed me a word or two, but I could only make out the general drift of the talk. The two women gravitated toward Kay, asking her over and over again by signs and stray words how she came to be here. They had never seen a white woman in the country at freeze-up time, and I suppose they wondered if she was going to live like an Indian always after this.

"Toganish squish," they called her from John's information, and their name for me was "mishnaygan napio," or teacher man.

Kay was buttering big slices of bread for the children, but they were very shy and hid away if anyone looked at them or tried to talk to them. They would not eat until their mother told them it was all right, and then how lovingly they dug into the *kushiwash* [sugar] for their tea. All but Poone. He began to shake his hands and cry with rage. Very gently, as always, his mother crooned, "Naneen, Poone," and the girl untied the little boy's long sleeves which were bound up at the ends with twine, in lieu of mittens. Poone was the only one of the children who wasn't shy. His bright eyes danced under his red wool cap and he laughed and fingered everything he could reach.

We said we were sorry we had no meat for them, but they answered that it made no difference, for, while camped five miles above us on an island they had killed a beaver. They knew we were here but we did not know they were anywhere near. They asked Kay if she liked beaver meat, and she, thinking they asked her if she had ever tasted it, said no. So we missed a "scoff" of beaver.

For half an hour John and the two men talked of signs of fur and what a late fall it was. The foxes would not take bait this year, the old man said, but next year they would be plenty. (They come and go in six- or seven-year cycles. For a year or two there are lots of them. They are fat and well fed and not afraid to cross a man's track or go after the bait in a trap. Then the mice, their principal food, commence to get scarce. The last year the foxes start to fight and eat each other. The next year there are none, not even the track of one. No one knows where they go. Gradually they start coming back again, but for the first few years they are lean and too cautious to go anywhere near a trap or a man's track. When they are starving hungry they will not go after the bait in a trap. When they are rolling in fat they will walk right into the jaws.) The father, who calls himself Mathieu André[32], said there was much sign of muskrat, mink and marten, also weasel. Soon there will be plenty

---

32 Mathieu André was the Innu who guided Joe Retty in 1937 to the deposit that would lead to the iron mines of Labrador West.

ptarmigan with the big snow-storms. In two risings and settings of the sun the river will freeze.

The family is going twenty-five miles farther down the river to fur for a month or two in the vicinity of Fred Goudie's. Fred will not like this much, but Indians fur anywhere they please, saying the country is theirs anyway. Generally, however, they prefer an isolated region where fur and game are sure to be more plentiful.

The Indians never get as much fur as the whites or halfwhites, for, even though they know the country and the ways of the animals infinitely better, they do not trap as intensively and haven't as many deadfalls or traps. They always bring so little food with them they have to spend more than half their time hunting meat.

Mrs. Mathieu dragged her long skirts down to the canoe and showed Kay a French Catholic calendar on which were printed for every day in the year the names of five saints. With this she showed the names of nearly all her children and indicated that she intended to name a new one in about a month, and one for her daughter-in-law in January. The girl is not a real Inu and they may not be able to travel for a week or more after she gives birth. They intend to come out at North West River for more food late in January.

I could not keep my eyes off Terese, a little girl about eight. For amongst her black-haired, swarthy brothers and sisters, she alone had blue eyes and brown hair. Her elder sister, Naneen, is so lithe and dark and beautiful she needs an eagle feather in her hair; she is the stuff legends are made of. But Terese is a lone marguerite in a field of clover. She made me think of a fair-haired child captured from the forts of the pale faces, or a Nordic infant kidnapped by gypsies. She, with her flower face and small hands, was more shy even than the rest and would not speak to me. I wonder where and how the white strain entered. Perhaps an English boy in the teepees on the shore of James Bay, perhaps far down the Mississippi, or beyond the Lake of the Woods, or an English girl captured from Deerfield.

Two winters ago this family camped on Lobstick Lake and it was there John met them and they christened him, Puckutushand. They always have their own name for whites they know. This one means something funny and scurrilous, I think. When John visited them on Sundays the woman sewed buttons on for him and mended his trousers. He traded them flour and cartridges for meat and moccasins.

Now he wants Mathieu to make him a sled, for the old man is a good hand at that.

Mathieu is unwilling at first, but at last he says he will for flour, much flour, for he has many mouths to feed. He goes to the scaffold and says, "Look, you are but three and have five bags of flour. With me are ten and we have only three."

John is willing to give him most anything he wants, but consults me, as we have agreed all the food here is to be ours jointly and while there is anything to eat we will share it equally, no matter that I paid for more of it at North West River and he paid for more of it on the portage. And I am not pleased to give the Indians much flour, for we cannot spare it. And I feel the air grow tense.

We agree to give him half a bag, but John is not content, and neither is the Indian. "If he wished to have more flour, he could have brought more, as we did, and started from the Gulf earlier to allow for the slower travel with heavier loads. Every year the Indians do this; shall we starve because it is their custom?"

But Mathieu will not make a sled for half a bag of flour. Well, we give him four double handfuls of beans and five of peas, one hundred .22 cartridges, six shotgun shells, a little sugar, and he consents.

The old woman shows us by putting her hands to her stomach how hungry the children will be this winter. She begs us for a pair of sealskin boots and demonstrates again and again how cold and wet the little ones' feet will be. So we give her an old pair of boots and a big piece of sealskin to patch many pairs with, and we do not think the family quite as quaint as before.

If our hearts are hardened against them it is because they do this same thing every year. Moreover they can live off the country, finding porcupine and beaver, rabbit and partridge, caribou, fish and bear better than we know how. Every winter they come out to the trading posts and they have been *sham sheevan* [very hungry]. And sometimes the strong men are staggering with weakness and must hasten back with food to their women and children who are keeping themselves alive on squirrels and mice and jays a week or two weeks back on the trail, where they dropped with hunger. And every year a family or two comes down Grand River and all down its length eats up the precious flour in the tilts, and their dogs smell out the lard that is buried in the snow against them. And always they say they were starving, and a starving man will fight or steal for his food and they could not help it. And the next year they do the same and the next and the next.

John knows this and still he would give them more. I know it, and I would give them less. I am glad he is a sunny, carefree one, and not surly and one to nurse a grudge. It is so easy in the woods to fight over food or little things, for a little thing as small as a match means the difference between life and death sometimes.

But now it is all arranged; the man will make a straightgrained juniper sled, so long, and so wide, with the bars lashed on with *babische* and will leave it at Fred Goudie's house. It is like sunshine after a shower, now the bargaining is done. The smiles come out and they are all, from the oldest to the youngest, happy children of the forest again, and not evil, threatening beggars.

The woman must needs take us to the canoe and unwrap her private store of treasures all done up in clean white rags inside a blanket. To John and me she gives a big, round soda biscuit each, and a small pack of pipe tobacco. There is more tobacco there too, though, oddly enough, none of the family smokes. In most Indian families everybody smokes the two or three pipes the family possesses and when a little girl of twelve wants a smoke, she reaches the pipe out of her mother's mouth and plants it in her own.

But this old lady is a canny one. She knows that trappers when they get out of tobacco will trade flour or anything else for it. A trapper has been known to trade a forty-dollar marten for a thirty-cent plug of tobacco.

To Kay she insists upon giving a small, white canvas bag, stitched all over with bright-colored tapes in the form of a star. Then, after a moment's hesitation, she decides she will entrust to her presents for Shwasheem's wife and her sister Pen-am-ee, who will come to North West River in January. They are, a tattered snapshot taken on the French shore, a string of imitation-pearl rosary beads, and an Indian woman's cap. This latter is a work of art made from red and black triangles whose points come together at the crown. The material costs twenty cents an inch at the post. The closefitting band, which is about two inches broad, is solid wampum made of red and blue and gray beads—the work of many weeks.

Child-like, the woman has to see where Kay is going to put these gifts for safekeeping on the long journey down. They are carefully wrapped in a clean towel, and stowed in Kay's "progbag" with her tooth brush, sewing bag, bandannas, pencil and paper, comb and three favorite little paper books. A progbag is to a trapper what a dittybox is to a sailor. In it he carries a few matches, a few candles and cartridges, a spare pair of sox, his pencil, an awl and crooked-knife, a snowshoe needle, sewing materials, deerskin and sealskin patches and other cherished encumbrances. The Indian woman recognizes this as the appropriate place and nods her approval.

Now Poone's cuffs must be tied up again and the flour put aboard. In the old man's canoe there is a pair of snowshoes no bigger than salad plates. Swiftly they step into their canoes, kneel and sit back on their feet. White men cannot sit that way all day. The paddles grind with a push on the pebbles, they hold their hands up and softly call, "Miami," and are gone.

They will have covered more than fifteen hundred miles before they get back to their "home" at Seven Islands, on the north shore of the Gulf of St. Lawrence where they spend summers. And the men, with their hunting, will have done twice that.

At Fred's they'll put their canoes up on scaffolds, for the river will be frozen when they get there. At the end of a month or two they'll start for North West River, hunting as they go. They'll trade their fur, then back again by way of Michikamau, hauling big loads. Toward May they'll be getting back here again to their canoes before the ice breaks up. It is bad to be caught by an early spring far from one's canoe. Or perhaps they'll get here early, make runnered sledges and haul their canoes over the watershed before the ice breaks up. Then down to Seven Islands on a fair tide.

These Montagnais have changed their ways a little since the days when they had no stoves, no canvas, no nails, no steel traps, no matches nor rifles, but not as much as one would think. The depletion of the caribou has changed them more than the coming of the whites. I think this is the last stand, and they don't intend to change any more.

In summer the men do practically nothing to avert the hardships of the coming winter. Perhaps they make a couple of extra pairs of snowshoes to sell, but these are never as good as the snowshoes they make for themselves. They could salmon-fish, or make canoes to sell, as the trappers have asked them many times, but they will not.

They dangle their legs and say the white men and halfbreeds are fools to live in the big houses that they must work on all summer and spend so much time providing firewood for. And in the fall when they start into the woods again, as often as not they camp within forty miles and eat up half their grub so they will not have so much to carry. And that winter they are *sham sheevan* again. They are children, careless of the morrow and forever scornful of the whites. One cannot but admire them in a way. It takes a certain kind of courage to forget tomorrow. They would rather die than change, and they are dying, I am afraid.

GOUDIE

In the early decades of the twentieth century, life on the Labrador coast had its rewards but was not easy. This was true for both aboriginals and non-aboriginals. Elizabeth Goudie describes a particularly trying and tragic time when she and her husband were trapping near Davis Inlet, today's Natuashish. While Goudie was a direct descendant of the earliest Europeans to settle in Hamilton Inlet, it took all the skill she had inherited from her European and aboriginal ancestors and all the courage she possessed to cope with a badly injured child with her husband so far away from home. In spite of the efforts of Grenfell, and more particularly of Harry Paddon, medical care on the Labrador coast at that time was distant and rudimentary. Such were the hardships in Labrador in those days. Husband and wife struggled to make a living from fur trapping in spite of the harsh economic rules of the Bay. Sometimes they won the fight for survival, but at other times they knew the awful pain of not only watching a child lose its battle for life but also the ultimate pain of having to bury in the dead of winter a child that has been lost.

The first to publish an account of her life on the Labrador was Lydia Campbell, an ancestor of Elizabeth Goudie. However, *Woman of Labrador*, from which this excerpt is taken, has been widely read and is the best local account of life in the early twentieth century.

Elizabeth Goudie

FROM *Woman of Labrador*, 1973 (ED. DAVID ZIMMERLY)

Treated by Sir Wilfred Grenfell

Three days after May was born, I took very sick for a week. I did not know anything that was happening. They told me after I got better that I was running a very high temperature. We heard Sir Wilfred Grenfell was coming up the coast and the day he came to Davis Inlet, my husband was out in the harbour waiting for him. Jim brought him ashore and when he examined me he said I had infant fever.[33] He went aboard his boat and got me some drugs and some oranges and soda biscuits to eat. He went on further north to visit the coast. Shortly after, I began to feel a little better but I was not well for a long time. That fall, I stayed in bed fifteen days altogether.

I had three other children to look after and my husband had to work every day or lose his job. I had to get out of bed the fifteenth day and try to look after the children. We were staying with Freeman Saunders and his family and his wife Nomi was expecting a baby. She could not help me very much so we were both in a helpless state. I used to get up for a while every day and take care of my baby and feed my children. Then, I would have to go to bed again. September passed by and we went back in the bay to prepare for winter again. I was still sick but I could manage to stay up all day. I had to go to bed early at night.

---

33 Infection of the uterus of a woman who has recently given birth—puerperal metritis.

Baby Bruce is accidentally burned

October passed by and Jim went setting his traps again. The first evening he was gone I was alone cleaning my floor. I looked around for my children. The girl Marie and the second boy Bruce were sitting by the stove watching the fire burning. I checked them to see if everything was alright and went on about my work. About ten minutes later, the whole house lit up with fire. I jumped to my feet and I was by Bruce's side in a minute. I did not know what to do; I saw a big coat close by and caught it and smothered out the flame. For a few seconds, he didn't move. I picked him up and the minute I moved him he went into a "rock of pain." I was a whole hour trying to keep him on my lap. That was between five and six in the evening; at about six-thirty, he fell asleep. Jim was still not home so I laid Bruce on a big wooden chest I had beside the table. I thought I would have something to eat because I expected to be up all night. I looked over his body as carefully as I could and I saw his right arm was burnt right to his body and one cheek, one ear and both his lips were burned, so I knew I had a terrible task on my hands. I tried to eat but couldn't. I walked the floor and the other children were afraid that their little brother would die and they were crying. Their daddy was not home yet.

About seven o'clock I heard the boat coming and I was there with my little boy all burnt. I did not know how his dad would take it. I thought that he might think that I had been careless and got him burnt so I just sat by my little boy and waited for Jim to come into the house. I told him what had happened. We sat beside our child and when he woke up he again went into a rock of pain. We walked the floor with him the whole night taking turns.

He could not even take a drink during the whole night. In the morning, he seemed to be better and asked for a drink. Then he fell asleep so we had a chance to look over his whole body. There were burns on his legs as well as his arm and face. We sat down and tried to figure out what we could do. The only thing we had in the house was a bottle of castor oil. I said to Jim, "You better get me a juniper stick and I will boil it and use the liquid to bathe the burns." I had no dressing. I had a couple of sheets and I tore them up for dressings. There was a small wound of open flesh on his elbow and I was really afraid that would become infected. I hoped and prayed it would be all right. Jim got the juniper stick. I went to work and boiled it four hours and started to bathe the wounds in the liquid.

On the second day, the spot on his elbow looked a bit red and infected. I took a piece of the stick and peeled the outside bark off and took the inside, the gummy bark of the stick, and beat it to a pulp. I sterilized my dressing by browning it on the stove and I placed a piece of the gummy pulp on his elbow. I greased the poultice with the castor oil and after six days he seemed to be getting a lot better.

There was a doctor at Nain with an explorer, Captain MacMillan from the United States. They were stationed at Nain but traveled all the time. MacMillan's doctor traveled to Hopedale and used to travel north to Okak, so we didn't know if he was in Nain or not. After eight days, my husband thought our little boy was better. Jim went out to Davis Inlet and waited for a day. On the second day, the doctor passed through Davis Inlet on his way to Nain.

Jim brought him up the bay the next morning. He looked at our boy and at what I was using and he said he was over the worst. He told me to carry on with what I was using. He gave me some dressings and I was very happy about what he told me. He said I had done a marvelous job so my mind was at ease then.

I was still sick myself from the infant fever and I had lost a lot of weight. The doctor said to me, "You should be in a hospital yourself." I was so frightened when the baby was burned that I hadn't eaten for four or five days. Jim stayed home with me for a month. It was three weeks before I could dress my little boy. I had three other children and the youngest was only two months old. We both worked night and day for about three weeks. With hard work we helped to save our little boy. We were both upset for a week because we did not know what was going to happen. You can't imagine what we went through that fall but the main thing is that we got through and our little boy got well again. Many, many times after, we both wondered how we had done it. But with God's help, we fought for his life together. For three weeks neither of us had a full night's sleep but the main thing was that he lived and we were both very thankful. When two people work so hard together to try to save a child, it is good to see him recover.

As time passed by, Bruce really began to get well again. His appetite came back and he began to go outside with the other children. By the end of November, he was back to normal again. Jim was waiting for the river to freeze over with ice to get in to his inland trapping lines. He lost most of that fall waiting for Bruce to get well. He got a few foxes and a few seals trapping around the bay. We had lots of wild ducks to eat and also Arctic hare which are bigger than rabbits and much better meat. They live on blueberries and off the shrubs on the side of the high hills. I could make a much more satisfying meal with Arctic hare than I could with the caribou meat.

Christmas 1927

Until December 1927, Jim stayed home waiting for our son to recover. The cold weather came quite early and froze over the river. He made a quick trip into the country and set up his traps and came back for Christmas. We spent our Christmas as a family together, the first one for a long time. It was a very quiet day.

The children hung up their stockings in those days. There were not many gifts. The boys had a rubber ball each and our little girl had a little doll and a few candies that had been saved in the fall for Christmas. There was an old man and his wife living near us and we took the children over to see them in the afternoon. We sang Christmas carols and read the Christmas story. We went home and had a quiet evening by ourselves. This was the way things went at Christmas in Labrador in the bays on the coast. We always visited with one or two families. The Christmas feast was made up of fresh baked partridges or baked rabbits or caribou steaks. The pastries were partridge-berry pies and the cake was made of molasses, raisins, currents, spices and baked in the oven like you bake a plain white bread. This was Christmas in Labrador and we were all quite contented with it.

Financial troubles

In January 1928, Jim went back into the country and had a haul on his traps. He did not get many furs so it did not look so good for us. We had a very cold winter. Jim kept himself busy on his trapping lines. We were getting behind. We were not getting enough furs to keep up with the bills we owed the Hudson's Bay Company. The winter was looking pretty grim.

March came again and the weather was getting a little warmer. The worst of winter was over for another year. On the tenth of March a man named Herbert Decker came to our house. He lived three miles away and his wife's aunt had died. He was looking for help. He wanted me to come and take care of their family while his wife was away helping with the funeral. I got the children ready and took them over to the Decker's. Jim went with Mr. Decker to help dig the grave. The ground was frozen very hard and it took them three days. I stayed with all the children.

Bruce dies

Marie, our little girl, went to Davis Inlet for a trip with her Uncle Arch and Aunt Lily. She came home sick, and three days later my oldest son and the little boy Bruce took sick. Twenty-four hours later Bruce died. I never knew what caused his death so fast. It was a type of sickness with very bad diarrhea, a lot of pain and a high temperature. Jim came home from the Decker funeral the day my little boy took sick. By midnight little Bruce could not recognize us. We were all alone with no help within two or three miles so Jim stayed with me until it was getting daylight and then went for Archie and his wife. Shortly after Jim left, Bruce got worse and kept getting worse. It was bad going for dogs and Jim took a long time. When he got back with help, my little boy was almost dead. When Archie's wife came in the house, she knew how bad it was. She moved Bruce to a table and straightened him out. He was gone in a couple of minutes. Our little boy we had fought so hard to save from burns died a few months later.

We were three miles from the graveyard. We had no place to put the little body. Jim and Archie built a scaffold about six feet from the ground. Jim and Archie and Mr. Decker made a casket for him and put it on the scaffold. The day after Bruce died we started digging the grave. We started out in the early morning. We had to go three miles on dog team to dig the grave and go back home every evening because Horace, our oldest boy, was very sick. We did not know if he was going to pull through or not. Archie's wife was looking after him for me in the day. I went with the men to cook their dinner to give them more time at the grave. The ground was frozen very deep. It took the men three days to dig the grave. The third day we took the little corpse with us. The only minister around was a long way away. There was an old English gentleman who lived near us who could have buried him for us, but at that time he was in bed with an abscess on his back and could not walk. We took the body into his house and he read a part of the burial ceremony for us. We went on to the grave about three o'clock in the afternoon and Jim and I had to finish burying him ourselves. The two men we had with us could not read and Archie said he could not bury him. We had no other choice but to do it ourselves. It was one of the hardest tasks I did in all my married life.

We went back to Archie's late that evening of the twenty-fifth and our oldest boy Horace was too sick to move. When we pulled up to the door it was after dark and we could hear him crying with pain. Archie's wife told us he was getting worse. We did not know what to expect. We took turns staying up with him all night. About twelve o'clock that night there seemed to be a change in him; his pain was leaving him a little. About three o'clock he fell asleep and at breakfast time he woke up and knew us and called us Daddy and Mommy.

The worst was over and he gradually got better. We had to stay at Archie's for a week until Horace was strong enough to take home. Our home was very lonely without our little boy Bruce. His playthings were scattered over the floor just the way he had left them about ten days before. I gathered up all his things and put them away where we could not see them because it made us both lonely.

Jim had to go into the country and put away all his traps for the spring. I was left alone again for a month. I had plenty to do trying to build up Horace and make him strong again. I caught some fresh fish for him and we had lots of fresh caribou. He was not very long getting back his strength. He could get outdoors and play. Everything was looking a bit brighter for us again. But the family chain was broken by the death of our little one. We would go to the table for meals and his place was empty and when we went to bed at night, it was the same thing. We spent a very lonely spring.

Financial troubles worsen

I missed my parents as I had been away from them now for four years. We only got letters from them about twice a winter and about three times in the summer. We were not making money to spare and there was no way of getting home for a trip to see them. Mail was delivered in winter by dog team and in summer by a steamer from St. John's. As each year went by we were a little more in debt. The Hudson's Bay Company was getting a bit more impatient with us.

In 1928, when we went to get our food again for the winter, the Hudson's Bay manager told us that if we could not payoff our bills that year, he would have to cut off our credit. Jim said we would have to do something. We needed a lot of things when our fourth child was born in 1927. We were living in a house in Davis Inlet with another family that summer because Jim had a job with the Hudson's Bay for a little while.

When fall of 1928 came around we went back to the winter place and we thought a lot about it. It was too late to go back to Hamilton Inlet to my father's and his brother's, although we knew we would get a little from them. We stayed on for another winter.

When Jim came out of the country the first time, he did very well with fur. We had to have food to eat and he put all he could against his bills. It was not enough. When he came back, he had his mind made up. He said if he could get enough furs to buy food for us and the dogs, we would get in touch with the mailman and travel down the coast with him because we did not know the way. Archie came to the house one day and Jim told him what we were going to do. Arch said that if we were going back home he was coming too. That was early in 1929. They both went back into the country and they came out March 20. Jim said he thought he had enough furs to buy food for the trip. I had to make a couple of pairs of boots for Jim and boots for the three children and a pair for myself. The trip we had to take was roughly a little over 300 miles by the coast. We both thought it was going to be pretty rough for me and the children but there was not much else we could do because we would not get any help from the Hudson's Bay Company for another winter.

We talked about it and at first I did not approve because I was worried about the children. We would have to go over quite a lot of land. It was up hills and down on the other sides and through valleys. I thought we might cripple our children. We only had six dogs. There were five of us besides our belongings, food and dog food. Jim said he would have to build a new kamutik. We had to be ready for the fifteenth of April because the mailman was making his last trip at that time.

HUBBARD

The year 2005 marked the one hundredth anniversary of Mina Hubbard's trek across the Labrador wilderness. No non-aboriginal had ever made the trip before. Much of it was uncharted or imperfectly charted. On the way, there were, as Byron Chaulk said in his song, "raging rivers and rapids," black flies that were persistent and unrelenting, and a ruggedly beautiful country that often yielded its game grudgingly. Yet Hubbard went where no white man or woman had gone before. She left the North West River post with four guides, one of whom had been part of her husband's tragic try, and one of whom, Bert Blake, was a young Labradorian who had grown up in the country on his family's trap lines. In the following weeks, she made her way up the Nascaupi River to the Height of Land and then down the George River to the northern coast. Her husband, Leonidas Hubbard, had perished in his attempt at this route when he mistook the Susan River for the Nascaupi. Now Mina was in a race to the George River with Dillon Wallace, her husband's companion, whom, she believed, had sullied her husband's reputation and character in his account of the ill-fated expedition, *Lure of the Labrador Wild*. She met the challenge by calling on stamina she never knew she had, and she found the courage to persevere in the face of seemingly insurmountable odds because she was determined to finish the aborted attempt of her dead husband. She deserves the various accounts of her trip and her life that have been published recently.

Here is an excerpt from the book of a true Canadian heroine who has received far too little attention. In this chapter, Hubbard records her historic meeting with the Barren Ground Innu. For centuries they had travelled the waterways from the Quebec north shore, where they had learned French from the Catholic missionaries, to the Atlantic coast. She had previously encountered the Montagnais (a name Champlain gave to those Innu whom he encountered near the mountains of the north shore); now she met the Barren Ground Innu, called by those to the south "Nascaupi," the uncivilized or merely far away. At the start of the twentieth century, the Innu already had been lured away from caribou hunting, which had been their way of life and sustained them for centuries, to the fur-trapping economy of the traders. However they still were in the woods and on the rivers they knew and loved, not yet herded into villages, not yet descended to the alcoholism and societal self-abuse that would bring them so much media attention in later decades. Hubbard's meeting with the Innu, particularly the women, is historic; here are women from two entirely different cultures who meet for the first time to discover they are so different and yet have so much in common.

Mina Benson Hubbard

"THE BARREN GROUND PEOPLE,"
FROM *A Woman's Way through Unknown Labrador*, 1908

On Sunday morning, August 20th, I awoke in a state of expectancy. We had slept three times since leaving the Montagnais camp, and unless the Barren Grounds People were not now in their accustomed camping place, we ought to see them before night. Many thoughts came of how greatly Mr. Hubbard had wished to see them, and what a privilege he would have thought it to be able to visit them.

It seemed this morning as if something unusual must happen. It was as if we were coming into a hidden country. From where the river turned into the hills it flowed for more than a mile northward through what was like a great magnificent corridor, leading to something larger beyond.

When Joe [Iserhoff] and Gilbert [Blake], who were usually the first to get off, slipped away down the river, I realised how swift flowing the water must be. It looked still as glass and very dark, almost black. The quiet surface was disturbed only by the jumping of the fish. We saw the canoe push off and turned to put a few last touches to the loading of our own. When we looked again they were already far away. Soon, however, we had caught them up and together the two canoes ran out into the widening of the river. Here it bent a little to the northeast, but two miles farther on it again bore away to the north. In the distance we could see the mountain tops standing far apart and knew that there, between them, a lake must lie. Could it be Indian House Lake, the Mush-au-wau-ni-pi, or "Barren Grounds Water," of the Indians? We were still farther south than it was placed on the map I carried. Yet we had passed the full number of lakes given in the map above this water. Even so I did not believe it could be the big lake I had been looking forward to reaching so eagerly.

As we paddled on at a rather brisk rate I sat thinking how beautiful the river, the mountains, and the morning were. I had not settled myself to watch seriously for the Nascaupee camp, when suddenly George [Elson] exclaimed, "There it is."

There it was indeed, a covered wigwam, high up on a sandy hill, which sloped to the water's edge, and formed the point round which the river flowed to the lake among the mountains. Soon a second wigwam came in sight. We could see no one at the camp at first. Then a figure appeared moving about near one of the wigwams. It was evident that they were still unconscious of our presence; but as we paddled slowly along the figure suddenly stopped, a whole company came running together, and plainly our sudden appearance was causing great excitement. There was a hurried moving to and fro and after a time came the sound of two rifle shots. I replied with my revolver. Again they fired and I replied again. Then more shots from the hill.

As we drew slowly near, the men ran down towards the landing, but halted above a narrow belt of trees near the water's edge. There an animated discussion of the newcomers took place.

We all shouted, "Bo Jou! Bo Jou!" (Bon Jour).

A chorus of Bo Jous came back from the hill.

George called to them in Indian, "We are strangers and are passing through your country."

The sound of words in their own tongue reassured them and they ran down to the landing. As we drew near we could hear them talking. I, of course, could not understand a word of it, but I learned later from George what they said.

"Who are they?"

"See the man steering looks like an Indian." "That surely is an Indian."

"Why, there is an English woman." "Where have they come from?"

As the canoe glided towards the landing, one, who was evidently the chief, stepped forward while the others remained a little apart. Putting out his hand to catch the canoe as it touched the sand he said, "Of course you have some tobacco?"

"Only a little," George replied. "We have come far."

Then the hand was given in greeting as we stepped ashore.

It was a striking picture they made that quiet Sabbath morning, as they stood there at the shore with the dark green woods behind them and all about them the great wilderness of rock and river and lake. You did not see it all, but you felt it. They had markedly Indian faces and those of the older men showed plainly the battle for life they had been fighting. They were tall, lithe, and active looking, with a certain air of self-possession and dignity which almost all Indians seem to have. They wore dressed deer-skin breeches and moccasins and over the breeches were drawn bright red cloth leggings reaching from the ankle to well above the knee, and held in place by straps fastened about the waist. The shirts, some of which were of cloth and some of dressed deer-skin, were worn outside the breeches and over these a white coat bound about the edges with blue or red. Their hair was long and cut straight round below the ears, while tied about the head was a bright coloured kerchief. The faces were full of interest. Up on the hill the women and children and old men stood watching, perhaps waiting till it should appear whether the strangers were friendly or hostile.

"Where did you come into the river?" the chief asked. George explained that we had come the whole length of the river, that we had come into it from Lake Michikamau, which we reached by way of the Nascaupee. He was greatly surprised. He had been at Northwest River and knew the route. Turning to the others he told them of our long journey. Then they came forward and gathered eagerly about us. We told them we were going down the river to the post at Ungava.

"Oh! you are near now," they said. "You will sleep only five times if you travel fast."

My heart bounded as this was interpreted to me, for it meant that we should be at the post before the end of August, for this was only the twentieth. There was still a chance that we might be in time for the ship.

"Then where is the long lake that is in this river?" George enquired.

"It is here," the chief replied.

We enquired about the river. All were eager to tell about it, and many expressive gestures were added to their words to tell that the river was rapid all the way. An arm held at an angle showed what we were to expect in the rapids and a vigorous drop of the hand expressed something about the falls. There would be a few portages but they were not long, and in some places it would be just a short lift over; but it was all rapid nearly.

"And when you come to a river coming in on the other side in quite a fall you are not far from the post."

There was a tightening in my throat as I thought, "What if I had decided to turn back rather than winter in Labrador!"

"Did you see any Indians?" the chief asked.

"Yes, we have slept three times since we were at their camp."

"Were they getting any caribou?" was the next eager question. "Had they seen any signs of the crossing?" George told them of the great numbers we had seen and there followed an earnest discussion among themselves as to the probability of the caribou passing near them.

"Are you going up?" we enquired. They replied, "No, not our country."

There were enquiries as to which way the caribou were passing, and again they talked among themselves about their hopes and fears. We learned that only three days before they had returned from Davis Inlet where they go to trade for supplies as do the Montagnais. They had come back from their long journey sick at heart to meet empty handed those who waited in glad anticipation of this the great event of the year—the return from the post. The ship had not come, and the post store was empty.

As they talked, the group about the canoe was growing larger. The old men had joined the others together with a few old women. As the story of their disappointment was told one old man said, "You see the way we live and you see the way we dress. It is hard for us to live. Sometimes we do not get many caribou. Perhaps they will not cross our country. We can get nothing from the Englishman, not even ammunition. It is hard for us to live."

All summer they had been taking an occasional caribou, enough for present needs, but little more than that, and the hunters on their return from the coast found the hands at home as empty as their own. Now the long winter stretched before them with all its dread possibilities.

We enquired of them how far it was to the coast, and found that they make the outward journey in five days, and the return trip in seven. They informed us that they had this year been accompanied part of the way in by an Englishman. All white men are Englishmen to them. As George interpreted to me, he said, "That must be Mr. Cabot."

Instantly the chief caught at the name and said, "Cabot? Yes, that is the man. He turned back two days' journey from here. He was going away on a ship."

When during the winter I had talked with Mr. Cabot of my trip he had said, "Perhaps we shall meet on the George next summer." Now I felt quite excited to think how near we had come to doing so. How I wished he had sent me a line by the Indians. I wanted to know how the Peace Conference was getting on. I wondered at first that he had not done so; but after a little laughed to myself as I thought I could guess why. How envious he would be of me, for I had really found the home camp of his beloved Nascaupees.

Meanwhile the old women had gathered about me begging for tobacco. I did not know, of course, what it was they wanted, and when the coveted tobacco did not appear they began to complain bitterly, "She is not giving us any tobacco. See, she does not want to give us any tobacco."

George explained to them that I did not smoke and so had no tobacco to give them, but that I had other things I could give them. Now that we were so near the post I could spare some of my provisions for the supply was considerably more than we should now need to take us to our journey's end. There was one partly used bag of flour which was lifted out of the canoe and laid on the beach. Then Job [Chapies] handed me the tea and rice bags. Two, not very clean, coloured silk handkerchiefs were spread on the beach when I asked for something to put the tea and rice in, and a group of eager faces bent over me as I lifted the precious contents from the bags, leaving only enough tea to take us to the post, and enough rice for one more pudding. An old tin pail lying near was filled with salt, and a piece of bacon completed the list. A few little trinkets were distributed among the women and from the expression on their faces, I judged they had come to the conclusion that I was not so bad after all, even though I did not smoke a pipe and so could not give them any of their precious "*Tshishtemau.*"

Mina Benson Hubbard

Meantime I had been thinking about my photographs. Taking up one of my kodaks I said to the chief that I should like to take his picture and motioned him to stand apart. He seemed to understand quite readily and stepped lightly to one side of the little company in a way which showed it was not a new experience to him. They had no sort of objection to being snapped, but rather seemed quite eager to pose for me.

Then came an invitation to go up to the camp. As George interpreted he did not look at all comfortable, and when he asked if I cared to go I knew he was wishing very much that I would say "No," but I said, "Yes, indeed." So we went up while the other three remained at the canoes.

Even in barren Labrador are to be found little touches that go to prove human nature the same the world over. One of the young men, handsomer than the others, and conscious of the fact, had been watching me throughout with evident interest. He was not only handsomer than the others, but his leggings were redder. As we walked up towards the camp he went a little ahead, and to one side managing to watch for the impression he evidently expected to make. A little distance from where we landed was a row of bark canoes turned upside down. As we passed them he turned and, to make sure that those red leggings should not fail of their mission, he put his foot up on one of the canoes, pretending, as I passed, to tie his moccasin, the while watching for the effect.

It was some little distance up to camp. When we reached it we could see northward down the lake for miles. It lay like a great, broad river guarded on either side by the mountains. The prospect was very beautiful. Everywhere along the way we found their camping places chosen from among the most beautiful spots, and there seemed abundant evidence that in many another Indian breast dwelt the heart of Saltatha, Warburton Pike's famous guide, who when the good priest had told him of the beauties of heaven said, "My Father, you have spoken well. You have told me that heaven is beautiful. Tell me now one thing more. Is it more beautiful than the land of the musk ox in summer, when sometimes the mist blows over the lakes, and sometimes the waters are blue, and the loons call very often? This is beautiful, my Father. If heaven is more beautiful I shall be content to rest there till I am very old."

The camp consisted of two large wigwams, the covers of which were of dressed deer-skins sewed together and drawn tight over the poles, while across the doorway hung an old piece of sacking. The covers were now worn and old and dirty-grey in colour save round the opening at the top, where they were blackened by the smoke from the fire in the centre of the wigwam.

Here the younger women and the children were waiting, and some of them had donned their best attire for the occasion of the strangers' visit. Their dresses were of cotton and woollen goods. Few wore skin clothes, and those who did had on a rather long skin shirt with hood attached, but under the shirt were numerous cloth garments. Only the old men and little children were dressed altogether in skins. One young woman appeared in a gorgeous purple dress, and on her head the black and red *tuque* with beaded band worn by most of the Montagnais women, and I wondered if she had come to the Nascaupee camp the bride of one of its braves. There was about her an air of conscious difference from the others, but this was unrecognised by them. The faces here were not bright and happy looking as at the Montagnais camp. Nearly all were sad and wistful. The old women seemed the brightest of all and were apparently important people in the camp. Even the little children's faces were sad and old in expression as if they too realised something of the cares of wilderness life.

At first they stood about rather shyly watching me, with evident interest, but making no move to greet or welcome me. I did not know how best to approach them. Then seeing a young mother with her babe in her arms standing among the group, near one of the wigwams, I stepped towards her, and touching the little bundle I spoke to her of her child and she held it so that I might see its face. It was a very young baby, born only the day before, I learned later, and the mother herself looked little more than a child. Her face was pale, and she looked weak and sick. Though she held her child towards me there was no lighting up of the face, no sign of responsive interest. Almost immediately, however, I was surrounded by nearly the whole community of women who talked rapidly about the babe and its mother.

The little creature had no made garments on, but was simply wrapped about with old cloths leaving only its face and neck bare. The outermost covering was a piece of plaid shawl, and all were held tightly in place by a stout cord passing round the bundle a number of times. It would be quite impossible for the tiny thing to move hand or foot or any part of its body except the face. As one might expect it wore an expression of utter wretchedness though it lay with closed eyes making no sound. I could make almost nothing of what they said, and when I called George to interpret for me they seemed not to want to talk.

Taking out my kodaks I set about securing a few photographs. Already the old women were beginning to prepare for the feast they were to have. Two large black pots that stood on three legs were set out, and one of the women went into the tent and brought out a burning brand to light the fire under them. Soon interest was centred in the pots. I had a little group ranged up in front of one of the wigwams, when the lady in purple, whose attention for a time had been turned to the preparations for the feast, seeing what was taking place came swiftly across and placed herself in the very centre of the group. All apparently understood what was being done and were anxious to be in the picture.

During the stay at camp I saw little sign of attempt at ornamentation. The moccasins and skin clothing I saw were unadorned. There was but the one black and red *tuque* with braided band, and the chief's daughter alone wore the beaded band on her hair, which was arranged as that of the women in the Montagnais camp. One woman coveted a sweater I wore. It was a rather bright green with red cuffs and collar, and the colour had greatly taken her fancy. I wished that I had been able to give it to her, but my wardrobe was as limited as I dared to have it, and so I was obliged to refuse her request. In a way which I had not in the least expected I found these people appealing to me, and myself wishing that I might remain with them for a time, but I could not risk a winter in Labrador for the sake of the longer visit, even had I been able to persuade the men to remain.

Already George was showing his anxiety to get away and I realised that it was not yet certain we should be in time for the ship. It might easily be more than five days to the post. I could not know how far the Indian mind had been influenced in gauging the distance by a desire to reduce to the smallest possible limit the amount of tobacco the men would need to retain for their own use. It was not far from the last week in August. Now I felt that not simply a day but even an hour might cost me a winter in Labrador.

When the word went forth that we were about to leave, all gathered for the parting. Looking about for something which I might carry away with me as a souvenir of the visit, my eyes caught the beaded band, which the chief's daughter wore on her hair, and stepping towards her I touched it to indicate my wish. She drew sharply away and said something in tones that had a plainly resentful ring. It was, "That is mine." I determined not to be discouraged and made another try. Stretched on a frame to dry was a very pretty deer-skin and I had George ask if I might have that. That seemed to appeal to them as a not unreasonable request, and they suggested that I should take one already dressed. The woman who had wanted my sweater went into the wigwam and brought out one. It was very pretty and beautifully soft and white on the inside. She again pleaded for the sweater, and as I could not grant her request I handed her back the skin; but she bade me keep it. They gave George a piece of deer-skin dressed without the hair, "to line a pair of mits," they said.

As they stood about during the last few minutes of our stay, the chief's arm was thrown across his little daughter's shoulders as she leaned confidingly against him. While the parting words were being exchanged he was engaged in a somewhat absent-minded but none the less successful, examination of her head. Many of the others were similarly occupied. There was no evidence of their being conscious that there was anything extraordinary in what they were doing, nor any attempt at concealing it. Apparently it was as much a matter of course as eating.

When I said, "Good-bye," they made no move to accompany me to the canoe.

"Good-bye," said George. "Send us a fair wind."

Smilingly they assured him that they would. In a minute we were in the canoe and pushing off from shore. As we turned down the lake, all eager to be shortening the distance between us and the post, I looked back. They were still standing just as we had left them watching us. Taking out my handkerchief I waved it over my head. Instantly the shawls and kerchiefs flew out as they waved a response, and with this parting look backward to our wilderness friends we turned our faces to Ungava.

DUNCAN

Well into the early decades of the twentieth century, seasonal fishermen sailed from Newfoundland each summer in search of cod. Well below the territory of the Innu and the Inuit, they encountered the "livyers," permanent settlers of Labrador who had steadily increased in numbers during the nineteenth century. In 1825 between 60 and 70 vessels from St. John's, and nearly 200 from Conception Bay, carried on the Labrador fishery employing nearly 5,000 men and women. Soon, Newfoundland schooners were going as far north as Saglek, leaving lasting signs of their presence through numerous place names: Cutthroat, Ironbound Islands, Windy Tickle, Fish Island, and Newfoundland Harbour.

It was these Newfoundland fishermen that Norman Duncan came to know and to capture in his fictional works. In 1895 he made his first trip to Newfoundland as a correspondent for *McClure's Magazine*. He made other trips to the island and Labrador between 1901 and 1906 while teaching at Washington and Jefferson colleges. Patrick O'Flaherty, in his study of Newfoundland and Labrador literature, *The Rock Observed* (1979), remarked upon Duncan's success in conjuring up "the real life of Newfoundland, its attractive features along with its cruelties and limitations."

Norman Duncan

"WITH THE FLEET," FROM *Dr. Grenfell's Parish*, 1905

In the early spring—when the sunlight is yellow and the warm winds blow and the melting snow drips over the cliffs and runs in little rivulets from the barren hills—in the thousand harbours of Newfoundland the great fleet is made ready for the long adventure upon the Labrador coast. The rocks echo the noise of hammer and saw and mallet and the song and shout of the workers. The new schooners—building the winter long at the harbour side—are hurried to completion. The old craft—the weather-beaten, ragged old craft, which, it may be, have dodged the reefs and outlived the gales of forty seasons—are fitted with new spars, patched with new canvas and rope, calked anew, daubed anew and, thus refitted, float brave enough on the quiet harbour water. There is no end to the bustle of labour on ships and nets—no end to the clatter of planning. From the skipper of the ten-ton *First Venture*, who sails with a crew of sons bred for the purpose, to the powerful dealer who supplies on shares a fleet of seventeen fore-and-afters manned from the harbours of a great bay, there is hope in the hearts of all. Whatever the last season, every man is to make a good "voyage" now. This season—this season—there is to be fish a-plenty on the Labrador!

The future is bright as the new spring days. Aunt Matilda is to have a bonnet with feathers—when Skipper Thomas gets home from the Labrador. Little Johnny Tatt, he of the crooked back, is to know again the virtue of Pike's Pain Compound, at a dollar a bottle, warranted to cure when daddy gets home from the Labrador. Skipper Bill's Lizzie, plump, blushing, merryeyed, is to wed Jack Lute o' Burnt Arm—when Jack comes back from the Labrador. Every man's heart, and, indeed, most men's fortunes, are in the venture. The man who has nothing has yet the labour of his hands. Be he skipper, there is one to back his skill and honesty; be he hand, there is no lack of berths to choose from. Skippers stand upon their record and schooners upon their reputation; it's take your choice, for the hands are not too many: the skippers are timid or bold, as God made them; the schooners are lucky or not, as Fate determines. Every man has his chance. John Smith o' Twillingate provisions the *Lucky Queen* and gives her to the penniless Skipper Jim o' Yellow Tickle on shares. Old Tom Tatter o' Salmon Cove, with plea and argument, persuades the Four Arms trader to trust him once again with the *Busy Bee*. He'll get the fish *this* time. Nar a doubt of it! He'll be home in August—this year—loaded to the gunwale. God knows who pays the cash when the fish fail! God knows how the folk survive the disappointment! It is a great lottery of hope and fortune.

When, at last, word comes south that the ice is clearing from the coast, the vessels spread their little wings to the first favouring winds; and in a week—two weeks or three—the last of the Labradormen have gone "down north."

Dr. Grenfell and his workers find much to do among these men and women and children.

At Indian Harbour where the *Strathcona* lay at anchor, I went aboard the schooner *Jolly Crew*. It was a raw, foggy day, with a fresh northeast gale blowing, and a high sea running outside the harbour. They were splitting fish on deck; the skiff was just in from the trap—she was still wet with spray.

"I sails with me sons an' gran'sons, zur," said the skipper, smiling. "Sure, I be a old feller t' be down the Labrador, isn't I, zur ?"

He did not mean that. He was proud of his age and strength—glad that he was still able "t' be at the fishin'."

"'Tis a wonder you've lived through it all," said I.

He laughed. "An' why, zur?" he asked.

"Many's the ship wrecked on this coast," I answered.

"Oh no, zur," said he; "not so many, zur, as you might think. Down this way, zur, *we knows how t' sail!*"

That was a succinct explanation of very much that had puzzled me.

"Ah, well," said I, "'tis a hard life."

"Hard?" he asked, doubtfully.

"Yes," I answered; "'tis a hard life—the fishin'."

"Oh no, zur," said he, quietly, looking up from his work. "'Tis just—just life!"

They do, indeed, know how "t' sail." The Newfoundland government, niggardly and utterly independable when the good of the fisherfolk is concerned, of whatever complexion the government may chance to be, but prodigal to an extraordinary degree when individual self-interests are at stake—this is a delicate way of putting an unpleasant truth—keeps no light burning beyond the Strait of Belle Isle; the best it does, I believe, is to give wrecked seamen free passage home. Under these difficult circumstances, no seamen save Newfoundlanders, who are the most skillful and courageous of all, could sail that coast: and they only because they are born to follow the sea—there is no escape for them—and are bred to sailing from their earliest years.

"What you going to be when you grow up?" I once asked a lad on the far northeast coast.

He looked at me in vast astonishment.

"What you going to be, what you going to do," I repeated, "when you grow up?"

Still he did not comprehend. "Eh?" he said.

"What you going to work at," said I, in desperation, "when you're a man?"

"Oh, zur," he answered, understanding at last, "I isn't clever enough t' be a parson!"

And so it went without saying that he was to fish for a living! It is no wonder, then, that the skippers of the fleet know "how t' sail." The remarkable quality of the sea-captains who come from among them impressively attests the fact—not only their quality as sailors, but as men of spirit and proud courage. There is one—now a captain of a coastal boat on the Newfoundland shore—who takes his steamer into a ticklish harbour of a thick, dark night, when everything is black ahead and roundabout, steering only by the echo of the ship's whistle! There is another, a confident seaman, a bluff, high-spirited fellow, who was once delayed by bitter winter weather—an inky night, with ice about, the snow flying, the seas heavy with frost, the wind blowing a gale.

"Where have you been?" they asked him, sarcastically, from the head office. The captain had been on the bridge all night.

"Berry-picking," was his laconic despatch in reply.

There is another—also the captain of a of a coastal steamer—who thought it wise to lie in harbour through a stormy night in the early winter.

"What detains you?" came a message from the head office.

"It is not a fit night for a vessel to be at sea," the captain replied; and thereupon he turned in, believing the matter to be at an end.

The captain had been concerned for his vessel—not for his life; nor yet for his comfort. But the underling at the head office misinterpreted the message.

"What do we pay you for?" he telegraphed.

So the captain took the ship out to sea. Men say that she went out of commission the next day, and that it cost the company a thousand dollars to refit her.

"A dunderhead," say the folk, "can *catch* fish; but it takes a *man* t' find un." It is a chase; and, as the coast proverb has it, "the fish have no bells." It is estimated that there are 7,000 square miles of fishing-banks off the Labrador coast. There will be fish somewhere—not everywhere; not every man will "use his salt" (the schooners go north loaded with salt for curing) or "get his load." In the beginning—this is when the ice first clears away—there is a race for berths. It takes clever, reckless sailing and alert action to secure the best. I am reminded of a skipper who by hard driving to windward and good luck came first of all to a favourable harbour. It was then night, and his crew was weary, so he put off running out his trap-leader until morning; but in the night the wind changed, and when he awoke at dawn there were two other schooners lying quietly at anchor near by and the berths had been "staked." When the traps are down, there follows a period of anxious waiting. Where are the fish? There are no telegraph-lines on that coast. The news must be spread by word of mouth. When, at last, it comes, there is a sudden change of plan—a wild rush to the more favoured grounds.

It is in this scramble that many a skipper makes his great mistake. I was talking with a disconsolate young fellow in a northern harbour where the fish were running thick. The schooners were fast loading; but he had no berth, and was doing but poorly with the passing days.

"If I hadn't—if I only hadn't—took up me trap when I did," said he, "I'd been loaded an' off home. Sure, zur, would you believe it? but I had the berth off the point. Off the point—the berth off the point!" he repeated, earnestly, his eyes wide. "An', look! I hears they's a great run o' fish t' Cutthroat Tickle. So I up with me trap, for I'd been getting' nothin'; an'—an'—would you believe it? but the man that put his down where I took mine up took a hundred quintal[34] out o' that berth next marnin'! An' he'll load," he groaned, "afore the week's out!"

When the fish are running, the work is mercilessly hard; it is kept up night and day; there is no sleep for man or child, save, it may be, an hour's slumber where they toil, just before dawn. The schooner lies at anchor in the harbour, safe enough from wind and sea; the rocks, surrounding the basin in which she lies, keep the harbour water placid forever. But the men set the traps in the open sea, somewhere off the heads, or near one of the outlying islands; it may be miles from the anchorage of the schooner. They put out at dawn—before dawn, rather; for they aim to be at the trap just when the light is strong enough for the hauling. When the skiff is loaded, they put back to harbour in haste, throw the fish on deck, split them, salt them, lay them neatly in the hold, and put out to the trap again. I have seen the harbours—then crowded with fishing-craft—fairly ablaze with light at midnight. Torches were flaring on the decks and in the turf hut on the rocks ashore. The night was quiet; there was not a sound from the tired workers; but the flaring lights made known that the wild, bleak, far-away place—a basin in the midst of barren, uninhabited hills—was still astir with the day's work.

At such times, the toil at the oars, and at the splitting-table, I whether on deck or in the stages—and the lack of sleep, and the icy winds and cold salt spray—is all bitter cruel to suffer. The Labrador fisherman will not readily admit that he lives a hard life; but if you suggest that when the fish are running it may be somewhat more toilsome than lives lived elsewhere, he will grant you something.

"Oh, ay," he'll drawl, "when the fish is runnin', 'tis a bit hard."

---

34 A quintal is, roughly, a hundred pounds. One hundred quintals of green fish are equal, roughly, to thirty of dry, which, at $3, would amount to $90.

Norman Duncan

I learned from a child—he was merry, brave, fond of the adventure—that fishing is a pleasant business in the sunny midsummer months; but that when, late in the fall, the skiff puts out to the trap at dawn, it is wise to plunge one's hands deep in the water before taking the oars, no matter how much it hurts, for one's wrists are then covered with salt-water sores and one's palms are cracked, even though one take the precaution of wearing a brass chain—that, oh, yes! it is wise to plunge one's hands in the cold water, as quick as may be; for thus one may "limber 'em up" before the trap is reached.

"'Tis not hard, now!" said he. "But, oh—oo—oo! when the big nor'easters blow! Oo—oo!" he repeated, with a shrug and a sage shake of the head; "'tis won-der-ful hard those times !"

The return is small. The crews are comprised of from five to ten men, with, occasionally, a sturdy maid for cook, to whom is given thirty dollars for her season's work; some old hands will sail on no ship with a male cook, for, as one of them said, "Sure, some o' thim min can't boil water without burnin' it !" A good season's catch is one hundred quintals of dry fish a man. A simple calculation—with some knowledge of certain factors which I need not state—makes it plain that a man must himself catch, as his share of the trap, 30,000 fish if he is to net a living wage. If his return is $250 he is in the happiest fortune—richly rewarded, beyond his dreams, for his summer's work. One-half of that is sufficient to give any modest man a warm glow of content and pride. Often—it depends largely upon chance and the skill of his skipper—the catch is so poor that he must make the best of twenty-five or thirty dollars. It must not be supposed that the return is always in cash; it is usually in trade, which is quite a different thing—in Newfoundland.

The schooners take many passengers north in the spring. Such are called "freighters" on the coast; they are put ashore at such harbours as they elect, and, for passage for themselves, families, and gear, pay upon the return voyage twenty-five cents for every hundredweight of fish caught. As a matter of course, the vessels are preposterously overcrowded. Dr. Grenfell tells of counting thirty-four men and sixteen women (no mention was made of children) aboard a nineteen-ton schooner, then on the long, rough voyage to the north. The men fish from the coast in small boats just as the more prosperous "green-fish catchers" put out from the schooners. Meantime, they live in mud huts, which are inviting or otherwise, as the womenfolk go; some are damp, cave-like, ill-savoured, crowded; others are airy, cozy, the floors spread deep with powdered shell, the whole immaculately kept. When the party is landed, the women sweep out the last of the winter's snow, the men build great fires on the floors; indeed, the huts are soon ready for occupancy. At best, they are tiny places-much like children's playhouses. There was once a tall man who did not quite fit the sleeping place assigned to him; but with great good nature he cut a hole in the wall, built a miniature addition for his feet, and slept the summer through at comfortable full length. It is a great outing for the children; they romp on the rocks, toddle over the nearer hills, sleep in the sunshine; but if they are eight years old, as one said—or well grown at five or seven—they must do their little share of work.

Withal, the Labradormen are of a simple, God-fearing, clean-lived, hardy race of men. There was once a woman who made boast of her high connection in England, as women will the wide world over; and when she was questioned concerning the position the boasted relative occupied, replied, "Oh, *he's* Superintendent o' Foreign Governments!" There was an austere old Christian who on a Sunday morning left his trap—his whole fortune—lie in the path of a destroying iceberg rather than desecrate the Lord's day by taking it out of the water. Both political parties in Newfoundland shamelessly deceive the credulous fisherfolk; there was a childlike old fellow who, when asked, "And what will you do if there *is* no fish?" confidently answered: "Oh, they's goin' t' be a new Gov'ment. *He'll* take care o' we !" There was a sturdy son of the coast who deserted his schooner at sea and swam ashore. But he had mistaken a barren island for the mainland, which was yet far off; and there he lived, without food, for twenty-seven days! When he was picked up, his condition was such as may not be described (the Labrador fly is a vicious insect); he was unconscious, but he survived to fish many another season.

The mail-boat picked up Skipper Thomas of Carbonear—then master of a loaded schooner—at a small harbour near the Straits. His crew carried him aboard; for he was desperately ill, and wanted to die at home, where his children were.

"He's wonderful bad," said one of the men. "He've consumption."

"I'm just wantin' t' die at home," he said, again and again. "Just that—just where my children be!"

All hearts were with him in that last struggle—but no man dared hope; for the old skipper had already beaten off death longer than death is wont to wait, and his strength was near spent.

"Were you sick when you sailed for the Labrador in the spring?" they asked him.

"Oh, ay," said he; "I were terrible bad then."

"Then why," they said, "why did you come at all?"

They say he looked up in mild surprise.

"I had t' make me livin'," he answered, simply.

His coffin was knocked together on the forward deck next morning—with Carbonear a day's sail beyond.

The fleet goes home in the early fall. The schooners are loaded-some so low with the catch that the water washes into the scuppers. "You could wash your hands on her deck," is the skipper's proudest boast. The feat of seamanship, I do not doubt, is not elsewhere equalled. It is an inspiring sight to see the doughty little craft beating into the wind on a gray day. The harvesting of a field of grain is good to look upon; but I think that there can be no more stirring sight in all the world, no sight more quickly to melt a man's heart, more deeply to move him to love men and bless God, than the sight of the Labrador fleet beating home loaded—toil done, dangers past; the home port at the end of a run with a fair wind. The home-coming, I fancy, is much like the return of the viking ships to the old Norwegian harbours must have been. The lucky skippers strut the village roads with swelling chests, heroes in the sight of all; the old men, long past their labour, listen to new tales and spin old yarns; the maids and the lads renew their interrupted love-makings. There is great rejoicing—feasting, merrymaking, hearty thanksgiving.

Thanks be to God, the fleet's home!

MERRICK

The large-scale Newfoundland fishery led to the first public steamship connection between Newfoundland and Labrador for the benefit of the transient fishermen. At first a boat ran between St. John's and Mannock Island, near Hopedale. By 1883 the connection extended to Nain, stopping there about twice a month. The service continued through the decades and still exists today, although many of its functions have been replaced by road and air service. In their day the coastal boats were a lifeline for both Newfoundland visitors and Labrador settlers. Perhaps the best-known and best-loved of all the coastal boats was the *Kyle*, a ship that became guest and friend to those who waited for her in their small and isolated communities.

In his own inimitable prose, Elliott Merrick describes her arrival and departure from Indian Harbour in 1933. He captures, as no one else can, the sights and sounds of a ship that meant so much to those who occupied and used the Labrador coast. Long before the end of the fifty years she served the coast, the *Kyle* was a legend north and south, as the following song by Henry John Williams of Cartwright attests:

We're heading for our fortune folks, to youse we'll say goodbye.
We've got our welcome now wore out and the beer kegs all gone dry,
So I think we'll jump the *Kyle* now, where fishermen do flop,
Who fished out their poor fathers' berths from the head to White
Point Rock.

Elliott Merrick

"THE KYLE COMES TO INDIAN HARBOUR,"
FROM *Among the Deep Sea Fishers*

In those days, twenty thousand men fished for cod in summer along the Labrador. Indian Harbour Hospital, halfway "down along," was the most northerly medical establishment on the Atlantic coast. This Grenfell Mission station had been built to serve fishermen, their main affliction being dreadful infections caused by fish hooks, fish-cleaning knives, fishbones, and the chafing of oilskins on wrists.

That summer I was a "wop" at the hospital, meaning volunteer With Out Pay. We two wops, Tom and I, were men-of-all-work, among whose duties was the job of watching for the steamer. Every two weeks or so, this salt-caked messenger from away south in St. John's, Newfoundland, anchored briefly in our harbor, with mail, freight and patients who had been collected for us along the coast. We also had patients to be sent south to better-equipped establishments. Because we had no radio to give us word of her whereabouts, and because her skipper was always in a hurry, we had to have some warning of the ship's arrival if everything was to be ready and our motorboat cranked up.

For all these reasons, I found myself one wide and beautiful afternoon up on the Indian Head's bare rock forehead. The spunyard clouds were adrift in the serene sky, the white icebergs adrift in the blue sea. Miles and miles out toward the Bear Islands a huge ice palace the size of a city block, all gleaming turrets and silver pinnacles, drifted south. A mere speck, a schooner was beating north against the breeze. In the other direction, George Island rose dripping from the water twenty miles away; and nearer, close below, fishermen in their punts were jigging cod along the sun's path. Right below my feet were the hospital roof and the harbor, where nine schooners lay at anchor. It was nearly always peaceful and blessed up on the Indian Head. Many times after a week of dirty weather, when that squat, ugly, beautiful hospital bed had been a besieged fort, warm and homely within, lashed without by rain and hail, beaten and rocked by the spray winds and wrapped close around with fog, we got downhearted and unfree. The air in the little ward where the fishermen lay in rows was heavy with pain, the pain of a clogged heart or a broken leg, but mostly the pain of sepsis-swollen fingers and bloated hands, and arms with the bright red streaks and the bulging armpits. Not their moaning and teeth-gritting and silence, not their living or their dying, but just their lying, big-eyed, in a bed got oppressive, so that Tom and I would draw lots to see who would go in there with an armful of wood for the greedy stove. Whoever lost went on tiptoe.

Maybe somebody had died that week and we had to dig him a grave with the others inside the rickety fence on the hillside, and make him a coffin out of old boards in the leaky shop where tools were scarce.

The fact was that Tom and I were the fellow slaves who did the dirty work of this establishment. We carried out the slops. Other times we caulked a boat and whitewashed the hospital with slaked lime that the next rain washed off. We got the water system going from the pond up on the hill and only flooded the kitchen once. We patched the roof and set up stovepipes and put in glass and unloaded countless barrels of flour and food and tons of freight at the wharf. We were hospital orderlies when the doctor was operating before the nurses came; and every rainy day somebody got out the glass and spied the wireless man's old trousers a-flap on the distant Marconi station pole and one of us had a mile to row and four miles of swamp to run through after a message.

Well, after a bad week along came one of those sun-and-silver days and all the schooners had their sails hoisted drying. Tom and I just said "yes" to the doctor and the intern and both nurses and the housekeeper and the cook. We put our hands in our pockets and went up on the Indian Head. We sat there drinking blue enchantment right fresh off the horizon, forgetful that anyone ever died since the world was born. And when we felt so free and wide we couldn't sit still any longer, we ran down the green south slope through the flaming fireweed and daisies and wild peas and bakeapple blossoms, over the black, striped ledges to the beach of white shell. We stripped and dove into the sea's clear liquid ice. It was so cold it burned like fire.

We came out purified and brand-new, and lay on a warm rock to let the salt dry on us. Tom generally told me about his girl, but I stuffed seaweed in my ears. Then we climbed the slope of our treeless island and had a last look from the top before going down to the civilized side where people worked.

Toward the end of the afternoon, with still no smudge of smoke in the north haze, the wind shifted and grew damp. The sky turned gray, the sea slate. A fog bank rose up out of the horizon and hung a few miles offshore. Our silver days were few and did not last long. Perhaps that is why we felt them so.

Tom came up over the edge of the rock, a leather jacket over his blue jersey to break the wind, denim trousers, rubber boots. He stood on the summit, one hand in his bosom and declaimed to encircling space: "Roll on, thou mighty Ocean, roll. Suppose I tell you to stop rolling? Ah, well may you ask what then.

"Supper," he said. "My watch for awhile."

I went down to supper in the square, high-ceilinged dining room where the floor creaked even when the doctor carved codfish. The jolly intern, the grizzled doctor, the housekeeper, and the least pretty of the nurses were there for the eternal codfish in one of its infernal disguises. The intern was telling about the malingerer: "After a week of most careful observation and tests, we have been unable to find anything wrong with him. He eats first-rate and sleeps like a top. So today I poked him under the left knee-cap and I said, 'When I press here do you feel a shooting pain just above your heart?' And he screwed up his face and moaned, 'O Doctor, I finds it wonnerful, right handy against me heart.' And would you believe it, I wiggled his right big toe and said, 'Can you feel a sharp ache in the back of your neck when I move your toe thus?' And he said it made a pain in the back of his neck that was worse than he could stand. He fooled his skipper into sailing him all the way from Nain to Hopedale so he could get down here and enjoy himself all summer."

"Well," said his senior, "we can't encourage that sort of thing, and I mean to speak to him privately. But I venture to say that a month in a Newfoundland fishing vessel would make a rest in bed and plenty of good food a pleasant prospect for most any of us. We'll send him south by the steamer. He lives in Bonavista Bay, I believe?

"And that reminds me, Bud," he said, turning to me. "We are sending that bad rheumatism case, Captain Willett, home by this steamer. He is absolutely helpless, his heart is in bad shape and he is in pain, so go easy with the stretcher. And will you make yourself responsible for Captain Willett's bag of clothes if the steamer comes tonight? See that it is placed in the bunk with him, as I understand there is some money in it."

The rain was beating against the window and the fire roared in the wind-sucked stovepipe while we ate our dessert of cheese and crackers. The back door slammed and we heard Joe, the hospital's young Eskimo helper, stamp the wet off his boots and giggle as he said to the cook, "Steamer's comin'—sometime."

The least pretty nurse went off to relieve the most pretty nurse. The medicos went to the ward. The mail was bagged and everything made ready for the zero hour.

At nine-thirty I stumbled through the rain to the doctor's shack where my bed was. It was a portable cottage guyed with steel cables to ringbolts leaded into the rock ledge. In the tearing wind it was trembling like a Japanese paper house. Doctor came in soon, and together we put up the wooden two-by-four props from wall to wall, an invention of his own designed to prevent the wind from crushing the building flat. I got into bed, leaving my trousers tucked in my boots close beside the chair with sweater and oilskins and mitts. Doctor set the kerosene lamp on a chair beside his bed and commenced to read *The Ring and the Book*. He always had to read himself to sleep, though one would have thought he would be tired enough to sleep standing up.

After an unusual gust, he laid the book on his knees and remarked, "By Jupiter, I've never in my life seen a place like this for wind. I wish you could have been here one night three summers ago. The harbor was boiling with solid foam picked right up off the water. Five schooners went ashore. Burdett had the *Kyle* hove to behind Pigeon Island. She had two anchors down and she steamed all night half-speed to keep them from dragging. No one could think of getting out to the steamer in the morning.

"Burdett was scared stiff, an odd chap, a timid soul, but not a bad skipper. If he were still master of *Kyle* we could depend on it he'd be snugged away in some harbor tonight. No fear of his showing up. But this fellow Clark! By George, the way he drives that ship is a miracle. Anyone else would pile her up twenty times a trip, running all night the way he does, fair or foul, in and out the narrow tickles, among the islands, fog, rain, ice, never a buoy or a light, making his stops as regularly as a suburban tram. There isn't a man on earth who knows this coast the way he does. Mark my words, he'll be along tonight about three o'clock when it's blackest. But you must get some sleep. It's your watch from twelve to two and Joe will call you." He went on with his book and I fell asleep.

Joe stood in the middle of the room, in his hand a lantern throwing shadows. Shining rain ran down his oilskins onto the floor and his round cheeks glistened. "Steamer's comin'," he chirped, and ran out the door. I looked at the clock. Ten of twelve.

Doctor was dressed before I was. He was buttoning his sou'wester under his chin when we heard her blow outside the harbor, "Whaw-w-w! Whaw-w-w-w!" Deep bass, ominous, making the already riven air tremble. A long monster afloat out there in the blackness, its scaly length lifted and rippled by the running combers, its yawning mouth agape, bellowing hoarsely for a victim.

We groped in the rain. Lights were springing up in the hospital. The prettiest nurse was in the ward fixing the stretcher for Captain Willett. Tom came in. I tied the Captain's clothes bag around my waist under the oilskins. He also had a suitcase, but that was already down at the wharf with the mail sack. Tom and I rolled him onto the stretcher and it hurt him badly.

The malingerer was there and dressed. I wondered if he knew we knew. The other patients were all awake, looking on with sleepy eyes. We covered the stretcher with a canvas, got him through the door and went down the long, slippery boardwalk. We walked as gently as we could, but he, poor fellow, gave a groan about every other step. The motorboat was at the wharf and Joe and the intern helped us lay the stretcher crosswise on the gunnels. He seemed to feel better with the boat rocking under him. Tom lifted a corner of the canvas. "How's that, Captain?"

"All shipshape, son," the sick man smiled.

Doctor came a-running, and with him at the tiller we shoved off. The intern and I stood on the foredeck hanging to the mast. Joe was at the engine, for he loved engines with a child's love of a marvelous toy. "Hang onto that stretcher," Doctor called cheerily. "We don't want to lose you, Captain."

"Twouldn't matter much," the Captain mumbled.

The shore dropped out as though it had fallen over the edge of an abyss. The rain stung and it was cold as winter. The booming surf on the point was all we had to guide us. Though the harbor was narrow, we might have been in mid-ocean for all we could see. The boat began to thrash and plunge as we got out onto the broader water. Now in the darkness round about we could hear the irregular, intermingled pung-pung-pung-pung-pung of fishermen's exhausts, coming from all the coves and bights and tickles within a mile or two to see the floating palace, the herald of the other world, the news-bearer, the steamer.

We could make her out now, a low, slim ship, something like a destroyer, outlined in lights, pawing there impatient. Shouts came out of the dark, the hiss of steam, the throbbing of her pumps. Fishermen's boats were clustered three deep alongside and astern, squeaking and crunching when they touched, a man in each with a boathook or a sculling oar, fending off; fishermen watching their chance to jump from one to the other as they rose and fell, fishermen swarming up the steamer's side and throwing a leg over the rail like attackers storming a citadel.

We rounded the stem and came up to the companion ladder slung on the port side. "Shut 'er off," Doctor called. We drifted in and our coiled painter sailed over the rail and hit the deck with a satisfying thwack. A sailor ran forward with it and brought us alongside the companionway, which was banging viciously. "Watch your feet," the sailor shouted. The boat rose half way up the wooden stair, then sank six feet below the bottom step.

Clark's huge head and shoulders loomed over the bridge wing above. "Go for'r'd and we'll hoist your man with the tackle!" he yelled.

The sailor on deck hauled us forward, passing our painter outside each stanchion as he went. When we were abreast of the hatch, the cargo boom swung over, the winch rattled and the hook descended, a chain barrel-sling dangling from it. With four doubles of codline we lashed each corner of the stretcher to the barrelsling. The bo's'n stood above holding the winch cable out from the ship's side. "Come up easy," he sang, and Captain Willett was whisked to the deck as smooth as glass.

Tom and I scrambled aboard on a line and carried him aft to the sickbay, which was also the steerage cabin. We fixed him comfortably in a bunk, and when it was over he sighed with relief. "You're a pair o' manhandlers all right," he grinned. "You lay another finger on me and I'll pitch you overboard, the two of ye." He had grit, and no mistake.

"Good luck, Captain," Tom said hurriedly.

"All right, b'y," he replied wearily.

The ship's doctor came in, an ancient pharmacist, and we told him Doctor would be there with instructions presently.

We hurried along the wet deck to the mailroom just forward, swung open the heavy oak door and stepped in. The mailman was a sandy-haired, ageless person with a cracked voice and every grain of gossip from eight hundred miles of coast on his tongue's tip. In one corner was his bunk, in the other a rack of open-mouthed mail sacks. Along the forward side of the cabin stood a long sorting table and opposite it a solid wall of pigeon holes, each bearing the name of one of the scores of little harbors and coves the steamer called at: Belle Isle, Battle Harbour, Cape Charles, Seal Islands, Fishing Ships, Hawke's Harbour, Occasional Harbour, Domino, Spotted Islands, Boulter's Rock, Gready, Cartwright, Rigolet, White Bear, Cut-throat, Ragged Islands, Emily, Holton, Makkovik and dozens more.

"Well, boys," he squeaked, "what's the news? I hear Jimmie Barnes' boy...."

"Yes," interrupted Tom, "he's in the hospital with an infected foot, but he's getting better. Got any mail for us?"

"Well, boys, all your mail's gone ashore in the boat to King's. But now here's something you won't see every day." With enormous enjoyment he handed Tom a letter postmarked Boston and addressed: Mr. Thomas Witherspoon Labrador.

"Why don't you tell your friends, your street and number, hey? Oh, ho, ho!"

Tom was duly flabbergasted and we left swearing eternal friendship. On the way by, we stopped to smell the heat and oil and look down through the slippery steel engine room companionway at the gleaming arms below and the polished massive metal in curious shapes. Next a glance into the little stokehole hell to see them open the doors and the red glare light the heaver's naked shoulders. One of them had a pinched-out cigarette behind his ear. He slammed the furnace door with his shovel and reached for the butt.

All of it was new to us, every trip. To see electric lights, steam condensers, engines, fittings of this floating, man-built stronghold was like polishing Aladdin's lamp. We had grown used to such things as wood and rock and a lopsided grindstone ashore.

Cascades of water were falling from the boat deck up above. Around the forward hatch searchlights shone warm and yellow. The winch chattered and stopped and chattered again. Barrels and boxes in slings came up through the hatch and disappeared over the side. The mate stood at the winch levers, and now and again he tightened or loosened a small wheel above the drum. The piston flew in and out and the drum unrolled and rolled itself in cable. The mate watched with cat's eyes, and the two levers in his hands guided the swinging loads with relentless precision, no matter that the ship was rolling. Jimmie, the bos'n, leaned over the side and signaled with his hand. It was easy to drop a puncheon through the bottom of a dancing trap boat, and it had often been done.

The crew had news of every schooner up along or down along, and while they worked they dished it out in snatches to the fishermen. Everyone was drenched, everyone was shivering, everyone was awake. If the crew of this ship ever slept, no one knew when.

Inside the first-class quarters beneath the bridge, the passengers had to be asleep, missing all this, for the white-paneled stateroom doors were tight closed. Below, in the brightly lit corridor, a heavy brass port had been unbolted and swung open for a few minutes in harbor. Tom and I went down the carpeted, branching stairs, feeling the smooth mahogany bannisters with pagan joy. Ostensibly it was to talk with Sam, the steward, in the spick-and-span dining salon and get him to sell us a couple of oranges. But really it was to contrast the white, speckless woodwork and the shining brass, this strong interior elegance, with the black, ruthless night outside. It satisfied a craving, as a spoonful of rich syrup might. Never unthreatened, buried under seas, wallowing over—how did they keep this inner jewel unmarked by the elements?

We had to run up the narrow companionway for a hello to Captain Clark on the bridge. In cowhide seaboots and a thick gray ulster bulged by his barrel chest, he stalked the bridge, pausing now and again to pull aside the canvas wind screen and glare at the foredeck, his cap pulled down over his red eyes. He was a walrus of a man, with a voice like the bass notes of a viol.

"Ha!" he growled, looking us over. "Your own mothers wouldn't know ye, ye two bloomin' Huskimaws. Got ye out of bed, eh? Do ye good. A dirty night, sure enough. A good trip? Yes, good enough. All right, two weeks next Thursday, God willing."

Down on the deck there was hurry. She couldn't stay much longer. The last gasoline drums were going over the side. The winch chattered furiously. From up above Captain Clark bellowed down into the searchlit hatch, "Hey! Get done!"

"Whaw-w-w!" A jet of steam jumped from the funnel and the hideous blare smote the night again. On the fo'c'sle head the anchor winch started to thump. Chain rattled in the hawsehole. Fishermen scrambled for their boats, the ship already underway.

Bells clanged in the engine room, half astern, wheel hard over, full ahead. The sea thundered under her counter. Lines were flying, men were leaping. Fishermen's boats began to pung. Last words shouted.

She steamed away into the inky night, masthead lights lurching, bound for another reef-guarded harbor of rock, as though she were steered by smell.

CRUMMEY

Michael Crummey's father was one of those Newfoundlanders who sailed to the Labrador. In the postscript to *Hard Light,* Crummey says it was his father's voice and his father's stories—more than anyone else's—that made him want to write these things down: the kinds of experiences that so many from Conception and Trinity bays and other parts of the Island had over many years of fishing "on the Labrador." Mostly it was for cod, either fresh or salted, or cod HOG-head on gutted. But there was "birdin'" and "woodin'" too. From time to time the sea would win its battle with some unfortunate ship whose crew would then be subjected to the inevitable salvage operation where one man's loss is another man's bounty.

The whaling station at Hawke Harbour was established in 1905 by Norwegians, but the fifty years of whaling had little effect on the region's economy. The Rangers were a paramilitary organization started by the Commission of Government in the 1930s to provide a police presence, and so much more, in rural communities around the Island and Labrador. The nurse in the story was one of many Americans who heard the call of Grenfell and volunteered to serve on the remote reaches of the Labrador coast, meeting a kindred spirit, as so many of them did.

Michael Crummey is an award-winning poet and novelist from Newfoundland and Labrador, one whose roots are on the Island but who also has lived in Labrador. His insights and writing are all the more perceptive because of it.

Michael Crummey

EXCERPT FROM *Hard Light*, 1998

The Law of the Ocean

Domino Run, Labrador, 1943

The Americans had dozens of boats on the coast during the war years, surveying the islands, mapping every nook. They had poles erected on all the headlands with little silk rags at the top, forty, fifty feet high some of them. We had no idea what they were there for, but we stole every piece of silk we came across, carrying them down the pole in our teeth, they were perfect to boil up a bit of peas pudding, or to use as a handkerchief.

We were out jigging one afternoon, mid-August, the weather fine enough until the breeze turned and a wind as warm as furnace exhaust came up. Took in our lines and headed straight back into the Tickle, knowing what to expect behind it. Passed one of those survey ships on our way, holed up in a shallow cove and they hadn't even dropped anchor, just put out a grapple. We stopped in to warn them but the skipper more or less laughed at us, and the squall came on just like we said it would, the wind wicked enough to strip the flesh off a cow.

Next morning that little survey boat was sitting on dry land, blown twenty feet up off the water. When word got out, every boat in the Tickle headed straight for the cove and we made pretty short work of it. Took anything that wasn't bolted down, food, silverware, bedding, books and maps, compasses, liquor, clothes. Got my hands on one of those eight-day clocks they had aboard, but I was too greedy to take it all the way to Father's boat; hid it behind a bush and turned back to the ship for something else. And I'll be goddamned if someone didn't go and steal it on me.

The Americans were standing alongside but they didn't say a word. Law of the ocean, you see, salvage. We were like a pack of savages besides, seventy or eighty men and boys climbing in over the side, what could they say? Cleared the boat in fifteen minutes, as if we were trying to save family heirlooms from a burning building.

The Americans sent up a tug later that day to take the ship off the land and we all helped out where we could, throwing a few lines around the masthead, rocking her back and forth until she shimmied free and slipped into the water like a seal off an icepan.

We kept waiting for another chance like that to come along, but the Americans got smarter afterwards or maybe they just got luckier. It's a job to say the difference between those two at the best of times.

Grace

Indian Tickle, Labrador, 1945

There's no saying why things turn out one way and not another. It could have been me easy enough.

We were out after a meal of birds, took the boat around the head and a little ways into the Bay where they had their nests. Four of us, myself and Ken Powell, Bill Delaney, and Sandy who was just home from overseas. He'd brought a rifle back with him, a sharp doublebarrelled thing with a German name, he could hit a turr at two hundred yards with that gun.

Sandy and Bill went ashore, and me and Ken pulled around in the boat to put the puffins to wing; they'd head straight for their nests and the other two would be waiting for them there. After half an hour or so we came into the shore to trade off, and Sandy passed me his gun as he stepped into the boat. Well, I can't say what changed my mind. I'd been after Sandy to let me use that rifle from the start of the season. Didn't like the way it sat in my hands and I stopped them just before they pushed off. "Here my son," I said, "I'm not used to this thing. Give me back the single." And Sandy passed it to me with this queer grin on his face, like he'd just won a bet with somebody.

We turned our backs and headed up the hill a ways, and then we heard it, a rifle shot but louder and not as clean, there was a grating sound like metal giving way. Sandy had seen a bird on his way off the shore, lifted the gun and fired. He threw it over the side and we never could find it to see what had happened exactly, but three of his fingers were gone, the bone of the first knuckle on his ring finger jutting from slivers of flesh as raw as a flayed cod.

The nearest hospital was in Cartwright, we took the boat and got started about six in the evening, going all night to Grady where we stopped in for a cup of tea. We pushed on right away though because Sandy's hand had come alive by then and he was throwing up with the pain, "my Jesus Christ," he kept saying, "the fucking thing is on fire." We had a bucket of salt water and that"s where he kept it, dipping up a fresh lot every half hour or so, tossing the bloody stuff over the side.

It was ten days before he came back on one of the hospital boats, they'd sawed off the bit of knuckle from his ring finger then sewed him up, and he went right to work. I did what I could to pick up the slack for him, it could have been me afterall. You'd see that queer grin on his face when his mangled hand couldn't do what he wanted, as if he was thinking about those three lost fingers, pale as plucked birds, rotting at the bottom of the Bay.

What We Needed
Battle Harbour, Labrador, Early 1930's
Mother always said I would never find a man tall enough to marry me. People worried about those sorts of things in Connecticut. I left for Labrador at twenty-three, a green nurse standing head and shoulders over every girl I trained with and still single.

The first Newfoundland Ranger posted on the coast arrived a year later, fresh from three weeks of instruction in St. John's. A boat dropped him at the Battle Harbour wharf in October with enough rough lumber to put a roof over his head. The weather had already begun to turn by then, most of the fishing crews had scuttled back to the Island to wait out the winter. He stood there a long time, staring at that stack of wood, wondering how he was going to make something of it before the snow settled in.

There were eight men from Twillingate on the wharf with all their outfit: nets and chests, a few quintals of cured fish, waiting to take the last coastal boat of the season home. They were sitting on their gear, a few of them with pipes, halos of tobacco smoke around their heads. It was a Wednesday afternoon and the *Kyle* wasn't due into Battle Harbour until the weekend. He nodded in their direction.

It took them three days to put up the house, just a stone's throw from the hospital. He bought a new iron stove and a couple of chairs from Slade's, used a piece of lumber laid across wood horses for a table. He had no other furniture and there was nothing more to be had until the *Kyle* started its run again in the spring. He took a picture of the men beside the nearly finished shack, their hands stuffed down the front of coveralls, a blond spill of sawdust on their shoulders. Saw them off on the *Kyle* that Sunday, slipping the skipper a bottle of rum for the trip back to Notre Dame Bay.

A lot of things were done that way on the coast: because they had to be done, because there was no one else to do them. When the doctor was called away to other outports, the nurses delivered children, amputated limbs on fire with gangrene, sometimes only an ordinary carpenter's saw pulling through flesh and bone.

On the last decently warm morning of that year he saw nurses setting up beds to lay the TB patients out in the fresh air. Every fine day saw a row of them on the hospital veranda, below the inscription on the building that read *Such as you have done to the least of these my brethren, so have you done unto me.* He put on his uniform and boots, stepped along the path to the hospital and asked the first nurse he encountered about any extra cots he might be able to borrow or rent for the winter. When I looked up at him the heat of a blush flooded my face. He stood six feet six inches tall, a little higher in his boots.

My bridesmaids were the other nurses, and two men from Twillingate stood for the groom, dressed in their coveralls. He was relieved of his position for failing to remain single four years after joining the police force, built a small schooner and worked the coast for the Grenfell Mission, bringing patients from as far away as Red Bay and Rigolet for treatment or surgery.

We didn't have much back then, but we had what we needed. A house, a stove for a bit of fire, some furniture. A four poster bed brought in on the *Kyle* the summer we were wed.

All the Way Home

Hawke Island Whaling Station, late 1930's

The *Kyle* went into Hawke's Harbour every season,
shallow bay stained the colour of wine;
storm of gulls over the water,
a racket like the noise of some enormous machine choked with rust,
grinding to a standstill.
Went ashore to have a look one year,
the whaling room about the size
of an airplane hangar but lower,
the air inside the building bloated
with the stink of opened carcass;
the one I saw was as long as a small schooner
maybe sixty or seventy feet,
five men in cleated boots scaling the back and sides,
hacking two feet through hide and blubber
with a blade curved like a scythe;
hook and cable attached to winch
it off in strips then, as if they were
pulling up old carpet from a hallway.
A man can get used to anything, I suppose.
I tried a piece of whale meat and liked it,
although it was coarse, and stringy
as a square of cloth.
One of the whalers showed me the harpoons up
close, explained how they explode inside the body
or open up to grapple bone and tissue.
He said a big one might drag the boat
half a day past Square Islands before
they could winch in and turn for the harbour,
a narrow trail of blood on the water's surface like a string they could follow
    all the way home.

Cousin

Saddle Island, Red Bay, c.1550

The world's largest whaling station, scores of Basque sailors hunting Rights and Bowheads up and down the coast in 16ft skiffs, six men at the oars and one straddled across the bow as they crest the back of a steaming whale, oak shaft of the harpoon hefted above his shoulder like a torch meant to light their way through night and fog. The weight of a falling man pierces the water's skin, the edgeless shape moving beneath it like a dark flame.

A speared Bowhead could drag a boat for hours, trailing blood and bellowing before it died of exhaustion or its wounds, the oarsmen rowing furiously to keep steady beside it, avoiding the piston slap of the animal's tail that could hammer the open skiff to pieces when it surfaced. Thousands hauled up in the lee of Saddle Island to be rendered every season, the enormous bodies like stolen vehicles being stripped for parts: the thick, pliant hide stretched across umbrella frames in France and Spain, the finest women in Europe corsetted with stays of whale baleen; tons of fat boiled down in copper cauldrons, a single schooner carrying 700 barrels of oil home in the fall.

The useless bones dumped in Red Bay Harbour—the curved tusk of the mandibles, hollow vertebrae, the long fine bones of the flipper: carpals, meta-carpals, phalanges, cousin to the human hand.

The remains of a hundred whalers interred on Saddle Island, their heads facing West, a row of stones weighed on their chests as if to submerge them in the shallow pool of earth, to keep them from coming up for air.

The corpses of several men often exhumed from a single grave, victims of a common misfortune. A seven man crew sometimes buried side by side, their livelihood their undoing; shoulders touching underground, long fine bones of the fingers pale as candle light folded nearly in the hollow of their laps.

The Women

There was one in every fishing crew of four or five, brought along to cook and keep the shack in decent shape, and do their part with making the fish when the traps were coming up full, cutting throats or keeping the puncheon tub filled

Michael Crummey

with water. They helped set the salt cod out on the bawns for drying in August, called out of the kitchen if a squall of rain came on to gather it up before it was ruined.

Most were girls whose families needed the wage, some as young as thirteen, up before sunrise to light the fire for tea and last to bed at night, the hot coals doused with a kettle of water.

Usually the girl had her own room beside the skipper's downstairs, the rest of the crew shoved into bunks under the attic eaves on mattresses stuffed with wood shavings. Sometimes it was only a blanket hung from the rafters that stood between her and the men.

When the work slowed after the capelin scull, a fiddle might be coaxed from a corner on Saturday nights, lips set to a crock of moonshine, followed by a bit of dancing, heels hammering the planks down in the bunkhouse. The single boys courted hard, they'd fall in love just to make it easier getting through the season. There was a carousel of compliments, of flirting, there were comments about the light in a girl's eyes or the darkness of her hair. There was romance of a sort to be considered: coals to be fanned alive or soused with the wet of a cold shoulder. The fire of loneliness and fatigue smouldering in the belly.

Most of it came to nothing but idle talk and foolishness, though every year there were marriages seeded on the Labrador islands, along with a few unhappier things. A child sailing home pregnant in the fall and four men swearing they never laid a hand upon her.

PADDON

Tony Paddon's father, Harry, was one of those who heard the call of Wilfred Grenfell and followed him to Labrador. Harry and his wife, Mina, became strong and prominent figures in Labrador, establishing the first medical and educational services and engaging in a much wider leadership. Both are still revered today in Labrador, and Harry Paddon's "Ode to Labrador" is still its unofficial national anthem. Sadly, Harry died in 1939 at the age of 58, leaving Mina to carry on alone at North West River and to administer the far-flung and growing medical service. For her outstanding work, she received the Order of the British Empire.

Following the war and his service in the Royal Canadian Navy in ships of the line, Tony Paddon, born in Indian Harbour, returned to take over his father's medical and social work. It was clear to him that many Labradorians, particularly the Innu and Inuit, were not comfortable going to St. Anthony, on the northern tip of the Island, for medical services and that the Labrador operation should be separate. He returned to North West River to set up a special zone of care for his people. He saw the Mission grow and develop as it entered the age of radio and airplanes. In northern Labrador his work was often in partnership with the Moravian Church, which had established Christian missions among the Inuit from 1770. Still, his prime highway was the North Atlantic, which constantly challenged him and his work. His medicine had to be practiced with ingenuity, optimism, and good luck, as he recounts in this excerpt from his memoirs.

Tony Paddon's contribution to Labrador life was recognized by the Royal Bank Award and by his appointment in the 1980s as lieutenant-governor of Newfoundland and Labrador.

W. A. Paddon

"Winter at Cartwright," from *Labrador Doctor*, 1989

We stayed a few days at North West River, where Mother was still holding the fort. While I was there, a tragic accident occurred—but with fortunate repercussions for us. During the previous winter, an American bomber had refuelled at Goose Airbase and taken off for Britain, flying down Lake Melville. But it could not gain sufficient altitude, and finally hit the ice a few miles east of North West River, breaking through and smashing its hull before sinking, apparently with all on board. The bomber was reported to have been loaded with supplies, including a large amount of penicillin for the American hospitals in Britain, where many U.S. military personnel were still being treated. One day, some children came in with some little glass vials, sealed with rubber caps. The labels had been washed off the vials. "Were they poison?" the youngsters wanted to know. "What were they for?"

Suddenly, I realized what they were for. "Where did you find them?" They had found several on the sandy beach, and thought more were washing ashore. "I'll give you two cents for each one, if you'll get me all you can find. They are real medicine if the doctor knows what to do with them." They hurried off to get more vials, and in the next few days brought me about 300 or 400 of them, all well preserved, despite weeks in the frigid depths of Lake Melville. Each contained 10,000 units of penicillin, which was then considered an adequate dose for any emergency. Today, we may use doses of a million units or more—sometimes much more—and occasionally even the biggest dose is shrugged off by older and wiser bacteria. As we had no refrigeration, we stowed it all in the hospital basement, which was cool all year round. I could not help wishing that I had had just a few of these vials back in 1939: they would almost certainly have saved my father's life.

Leaving North West River, we made our way north. It was a joy to see the people of Rigolet, Indian Harbour, Makkovik, Hopedale, Davis Inlet and many other villages and fishing stations I had come to know well while working during summers aboard the Maraval with my father. But it was also sad to see tuberculosis still spreading: the hollow cheeks with their bright red flush; the emaciated hands extended to shake mine; the ceaseless coughing. I thought of my penicillin supply from the sunken bomber: it was no use against tuberculosis, but surely a variation was not far from discovery—something that would do the same thing for tuberculosis that penicillin was doing for other infections.

One morning before breakfast, we entered Nain and the air horn shook the village to life. First to the ship was Bill Peacock, a Moravian missionary and well-loved friend. I met him at the ship's ladder and started to greet him, when he interrupted: "Our little daughter, she has pneumonia, I think. Come, quick. She's in an awful state!" It took no time to grab a handful of our salvaged vials, a syringe, and some needles. We went ashore as fast as the motorboat would take us, and up to the missionary's residence. There we found a desperately sick little girl, listless and fretful, her skin starting to look blue. It was pneumonia, and both sides of her chest were involved. She was so weak that she didn't even struggle when the first needle went into her buttock; and she got four ampoules, which I felt would help. There was nothing else I could do for the moment, so Bill joined me aboard for the rest of the morning, acting as my interpreter for the mainly Inuit patients who came through our clinic, hour after hour. With a daughter in critical condition at home, he decided it would be better for him to do something useful than watch her struggle for breath. Bill spoke the Inuit language fluently, knew everybody in the village, was aware of their health, and was invaluable in the clinic.

As we worked together, progress reports about Bill's daughter reached us frequently. The first message was that the little girl was "alright still," and a while later, we heard that she seemed a little better. At noon, I was standing over the child, and Bill's wife, Doris, was saying that her daughter had started to improve ever since the first interminable hour. Indeed, the child was pink, breathing more easily, and clearly making a fine response to the antibiotic.

It was my first meeting with her mother, who, along with Bill Peacock, would become long-time friends to my wife and me. Their collective knowledge of the people they served would always be made available to me in my work: we would always share our insights and work toward common ends; and we would always be welcome as guests in each other's homes. As missionaries, the Peacocks practised what they preached, worked completely for the benefit of the people they served, and were tireless in their efforts to help the Inuit preserve their language and identity. They adjusted skilfully to the influx of new people and customs flooding into Labrador after the war, and they encouraged the Inuit to hold onto as many of the benefits of the old ways as possible: this would win them the deep respect of these indigenous peoples as painful change threw their lives into turmoil.

The *Maraval* went as far north as Saglak Bay, famous for char fishing. The arctic char is a beautiful trout which spends much of its life in salt water, but makes a complex series of journeys back to fresh water during the year. Although it is a gourmet delicacy, it was then being salted and shipped in barrels as a fairly lowgrade fish food, but subsequent efforts to freeze it, and ship it to markets where it would fetch its true value, have since been successful.

The Inuit in the northern grounds lived in tents, which were dwarfed by towering cliffs that dropped 2,000 to 3,000 feet, almost vertically, to the shore. They all came out in their boats for clinic aboard the ship, and when we examined them, they looked well and vigorous—they were always happier following the old ways than in town. But appearances were deceiving. It was the last summer we would be working without X-ray machines aboard, and not until the following summer did we find on X-ray survey that 37 per cent of the Hebron Inuit had advanced open tuberculosis.

On the way south, we visited the Innu settlement of Davis Inlet, where, for the first time in eight years, I saw Joe Rich, the long-time chief. He had much to tell me. Evidence of increasing tuberculosis among his people was painfully obvious, and the urgent need for an X-ray machine even more so.

The ship continued south to St. Anthony, after letting me off back at North West River. There would be a second trip north in September, to check on patients I had already seen, and to carry south as many patients as we could squeeze into the ship, plus any children who were to spend the winter in the dormitories and schoolrooms of North West River.

At North West River, a new barn was rising rapidly. It would house six cows plus a number of hens, and though it was less palatial than Dr. Curtis's splendid building, it would prove warm and efficient. Staff contributions paid for most of the work, as association money was scarce at that time.

Summer volunteers were busy with the usual work of hauling great booms of wood—mostly black spruce and birch—for the winter. The two small dormitories and the worn-out little school building were deteriorating rapidly after twenty years of having lively youngsters as inhabitants; in fact, they were so worn that a great deal of firewood had to be burned to keep them warm. But the most serious cause for worry was the hospital. Considering the severity of the climate, it had lasted well, but twenty-two years had been particularly hard on the shingled roof, which was vulnerable to great ridges of ice that formed along the eaves, and cradled pools of water when the weather was mild. This water then generally ran into the attic, where my mother had strategically placed a large number of buckets. The attic also served as a storeroom for medicines, and as the "clothing store." The association was still soliciting good used clothing, which was shipped north and distributed to those in real need, in exchange for some game or trout, a gallon of berries, or handicrafts of various sorts.

The little operating room generally contained six beds for tuberculosis cases—always full—so operations were performed wherever there was room. The nurse's bedroom was usually the choice, and Mother frequently stripped the room of her belongings before we set up our rickety old operating table there.

There was a large room at the back of the hospital on the ground floor. It was called the Social Room, and part of it became the dental area and clinical laboratory—where I could do my blood counts or typings, hunt for tuberculosis organisms, or do white blood counts. In 1948, we added a portable X-ray machine, with its own darkroom in the back porch. The arrangement worked out

W. A. Paddon

much better than we had any reason to hope for: my technical facilities were partitioned off by a wall, so that the Social Room could still be used for village functions and parties. As for the staff, my mother was still extremely helpful, and we also had an excellent nurse and midwife, Margaret Ormerod. But the luxury of having two nurses couldn't last forever: one day, Mother administered her final anaesthetic and announced her retirement. I don't know how many she had given for Father, for me and for many other doctors, but all her patients had regained consciousness uneventfully.

It was with a certain amount of reluctance that I prepared to leave familiar North West River and go south on the *Maraval* to Cartwright. On our trip, we visited each community as we reached it, held clinics, and picked up patients. When we finally arrived at Cartwright, I received a warm welcome from the Forsyths.

Dr. Forsyth served with the association from the early 1930s, mostly in the same area. A quiet man who deserved much more credit than he ever received, he ran the Cartwright station very well, and after the death of my father, he also managed to visit the northern district by dog team from time to time, which was much appreciated, since his own district extended to the Straits of Belle Isle and required a good deal of travelling. He married Claire Ruland, a vigorous and efficient nurse, and together they did a fine job of promoting education as well as health. Many of their students, educated in a large boarding school, later made very important contributions to Labrador, confirming the views of Sir Wilfred Grenfell and my father that knowledge offered quite as much to the people of Labrador—even to their health—as medical and surgical treatment.

At Cartwright, Dr. Forsyth took me through the station, demonstrating the eccentricities of the antique sterilizer, the emergency lighting plant and the little portable X-ray; we also made rounds, and he enlightened me about the patients then in hospital. Most were tuberculosis cases, and few, sadly, were to live the extra year that would have brought them streptomycin and a good chance of recovery. All in all, it was a much more modern and better-equipped facility than North West River—and I suspect that Dr. Curtis hoped it might lure me away from North West River. None the less, there were some important equipment shortages: like me, Dr. Forsyth probably encountered the association's trend toward centralization of resources. The next day, he and his wife were on their way, and it was pleasant to be suddenly promoted from the most junior doctor in the place to the most senior, even if the only, doctor.

Since Dr. Forsyth travelled a good deal, my main staff, nurses Margaret Darby and Edith Miller, were used to being self-sufficient. They provided ante-natal care, delivered babies, and altogether ran a spotless ship. A Miss Yellowlees ran the dormitory unit with a very firm but friendly hand. Unlike North West River, this station had full water and sewage, although the electrical power, as in North West River, came from a gasoline generator and was turned off at 10:00 p.m. In emergencies, it was customary to turn on the generator that supplied power to the X-ray machine; and there was a switching system which connected the lines supplying wards, the operating room and other essential areas. For the rest, it was kerosene lamps in emergencies, and every night from 10:00 p.m. until daybreak. This system was to play a leading role in my first operation.

Several days after arrival, I was awakened one night to a report that one of our patients, Mr. Mesher, was having a bad attack of something. Dr. Forsyth had told me about him—chronic recurring gall bladder. He did not want surgery, I was told, and usually calmed down on sedation and atropine. Forsyth had repeated the same pronouncement my old surgical chief had used, saying, "These cases look very dramatic, but they virtually never rupture their gall bladders, and expectancy is the best treatment." When I reached him, the patient was pale, somewhat shocked, and in acute pain, his abdomen rigid. Suddenly awakened from sleep by agonizing cramps, he had screamed with pain for several minutes.

Clearly, there had been some kind of catastrophe inside, and despite what I had been told, I had a fair idea what it was. Further inspection and exploration seemed only to confirm my suspicion. The two nurses waited expectantly. During my entire stay at St. Anthony—and despite the innumerable operations performed there—I had never been given a single one to do myself. Indeed, the only major unsupervised operation I had ever performed had been on a destroyer in the North Atlantic.

Well, if I could manage then, I could now—though heaven knew what I would find inside Mr. Mesher. The familiar routine—the scrubbing up, the gowning, the sight of the shining instruments—produced confidence. A bit of pentothal, then ether administered by nurse Miller, who had had plenty of anaesthetic experience, and off we went. There was no blood-typing sera on hand, but two units of whole dried plasma (liberated from a good-natured American surgeon at Goose Bay) were waiting in a sterile package. All went splendidly: the patient's blood pressure returned to a respectable level, nurse Darby assisted efficiently, the abdominal wall was open—and we were suddenly in pitch darkness!

There are few things better calculated to provide a challenge to any surgeon than sudden darkness. It certainly had me flustered. "Darby, a flashlight! No lamp near that ether! Edith, keep him light (meaning lightly anaesthetized). I'll go down and start up the X-ray generator."

"Doctor, I'll run and call Harvey!" But Harvey [Bird], the station foreman, lived some distance from the hospital, whereas the "surgeon of the day" was familiar with balky lighting plants, had studied this one, and had no time to waste. Down I went, with flashlight and plenty of hope. Generator won't start! Fuel? Enough. Sparkplugs? Have to change them. Wrench, Nurse. (Damn. Should have brought her.) Ah, here's the wrench. Plugs in the engine very bad—and carbonned up. No new ones. Search around. A saucer with half a dozen used ones. Put two in, after a quick scrape and a brush. Try again. It catches, hesitates, backfires, picks up and—settles down to its usual industrious hum, which causes voices upstairs to shout, "They're on!" Back in O.R., the patient still asleep. Discard the filthy gown at full speed—gloves, and so on. Hand wash in strong bichloride of mercury; no time to scrub. Fresh gloves, cap, mask, and back to work. Frankly, I was appalled, but in the back of my mind was the humorous idea: What would they think of this at St. Luke's?

The moment the abdomen was open, a sudden upwelling of something pitch-black further unsettled me, until it was apparent that these were hundreds of little black gallstones, from split-pea size to about twice that circumference. I bailed them out with a beaker, but more came; enough to fill three large coffee cups. At last, the stream ended; my assistant and I picked up as many as we could—they seemed to be everywhere—and time started running out. "Blood pressure dropping," said Miller.

"Tilt the table down a bit, get me the plasma and distilled water and a l00-cc. syringe, oh—and your biggest needle! Don't let him wake up." I hoped the big syringe would not stick; plasma can be like glue. But it was a large-bore needle; no trouble at all. The plasma flowed easily. This was before the day of ready-made intravenous units; we would normally pour serum into a glass vessel and place it on a stand, allowing gravity to draw it down an intravenous needle. But there was no time for that. One hundred cc. of plasma into a large vein, then another hundred, and another. After 500 cc., the blood pressure was rising. Another 200, and it was acceptable. I still don't know if this unorthodox treatment was correct, but if it was not, it didn't do any harm. As I finished up my first cholecystectomy, the patient seemed to be in good condition. Perhaps the five-minute delay, during which the engine in the basement had monopolized the available medical talent, had done him no harm. Anyway, a drain was inserted and it drained diligently for us. When the patient awoke, he complained of being cold and thirsty— although he had had adequate intravenous fluids—but reluctantly conceded that maybe we "done him good." But he wanted to be back in a real bed, fast asleep. I couldn't have agreed with him more.

As it turned out, we didn't get all the stones. The next morning, several escaped from beneath his dressing, and each day thereafter, there were more. The supply finally dwindled, but a month later, when he had been home for a fortnight, I visited him in his own village and he told me, "I'm still spittin' the damn things out." He finally ran out of ammunition, and turned up thirty years later in North West River requiring some minor in-patient treatment in hospital.

Shortly after that episode, we encountered a difficult delivery of a woman in her first labour. She was old to be starting a family, but seemed all right until a little more than half of her labour was completed, when she suddenly began to have repeated convulsions. Despite almost no clinical evidence—only a slight increase in blood pressure and nearly normal laboratory tests—she was clearly in eclampsia. The convulsions continued until she was given pentothal (an anesthetic). A Caesarean section was indicated but I had little experience with this procedure; besides, we were not really prepared. Nevertheless, there was no choice—we went ahead. A healthy boy eventually arrived and the mother woke up in good shape.

Due to a good deal of rickets on the coast, quite a few normal deliveries were impeded or made impossible because the mothers had small pelvic bones (or distorted ones). Apart from the woman with eclampsia, my choice for dealing with difficult deliveries was Caesarean section. At the time of the birth of Julius Caesar, the first prominent citizen known, as Shakespeare expressed it, to have been "ripped untimely from his mother's womb," the operation was usually fatal. Even if the patient survived, she was thereafter sterile. But the modern operation usually permits the mother to safely have another child later: I did three on one mother. Fortunately, my father's cod-liver oil regime sharply reduced the vitamin D deficiency that led to rickets, and within a few years, the problems preventing them from delivering had all but disappeared. Although I felt myself rather thinly spread over a very large territory, I was finding my time in Cartwright both instructive and pleasant. The staff was everything I could have wanted. The station foreman, Harvey Bird, was the Cartwright equivalent of Jack Watts[35]—a splendid man on a boat, most conscientious, and a natural mechanic who could make missing parts of machinery and repair anything. He was the second of three generations of a family who devoted their lives to the association, and at the same station.

Most of all, I was free from constraint, free to adopt what I perceived as the best solution to a problem, and, at last, free to do some of my own surgery and medicine. During my stay, the O.R. saw various fractures reduced; colostomies, hernias and the like repaired, and—of course—Mr. Mesher's brilliantly staged extravaganza. I was growing increasingly confident of my ability to cope with any emergency.

---

35 Jack Watts. General works superintendent for the Grenfell Mission in Labrador.

SMITH

Nothing makes the people of Newfoundland and Labrador angrier than recalling the deal that was made with Quebec for the transmission of power from Churchill Falls to the Quebec and U.S. market. Every year, Quebec takes in a king's ransom while its neighbour to the east makes a pittance. Without federal support for cross-border transmission in the national interest, Newfoundland and Labrador was left to bargain with Quebec for the amount of toll—a terrible long term bargain that was exacerbated by the OPEC oil crisis in the early 1970s. As a result, Canada's newest province has been relegated to perpetual penury, while Canada's oldest province captures a windfall from a resource on someone else's territory. Indeed, the waters flow through the woods and marshes that the Innu historically travelled in their quest for caribou, and no one ever attempted to engage them in a discussion of how the waters were to be used or to compensate them for the loss of habitat. While the courts have ruled that a contract is a contract, it is still an open, abiding, and painful sore on the body politic.

Philip Smith in *Brinco* recounts how the deal was made, or, more accurately, how the province of Newfoundland and Labrador, through Brinco, was forced into a deal or left to walk away from the table. In this excerpt, he tells the tale of the river and the aboriginal and non-aboriginal men and women who used it and explored it and witnessed its beauty, magnificence, and power before Joe Smallwood decided that it must be harnessed.

Philip Smith

EXCERPT FROM *Brinco: The Story of Churchill Falls*, 1975

An English poet laureate, Robert Southey, once demonstrated the inadvisability, if not the utter impossibility, of trying to capture in mere words the sight and sound of a waterfall. Inspired by the comparatively modest Cataract of Lodore in the English Lake District, he unwisely ventured too near the brink and was swept away in a cascade of excruciating lines of which the following are only a brief sample:

And pouring and roaring,
And waving and raving,
And tossing and crossing,
And flowing and going,
And running and stunning,
And foaming and roaming,
And dinning and spinning,
And dropping and hopping,
And working and jerking,
And guggling and struggling…

The first white man to see the much more dramatic Great Falls of Labrador was more restrained in his description of them, as befits a Scot who spent twenty-five years trading with the Indians in the service of the Hudson's Bay Company. John McLean, born on the Isle of Mull in 1799, had served in the Ottawa Valley and the wilds of what is now British Columbia when he was ordered in 1837 to the recently opened company post at Fort Chimo, on Ungava Bay. The company hoped to develop a fur trade in the unexplored interior of Labrador and McLean was told to find an overland route by which Fort Chimo could be supplied from the post at North West River, near the mouth of the Hamilton.

He set off with a party of four on January 2, 1838, and seven weeks later arrived at North West River, having accomplished one of those incredible journeys which make up so much of the history of the North—more than four hundred miles as the crow flies, and nearer to six hundred as McLean travelled. Without tents, he and his party slept beneath the stars, rolled up in their blankets in the shelter of trees where they were lucky enough to find them, burrowing into the snow when, as often, there were no trees within miles. On clear days, though occasionally suffering from frostbite, they were able to make as much as twenty miles on their snowshoes. On others, trudging knee-deep through fresh snow and stopping every few feet to manhandle their sleds, they were able to cover only a mile. Sometimes, the blizzards were so fierce they dare not travel at all and were forced to remain huddled in their blankets all day.

After two weeks' rest at the post, revelling in the luxury of a roof over their heads, they embarked on their equally arduous return journey, during which, when one of his men fell sick, McLean pushed on ahead to get help. Before he reached Fort Chimo on April 20, he ran out of food and had to eat his sled dogs to survive.

His spectacular trek convinced him that the rugged country he had crossed could never serve as a supply route for Fort Chimo from the Atlantic coast. Furthermore, his inability to live off the land (his party rarely encountered any game which might have supplemented the rations they dragged with them on their sleds) prompted him to write to the Governor of the Hudson's Bay Company predicting that there was scant prospect of establishing a profitable fur trade in the interior of Labrador.

However, despatches from an outpost such as Chimo might take two years to reach their destination in those days, and in the meantime McLean dutifully continued to try to follow his instructions. Soon after his return he heard from some passing Indians of a "Michipou," or big river, which ran from west to east some distance south of the route he had taken, eventually emptying into Esquimaux Bay, as Lake Melville was then known. So the following summer, as soon as the ice cleared from around Fort Chimo, which was not until June 24, he set off to find this big river and follow it to its mouth to discover whether canoes could navigate it in the opposite direction and thus bring supplies up from the coast.

McLean described his various journeys in a book called "Notes of a Twenty-Five Years' Service in the Hudson's Bay Territory." By the middle of August 1839, he and his companion, Erland Erlandson, were paddling peacefully down the Hamilton "when, one evening, the roar of a mighty cataract burst upon our ears, warning us that danger was at hand. We soon reached the spot, which presented to us one of the grandest spectacles in the world, but put an end to all hopes of success in our enterprise."

The sight McLean saw—the water leaping out in a cloud of spray and falling into a steep-sided gorge far below—certainly seemed an insuperable obstacle to any canoe trying to travel upstream. He wrote that the river, several hundred yards wide before it enters the rapids above the falls, "finally contracts to a breadth of about fifty yards, ere it precipitates itself over the rock which forms the fall; when, still roaring and foaming, it continues its maddened course for about a distance of thirty miles, pent up between walls of rock that rise sometimes to the height of three hundred feet on either side." (He overestimated the length of the gorge, and underestimated the height of its walls, at least toward its lower end.)

After carrying their canoes and supplies through bogs and swamps for a whole day, trying vainly to find a way down to the river below the falls, McLean and Erlandson gave up their attempt to reach North West River by this route and "with heavy hearts and weary limbs" retraced their steps. But after his return to Fort Chimo, McLean learned from an old Indian that there was in fact a portage route around the falls—up a steep gully later to be known as Big Hill, which climbs a thousand feet in little over a quarter of a mile and reaches the plateau where the town of Churchill Falls now stands.

During the next few years he made at least one successful journey to North West River by this route, and it was later used briefly by the Hudson's Bay

Company to supply two posts set up in the interior, one near the present site of Schefferville, in Quebec, and the other on the shore of Lake Michikamau, largest of the hundreds of lakes now incorporated into the Churchill Falls reservoir. Neither post survived for long, because there were too few inhabitants of the interior to keep them supplied with furs.

McLean estimated that the Indian tribe inhabiting the interior of Labrador, the "Nascopies," numbered "about one hundred men able to bear arms." This was probably an underestimate, but a government count half a century later put the total number of Indians in the interior at only a thousand. The tribe is more generally known today as the Naskaupi, an uncomplimentary name meaning "uncivilized" bestowed on them by their neighbours to the south, the Montagnais. The Naskaupi, who speak a dialect of the Cree language, refer to themselves as "Nenenat," meaning "true people."

The tribe was probably forced on to the inhospitable hunting grounds of the Labrador plateau by pressure from the much more numerous Montagnais to the south and west, and their alleged traditional enemies, the Eskimos of the coast. McLean described them as "a peaceful, harmless people," but added that "they cherish the unprovoked enmity of their race towards the poor Esquimaux, whom they never fail to attack, when an opportunity offers of doing so with impunity. Our presence, however, has had the effect of establishing a more friendly intercourse between them; and to the fact that many of the Esquimaux have of late acquired fire-arms, and are not to be attacked without some risk, may be ascribed, in no small degree, the present forbearance of their enemies."

In McLean's day, and for long afterwards, the Naskaupi survived precariously by constant roaming in search of food, wandering over the interior in the short summer season and, like the Montagnais, retreating to the milder coast when the winter closed in. They caught salmon in the coastal rivers and seals on the ice of the Gulf of St. Lawrence; picked berries wherever they could; brought down ptarmigan, ducks or geese with their arrows; and speared muskrat or beaver with their long, barbed lances. Most of all, though, their existence depended on the vast caribou herds which used to travel across the interior. Caught in carefully planned ambushes, the caribou provided meat, hides for clothing and tents, bone for weapons and tools, sinews for thread.

As the caribou herds dwindled, the Naskaupi moved out of the interior to the settlements; since the opening of the iron-ore deposits in Labrador and nearby Quebec, many of them have congregated around Schefferville.

After their description by McLean,[36] the falls reverted to their original obscurity. Between 1866 and 1870 an Oblate missionary named Father Babel lived with the Indians in the interior, exploring stretches of the Hamilton and making what was probably the first map of the area. But it was almost the turn of the century before there was any more interest in the Labrador plateau. In 1891, several newspapers in the United States carried a report that Indians and voyageurs claimed the existence in the interior of Labrador of a towering waterfall fifteen hundred feet high. Intrigued by, but apparently skeptical of, this "attractive piece of geographical news," Henry G. Bryant, recording secretary of the Geographical Club of Philadelphia, recruited a friend, Professor C. A. Kenaston, of Washington, DC, and set off in search of this natural phenomenon.

Like most explorers who followed McLean, Bryant and Kenaston decided to push inland from the coast, ascending the river from Hamilton Inlet and Lake Melville, at its mouth. They arrived at North West River by sea on July 27, 1891, hoping to engage Indian guides. But when they announced their intention of travelling the 210 miles from the mouth of the river to the falls, they could find no Indians willing to go with them. As Bryant said in an account of their journey published in the *Century Magazine* in September 1892, "They believe the place to be the haunt of evil spirits, and assert that death will soon overtake the venturesome mortal who dares to look upon the mysterious cataract."

There are several versions of the old Indian legend attaching to the falls, which were known as Patses-che-wan, or "The narrow place where the water falls." Essentially, it seems, two Indian maidens were either swept over the falls while

---

36 John McLean resigned from the Hudson's Bay Company in 1845, when he was once again posted to the West, and settled in Guelph, Ontario, where he became first a bank manager and later clerk of the Division Court at nearby Elora. Almost forty years later, still tall and fit, he returned to the West to live with his youngest daughter in Victoria, where he died in 1890, at the age of ninety-one.

fishing from a canoe or fell in while gathering firewood too close to the brink. Death by drowning was a horrible fate for an Indian because it was believed his spirit would be trapped forever beneath the water, screaming for an escape which never came. The Indian maidens were thus condemned to live beneath the falls, endlessly processing caribou hides. As time passed, their beauty faded and it was said they would occasionally climb to the brink of the falls, their white hair streaming in the spray, and try to lure careless mortals into joining them in their servitude below.

Unable to overcome the Indians' fears, Bryant persuaded a Scots trapper named John Montague and an Eskimo named Geoffrey Ban to guide them. They left North West River on August 3 in an eighteen-foot river boat with sail, towing their sixteen-foot canoe behind them, and on the third day encountered the first of the many obstacles in their path, Muskrat Falls. It took them a day and a half, with the aid of block and tackle, to manhandle their unwieldy 500-lb. boat up the steep banks and regain the river, a hundred feet above.

For the rest of their journey, because of the swift current bearing down on them, they were seldom able to use their oars or paddles, let alone their sail. For the most part, they had to resort to the form of travel the trappers called "tracking"—towing their boats upstream by means of ropes tied to leather bands into which they could lean their shoulders. Since there are many rapids on the Hamilton, and its banks are often strewn with boulders, it was an exhausting way to go. But they pressed on, across Gull Island Lake and round Porcupine Rapids, Gull Island Rapids[37] and Horseshoe Rapids until, after almost four weeks, they came to another set of rapids which they judged to be the foot of the gorge in the area of Big Hill and the portage around the falls.

Leaving Geoffrey with the boat, the other three set out carrying the canoe and a week's provisions, and after a long search found the trail and climbed up the hill on to the plateau. They were now fifteen hundred feet above sea level (which prob-

---

37 John Montague, who hailed from the Orkneys, drowned some time later while tracking a canoe through
    Gull Island Rapids on a trapping expedition. His grandson, Harry Montague, who used to be a trapper
    in the same area, later became a janitor at Churchill Falls. And two of his sons (John Montague's great-
    grandsons) also worked at Churchill: Ed, as project geologist, and Clayton, as a driver.

Philip Smith

ably accounts for the garbled press report Bryant had read), on an apparently endless plain strewn with lakes and bogs and boulders. Three days travelling across a chain of six lakes, with portages between them, brought them to a point at which they could strike off across the rough, mossy ground to the southwest and reach the banks of the Hamilton near the falls, which they did on September 2.

"A single glance," wrote Bryant, "showed that we had before us one of the greatest waterfalls in the world." While Bryant made a risky descent down the sheer side of the gorge in an unsuccessful attempt to photograph the falls, Professor Kenaston tried to measure their height by the ingenious but none-too-scientific method of tossing a "heavy billet of green fir" over the edge, attached to a long length of rope he had thoughtfully provided for this purpose. He arrived at a height for the falls of 316 feet. This was considerably less than they had been led to expect, but considerably more than the falls' actual height, which is 245 feet—85 feet higher than the Horseshoe Falls at Niagara.

No doubt to his disappointment, since priority is important to explorers, Bryant discovered as he was leaving the falls that another American party had by coincidence beaten them to the scene by a mere two weeks. Tied to a spruce tree which had been cut off about four feet from the ground he found a glass fruit bottle sealed to keep its contents dry. Inside was a paper recording the arrival at the falls of Austin Cary and Dennis Cole, two recent graduates of Bowdoin College, in the state of Maine.

Bryant added the names of his party to the bottle, thus beginning a tradition that later visitors perpetuated. When the bottle was retrieved by Brinco and presented to Joey Smallwood in 1960, it contained the names of eighty-four visitors or groups of visitors; and it is a telling commentary on the isolation of the falls that most of them were those of surveyors and engineers sent into the area by Brinco during the preceding six years.

Cary and Cole were members of a nineteen-man scientific expedition sent to Labrador by Bowdoin College in 1891, thus initiating a longstanding connection between the area and the states of Maine and Vermont which they commemorated by naming the gorge below the falls Bowdoin Canyon and a nearby mountain and lake Mount Hyde, in honour of the president of their college.

While most of the members of the expedition sailed up the coast, Cary and Cole and two colleagues, W. R. Smith and E. B. Young, pushed up the Hamilton in two fifteen-foot cedar boats, without benefit of guides.

Perhaps because of this collegiate over-confidence, one of the boats soon overturned and they lost about a quarter of their supplies. Then Young injured his hand and he and Smith turned back. Worse was to come for Cary and Cole. Forging upriver until they were stopped by what from their adventure became known as Disaster Rapids, they then left their canoe, carrying packs with only two days' supply of food. Thus unencumbered, they managed to climb out of the gorge and reach the falls. But on their return they found to their horror that they had not properly extinguished their riverside camp fire and it had spread and destroyed not only their boat but most of their supplies for the return journey.

Left with a quart of rice, three quarts of mixed meal, a little tea and some partly burned flour and rice, their clothes and boots already the worse for wear, they might have been expected to starve to death. Incredibly, they managed to walk out to Lake Melville in seventeen days, shooting an occasional squirrel or partridge with a .22 pistol which providentially escaped the flames, and fortified by a couple of food caches they stumbled across along the way.

Others who took the Labrador bush too lightly were not so fortunate, including an American magazine writer named Leonidas Hubbard who tried in 1903 to find a new route into Lake Michikamau. Since the only existing maps of Labrador were hopelessly inadequate, Hubbard was soon lost. Wearing only thin summer clothing and running short of food, with winter fast closing in, he became weak and ill and his two companions, a fellow-writer named Dillon Wallace and a Scots-Cree guide named John Elson, built a camp for him and left him behind while they headed for the coast and help. A rescue party of four trappers found his frozen body late in October.

Two years later, Wallace himself almost died on another and even longer trek across Labrador, though in that same year Hubbard's wife, who must have been both more determined and wiser than her husband, since she provided herself with four guides, managed to complete the journey he had set for himself.

These and later wanderings by amateur explorers from the United States extending almost up to the Second World War, contributed little more than further Southey-esque effusions to the outside world's knowledge of the Labrador plateau, and in particular Grand Falls. The first real scientific information about the area was provided by a young Canadian geologist named Albert Peter Low, who deposited his name in the bottle at the falls in 1894, three years after Cary and Cole had left it there.

Low had graduated from McGill University in Montreal in 1882 and joined the Dominion Geological Survey.[38] In 1893 he began a crisscrossing expedition across Labrador which was eventually to last sixteen months, during which he only once received mail from the outside world. By the time he returned to Ottawa he had made detailed surveys of more than two thousand miles of rivers and lakes and collected more than two hundred rock samples.

He reached Grand Falls on May 2, 1894, and described his impressions in the report of the Geological Survey for 1895. "The noise of the fall has a stunning effect," he wrote, "and although deadened because of its inclosed situation, can be heard for more than ten miles away, as a deep, booming sound. The cloud of mist is also visible from any eminence within a radius of twenty miles."

Like McLean, Low overestimated the height of the falls—he put them at 302 feet—but his guess at their volume was closer than some estimates made many years later with the advantage of more advanced measuring techniques: he put their discharge at 50,000 cubic feet per second, "or nearly the mean volume of the Ottawa River, at Ottawa." He did not speculate at this time on a potential use for all this water, and more interest was probably aroused by his discovery in several places of "immense deposits" of iron ore. In some areas, he reported, there were so many outcrops of iron-bearing rocks that "the ores will be found in practically inexhaustible quantity."

He returned to this theme some years later, in 1907, when a committee of the Senate held a series of hearings whose proceedings were later published

---

38 Low was appointed director of the Geological Survey in 1906 and when the Federal Department of Mines was established a year later became its first deputy minister. Ill health forced his retirement in 1913 but he lived on in Ottawa until 1942.

under the title of "Canada's Fertile Northland." Low told the committee there was "a great supply of iron" in Labrador "which will probably be valuable in the next twenty-five years." The greatest difficulty in making this iron ore commercially valuable was the problem of transportation, he said, "but there are several millions of horse-power in the Grand Falls of the Hamilton River, and in addition to mechanical horsepower it would also furnish the heat whereby by an electrical process, the reduction of the ore by electricity might be performed. Transportation might also be provided by electric power."

The fact that this never came about does not detract from Low's prescience: proposals for using Hamilton Falls power for the electrical reduction of iron ores (a process used successfully in Europe but never adopted in North America) were still being advanced in the late fifties and early sixties.

The next scientific survey of the falls was made by a French-Canadian engineer named Wilfrid Thibaudeau, who worked in Europe for three years after his graduation from Laval University in 1883 and then spent the next twenty-five years on various surveys and construction projects in western Canada, serving for a time as superintendent of public works for the Yukon Territory. In 1912, Thibaudeau surveyed the St. Maurice River for the newly formed Commission for the Management of Running Waters in Quebec, and in 1915 turned his attention to the upper basin of the Hamilton. Though copies of his report no longer seem to exist, he is credited in the early surveys commissioned by Brinco with being the first man to suggest, in a general way, the "Channel Scheme" which was eventually used to develop the falls.

It was not until 1947 that a preliminary survey of the river and falls was carried out for the Newfoundland government, by a party of four men under Commander G. H. Desbarats, a retired Royal Canadian Navy officer. Desbarats, too, was impressed by the falls' potential and reported: "Some day a use will be found for this power, pioneering men and women will move northward, and another frontier will be rolled back."

The development foreseen by Thibaudeau and Desbarats was made possible by a peculiarity of the topography of Labrador which is not apparent to a lay observer gazing at the falls; nature, in fact, was the first engineer on the Churchill Falls project. Before the last Ice Age, the rivers of Labrador ran through deep gorges worn in the granite over millions of years. Then the glaciers came and what is now the Labrador plateau was crushed under a mass of ice a mile high. As the glaciers receded, the awesome weight of the ice ground off the tops of the hills, filling up the ancient river beds with boulders and gravel and leaving behind a plain which is not quite level but is lower at the centre than at its rim, like a saucer. The gouging action of the ice on this plain also created hundreds of lakes; if you fly high enough over Labrador in the summer you can see the pattern left by the retreat of the glaciers in the way the lakes generally seem to run in the same direction, as if they had been scratched out by the claws of giant bears.

The melting ice and the return of the rains filled up the lakes and new rivers formed between them. Unable to find the old channels, these rivers meandered about the plain seeking weak points on its rim through which they might escape down to the sea. Fortunately for the builders of the Churchill Falls project, the rim sprang few leaks and most of the water from the plateau ultimately came to drain through the weak spot found by the Churchill River. This weak spot was not simply the falls themselves, grand though the early travellers found their 245-foot drop to be.

Before the river was diverted, it began to run down off the plateau five miles above the falls, when it entered a series of rapids. By the time it reached the falls it had already dropped more than two hundred feet and at this point was foaming downhill in a sort of chute at an angle of forty-five degrees. The chute, and the lip of the falls, which curved upward, could be compared to a ski-jump. The action of the upcurved lip hurled the water out into space for a free fall into the churning pool below.

From there, the river turned sharply to its left and surged away down the five-mile-long Bowdoin Canyon, fortuitously providing the best vantage point for viewing the falls, from a clearing on top of a 300-foot cliff directly opposite them. Few early travellers saw the falls from this spot—dubbed "the Meadow" by Brinco employees—because it is on the far bank of the river.

At the foot of Bowdoin Canyon, where it is joined by a tributary, the Valley River, the Churchill turns sharply left again and continues to run downhill through another series of rapids in a deep gorge. In the twenty-two miles between the pool at the foot of the falls and the end of the rapids, where the trappers began their portage up Big Hill, the river drops a further 580 feet. At that point, it is thus more than a thousand feet below its original level up on the plateau.

The amount of power that can be generated by a hydro-electric plant depends not only on the volume of water available to turn the turbines (which are in essence water wheels) but on its "head": in other words, how far the water falls before it hits the blades of the turbines.

A layman looking at the falls might have assumed that to harness the river you would need a powerhouse at their base. Thibaudeau was the first to realize that if the water could be diverted before the river entered the rapids above the falls and somehow conducted back into it twenty miles downstream, the "head" would not be the mere 245 feet existing at the falls themselves but more than a thousand feet.

In its simplest outline, this is what was done at Churchill Falls: the forty miles of strategically placed dykes built with rock and glacial rubble available on the spot (there was no need for towering and expensive concrete dams) plugged the low spots in the rim of the Labrador saucer and formed a huge reservoir almost half the size of Lake Ontario. From the reservoir, the water flows through a natural canal formed in effect by raising, and thus linking, the lakes that used to make up the portage route around the falls. Then it is channelled down tunnels bored into a hill on the rim of the plateau. One thousand and forty feet below—a "head" to make an engineer's eyes shine—it spins the turbines in the underground powerhouse. From there, its work done, it rejoins the river through two mile-long tailrace tunnels near the place where the voyageurs and explorers and trappers used to begin their steep climb to the plateau above.

BERTON

It was Mathieu André, an Innu guide from Sept Isles, who in 1937 alerted Joe Retty, acting on behalf of Labrador Mining and Exploration, to a mineral showing 80 kilometres west of Churchill Falls. André was eventually given a $7000 finder's fee—a far cry from what aboriginals will undoubtedly receive today from the discovery of nickel in northern Labrador or the development of the Lower Churchill. The second major demographic shift in Labrador came with the development of the iron mines in the west, a development that had its roots in the days of Newfoundland's Commission of Government in the 1930s.

It was C. D. Howe who pointed out to Jules Timmins, then owner of Labrador Mining, the necessity of a railroad to bring the ore to tidewater. Howe suggested Timmins hire Bill Durrell, who at the time was supervising the construction of Goose Airport. In 1948 Durrell began planning and overseeing the construction of the Quebec North Shore and Labrador Railway, linking the port of Sept Isles with the iron ore deposits at Knob Lake, later Schefferville. In 1958 the Iron Ore Company announced that it would develop the Carol Project, which later became Labrador City; spurs of the railroad were built to it and later to the nearby mining town of Wabush.

For Pierre Berton, Labrador is a unique part of the Canadian north, sharing its mystique, its place in our imagination, its problems and its potential. In *The Mysterious North,* he tells of the railroad and the great untapped resources of Labrador. Berton deals not just with iron ore but also with the many resources found in Labrador, not the least of which is the semi-precious stone Labradorite. He indicates that Tiffany's considered it too brittle to work with, but John Goudie of North West River has had the talent and the sensitivity to bring to life beautiful Labrador images from this unique stone.

Pierre Berton

"IRON IN THE LAND OF CAIN,"
FROM *The Mysterious North*, 1956

A month later I was back in the heart of the iron country, deep in the gloomy interior of the Labrador Peninsula, whose somber cliffland, rising from the chill ocean mists, cast a pall on Jacques Cartier, the Breton explorer. The discoverer of the St. Lawrence stared up at the forbidding shoreline and called it "the land God gave to Cain," then passed on upriver in a vain search for the jeweled mountains of Cathay. In the four centuries that have passed since that day, the great peninsula has resisted those who followed in Cartier's wake, to remain an inaccessible and rarely traveled wasteland of rock and muskeg. Only in the days since World War II has it begun to yield up its secret treasures; but these are easily as rich as all of Cathay's legendary gems.

I started out from the little port of Seven Islands, on the north shore of the Gulf of St. Lawrence, across the water from Mont Joli. The iron country lay four hundred miles due north, and because of its development the tiny town of six hundred persons, which had slumbered for three centuries among the Laurentian rocks, was now a booming seaport of six thousand, where lots had jumped to as high as thirteen thousand dollars apiece and freighters, each capable of loading thirty-two thousand tons of ore, lay moored against the new docks. The streets were only now being paved, the sewers only now being laid, but the Cadillacs and the cocktail bars and the bright new company homes told the story of Seven Islands' sudden prosperity.

At seven o'clock one morning I boarded one of the little passenger cars of Canada's newest railway, the Quebec North Shore and Labrador, a three-hundred-

and-sixty-mile line that knifes across the Precambrian plateau to connect the iron country with the sea. Completed in 1954, it represents a prodigious feat of engineering. We had traveled hardly a dozen miles across the gray expanse of muskeg and stunted spruce before we reached the outer edges of the great Laurentian Scarp, a granite barrier three thousand feet high, which walls off the interior of the peninsula from the outside world and defied the railway-builders. Bored into the face of this natural bastion was a tunnel, dripping with water, through which the train plunged. Half a mile farther on, a pinpoint of light appeared and we burst from the bowels of the mountain to find ourselves suspended in mid-air seven hundred feet above the canyon of the Moisie River. The train snorted across the slender orange trestle and then clung to the dynamited flanks of the sheer rock cliffs, climbing wearily for mile after mile toward the plateau of iron.

We had entered an unearthly world, half fairyland, half purgatory. Here were boiling rivers, harsh canyons, piles of granite rubble blasted from the hills, and camel-backed mountains with sheer faces that seemed to have been split in twain by a giant cleaver. Here among the spiky black spruce were thin mists of deciduous green where the birch and larches heralded the onset of spring. And from the rocky heights above, a thousand waterfalls dropped in lacy cascades. Indeed, there was water everywhere. The black cliffs were wet with it; the forests gurgled with it. Foaming torrents poured under the railway culverts and tumbled on down the steep slopes. Falls, still imprisoned in the grip of a dying winter, hung like enormous icicles from the granite scarps. And far below, the river hissed and roared as it cut its way through the mountain barrier.

The track clung to the cliff edge. Only the riches of the Labrador-Ungava iron country could force as ambitious an engineering venture as this one: a quarter of a mile of docks, thirteen airfields, two hydroelectric plants, a new city, and this spectacular line of track. The total bill came to $235,000,000, and the Iron Ore Company of Canada, which controls it all, had to have forty years of ore production in sight before the scheme was feasible. Before the trains began to move, everything from bolts to bulldozers was flown into this country by air, so that the mining company found itself operating one of Canada's largest airlines, shifting as much as three hundred tons of goods a day north to the land of Cain.

At the peak of its operation the airline had seventy-five pilots in its employ, and sometimes its planes were taking off at the rate of one every five minutes to supply the railway-builders.

Slowly the train heaved itself out of the gorge and river country and we found ourselves sliding across the tabletop of the great Labrador plateau in a monotonous land of lakes and muskeg, moss and lichen, harsh brown sand, soiled patches of snow, and a single variety of tree: the black, stunted spruce, whose twisted body seems racked continually by some inner torture. The Labrador Peninsula, which takes in most of the province of Quebec and all of the territory of Labrador (part of Newfoundland), is more than half a million square miles in size and most of it looks like this. It is, indeed, a great rigid block of Precambrian rock, unmarked by hills, except for the spectacular mountain ranges along its eastern and southern coastlines. Its surface is carpeted in a foot-thick blanket of moss and lichen and a fragrant shrub called Labrador tea, which turns bright orange in the fall. From this spongy floor the gaunt trees protrude like posts, many of them almost devoid of leaves or needles, growing so slowly that it takes them almost a century to reach their full height. Through the rock the rivers cut in dizzy gorges, many of them one thousand feet deep, for this continental cornerpost has slowly been rising over the ages as the rivers worked their way down.

It is this downward erosive action that has produced the bare jagged peaks of the Torngat Mountain range at the northeastern tip of the peninsula. "Torngat" is an Eskimo word meaning "evil spirits," and evil spirits they seem to be, horn-shaped and saw-toothed, many of them five thousand feet in height. They spring abruptly from the fiords or the ocean, the most rugged mountain range on the east coast of the continent, rivaling the Alps of Switzerland and the Selkirks of British Columbia, stretching in a long gap-toothed line for one hundred and fifty miles, bejeweled with ice cornices, decked with green lakes, and gouged by immense glacial gulleys.

Farther to the south lies another mountain range, equally terrible, equally majestic. They are really mountain stubs, created by molten rock surging up from the bowels of the earth within the body of earlier mountains. The outer flesh of crystalline rock has long since been torn away by the elements so that only the ebony core remains, bare of vegetation. This rock, called gabbro, contains a feldspar of great beauty known as "labradorite," whose glassy surface, prism-fashion, breaks up white light into its colored components so that it seems to flash with purples, violets, blues, and occasionally yellows, oranges, and reds. It is undoubtedly this phenomenon that has caused the Montegnais Indians of the coast to talk of flashing fire rocks and the Nascopies of the interior of fire mountains along the height of land. One explorer tried to market the labradorite as a precious gem, but Tiffany's found it too brittle to work with. It occurs in various places throughout the plateau.

All around us as we crossed the tableland were the shapes of the lakes that lie in the hollows of the rocks. There are parts of Labrador that are almost three-quarters water, for this is old glacier country, and the dikes of glacial rubble have dammed up the old watercourses so that there is no recognizable pattern of drainage. Thus the rivers seem to run in all directions, twisting and corkscrewing around the obstacles left in the wake of the receding ice sheets. Vast sections of the peninsula, especially toward the southeast, are pocked with kames and kettles. The kames are round little knolls of glacial till; the kettles are small bowls in the earth that mark the last resting place of scattered ice-blocks—remnants of the great glacier. Because these hummocks and hollows are scarcely marked by erosion, many geographers believe that this was the final domain of the Labrador icecap. Some think, indeed, that it is only a brief two thousand years since the glacier vanished from this corner of the peninsula.

As the train rattled north, long fingers of ice began to appear on the lakes, and the patches of snow, caught in the hollows of the hills, increased in number. It was June, but spring had scarcely arrived. Labrador is no closer to the Arctic than northern Saskatchewan or the warm valleys of British Columbia, or the entire cultivable portion of the U.S.S.R. and yet in its temperature it is wholly Arctic or sub-Arctic. With the possible exception of eastern Siberia, no other region of Arctic climate extends so far south. It has only one frost-free month, July, though the latitude of its heartland corresponds with that of Dublin, Liverpool, Hamburg, and Berlin. For the great peninsula is caught between two natural refrigerators. A river of ice, the Labrador Current, pours down from the Arctic to cool the eastern coastline. A stream of polar air sweeps across from northwest Canada, growing colder over the frigid surface of Hudson Bay to chill the

Labrador interior. The plateau itself, two thousand feet above the sea and almost devoid of obstacles, is swept by icy winds that often reach one hundred miles an hour. (At the iron mines in Knob Lake the winds averaged sixty miles an hour for twenty-four hours on one winter's day in 1955.) F. K. Hutton, an old Labrador hand, has written of the howling northwest wind, the attuarnek of the Eskimos, which "storms along with a ceaseless roar over the frozen plains and valleys and fills the air with powdered snow as thick as a London fog. No living thing can face it, buildings shake, snow huts are worn thin. When the snow drift is thick one can scarcely see anything half a dozen yards away. On some days one cannot see the dogs. One is lost somewhere in Labrador."

Indeed, since Cartier's day, travelers, explorers, writers, and scientists have strained for imaginative phrases to describe the harshness of Cain's land. The Labrador Peninsula is one of the world's three largest outcroppings of continental land, and like the other two, Alaska and Arabia, it has been regarded until recently as virtually sterile. Cartier remarked with a sneer that "there was not one cartful of earth in the whole of it." Hesketh Prichard, a traveler at the turn of the century, called it "a menacing wilderness" and added that "a desolation more appalling cannot be conceived." Two of his predecessors were equally emphatic. "A country formed of frightful mountains and unfruitful valleys…a prodigious heap of barren rock," wrote Lieutenant Roger Curtis. "God created this country last of all and threw together there the refuse of his materials as of no use to mankind," wrote Captain George Cartwright, who spent sixteen years on the Labrador coast. Elliott Coues, a naturalist from the semi-tropics, set down his own equally graphic impressions of the peninsula:

"Fog hangs low and heavy over rock-girdled Labrador. Angry waves, paled with rage, exhaust themselves to encroach up her stern shores, and, baffled, sink back howling into the depths. Winds shriek as they course from crag to crag in a mad career, and the humble mosses that clothe the rocks crouch lower still in fear."

The land has lived up to its billing. One famous American naturalist, Alpheus S. Packard, came to the tableland to study insect life, but the insects were so fierce they drove him from the country. One explorer of note, Leonidas Hubbard, Jr., who tried to make his way northwest across the peninsula from Hamilton Inlet on the east coast to Ungava Bay in the north, starved to death by inches in the valley of the Susan. Hubbard, who died in October 1903, a march or two from safety, waiting for his two comrades to bring help, left a diary, which graphically describes the hardships that face the unwary wanderer in the Labrador wasteland. The final item was written after Hubbard had gnawed on a caribou-skin moccasin to give him strength to scribble it down:

"Tonight or tomorrow perhaps the weather will improve so I can build a fire, eat the rest of my moccasins and have some more bone broth. Then I can boil my belt and oil-tanned moccasins and a pair of cowhide mittens. They ought to help some. I am not suffering. The acute pangs of hunger have given way to indifference. I'm sleepy. I think death from starvation is not so bad…."

Undaunted by her husband's death, Hubbard's slender and handsome widow, who had waited for him at home, decided to complete the journey that he had attempted. Alone, except for two Indian guides, heavy-skirted and bloomered, with a revolver on her hip and a knife at her belt, this remarkable young woman trekked through almost a thousand miles of river, bush, rock, and tundra successfully to attain her objective and meet the challenge of the peninsula.

Now, half a century later, others are meeting the same challenge. For, paradoxically, the very factors that have given Labrador its reputation for bleakness and unfriendliness are now proving to be its greatest asset.

—The harsh climate causes trees to grow with maddening slowness so that the growth rings are so close they are hard to distinguish one from another. Yet this very phenomenon is the reason for the long fiber in the pulpwood the papermakers cherish. There are enormous stands of these dense spruces across the rockland of Labrador, and there is little doubt now that they will soon be harvested.

—The fierce, impassable rivers that make the peninsula so difficult to navigate by canoe are now proving to be the source of a vast hydroelectric potential. The myriad lakes, dammed up by the glaciers of old, hold an enormous storage of fresh water waiting to be tapped. There may be as much as twelve million horsepower in Labrador, or about five times as much as is produced by the Grand Coulee Dam.

—The naked ocean of rocks that looked so barren to Cartier hold, locked within them, a fortune in iron ore, not to mention copper and other base metals.

Already a huge company, the British Newfoundland Corporation, backed by Rothschild millions, is exploring a fifty-thousand-mile tract of Labrador under an arrangement with the province of Newfoundland. The company's objectives include a search for metals and pulpwood, but its main energies are focused on the spectacular Grand Falls of the Hamilton River, where, it is believed, four million horsepower can be developed at low rates. This enormous cataract is reckoned between 245 and 305 feet high; it defies proper measurement because the tall column of spray, visible for fifty miles, obscures its lower portions. The river, frustrated in its former course by glacial dikes, has cut its way down through the soft alluvial rubble in a writhing pathway that leads it eventually to the preglacial stream bed. In a dozen miles of this tortuous journey the level drops seven hundred feet, and it is this section of the river, as swift as a millrace, that the engineers hope to develop.

Our train stopped at Mile 224, where a roadway to the Grand Falls is already being surveyed, and here a group of men disembarked heading for the Hamilton River. Then the train rumbled on into a dead gray world—a burned land where the very lichens had been charred from the rocks, and the trees were ashen poles rising from the lifeless terrain. There are thousands of square miles of this burned country on the Labrador Peninsula—more perhaps than anywhere else in the north, for it takes close to a century to renew it. Burned areas reported by geologists in 1892 were still unforested in 1955. In the middle of the last century an observant explorer, Henry Youle Hind, came upon an enormous desert of this burned country in the tableland above the Moisie River—the same country through which the railroad now cuts. Appalled at the hundreds of miles of ruined forest, he suddenly recalled the queer "dark days" that had fallen over eastern Canada fifty and sixty years before. The darkness had extended from Montreal to Fredericton, New Brunswick. It was so dark on some days that it was impossible to read a newspaper at ten in the morning. Eyewitnesses wrote that the darkness seemed to come out of Labrador. At Seven Islands the atmosphere had gone red and fiery, and the sea water became black as ink. The scientists of the day blamed a volcano, somewhere in the unexplored midriff of the peninsula, but later research has uncovered no volcanic evidence. Hind reasoned, probably correctly, that the real explanation lay in these vast acres of smoldering

Pierre Berton

caribou moss, ignited by spontaneous combustion, sending up clouds of ashes and wood smoke.

A long train speeding south rattled by us, each of its open cars piled with the red-brown iron ore. In the fourteen-hour trip between Seven Islands and Knob Lake we passed six of these trains. Each pulled one hundred and five cars; each car held one hundred tons of iron ore. We were entering the iron country. Around us, as we moved north, the trees were growing sparser and more stunted; the ice was growing thicker on the lakes; and the soil was growing redder.

It was this red soil that told us we had entered the great Labrador Trough, the geological key to the development of the entire peninsula. Here is the promise of the land of Cain, a king's ransom in iron that has lain undisturbed for half a billion years. From the air, or on the map, the trough is easily recognizable, for the lakes run north and south in long, parallel shreds for almost six hundred miles.

The trough represents an ancient arm of the sea—a shallow inlet a hundred miles in width that invaded the Precambrian rockland in Proterozoic times, before life existed on the face of the earth. The sea swept down from Ungava almost splitting the peninsula in two, and there it lay for millions of years eroding the soft sandstones and muds that flanked it. These sediments formed an enormous weighty layer thousands of feet thick. The top eight hundred feet consisted of iron and silica in bands of varying width. How these iron deposits were formed is still something of a mystery to scientists; all that is known is that at this period, all over the world, a set of conditions existed which allowed iron and silica to be deposited in this manner. In South America, in India, in the United States (where the Mesabi Range was building), and along the shores of Lake Superior, where the great Steep Rock mine has been developed, iron oxides were being laid down in this way.

New forces came into play. The ocean retreated and the sediments, being weaker than the surrounding granite, were caught as in a vise between the teeth of the Canadian shield. As the earth's crust cooled and wrinkled, enormous pressures from the northeast squeezed the softer rock against the unyielding buttress to the south. Caught in these natural forceps, the floor of the trough warped and buckled and split until it was forced up into a mountain range. Over the ages the mountains were gnawed away by the tooth of time until the land was again as flat as a billiard table. But the ceaseless rains, washing through the crevices in the soft rocks, had leached away the surface silica, leaving almost pure iron behind. Without this historic washing action, the iron of Labrador would be scarcely worth mining, for, mixed with vast quantities of silica, the ore would not be rich enough to freight south. But wherever the water could get at the rock, there are high-grade deposits. The very process that produced the ore makes it easy to mine: because the water action took place in pockets and fissures near the surface, the ore can be dug without tunneling, by an open-cut process. Because the silica has been removed, the ore is porous—like a cheese full of holes—which means it crumbles and digs easily.

Exploration parties in the vicinity of Ungava Bay, far to the north of the richest iron deposits, are now beginning to suspect that the geological upheaval that shaped the land brought more than iron. In the days when the mountains were heaved up, great faults split the rock on the northeast side of the trough, in the area where the pressure was the greatest. It was as if the lid had been removed from a bubbling caldron. Up through these crevices from the molten womb of the world, in the form of hot solutions and steaming vapors, came various metals, notably copper. Concentrated in tiny fractures in the rocks, they cooled and formed deposits. These deposits are now slowly coming to light in the area of Chimo, the old Hudson's Bay Company fort on Ungava Bay.

The first man to outline the shape of the trough and to suspect the presence of iron in the land of Cain was a remarkable Canadian government geologist, A. P. Low, a hefty scientist whose curiosity was as prodigious as his physical stamina. Low stands today as the only man who has trekked across Labrador from north to south and from east to west. He traversed seven thousand miles of country by foot, canoe, and snowshoe, living off the country and scribbling ceaselessly in his notebook. One year he and a fellow surveyor probed deep into the heart of the peninsula and then fell to arguing about who was the proper leader of the expedition. Finally Low decided to settle the quarrel. "I'll walk to Ottawa and find out," he said. And he did—in three weeks. On his journeys through Labrador, Low produced complete notes on mineral wealth, power sites (including the Grand Falls), topography, fish, flowers, birds, and mammals. And in 1893 he noted the presence of an iron formation along the length of the great trough.

But it was more than half a century before anyone bothered about the iron that Low reported. Other geologists, most of them looking for gold, found more definite showings, but there was little reaction. One of the areas now being mined by the Iron Ore Company was actually discovered by two Montreal geologists in 1929. Their company soon ran out of funds. Then in 1936 there was the familiar touch of romance that seems to precede all great northern mining developments. A gnarled old Indian chief of the Montegnais emerged from the heart of the peninsula with a piece of "pretty rock" and showed it to Dr. Joseph Retty, a geologist who was already exploring the area for a development company. The rock looked very pretty indeed to Retty: it was dark blue in color and it was almost solid iron. It came from a spot not very far from the area that the Montreal men had found years before. Retty's company, which owned a huge concession on the Newfoundland side of the Labrador-Quebec border, was taken over during World War II by Hollinger Consolidated, the biggest gold concern on the continent. Retty, who had been exploring the area, recommended that the company also get a concession on the Quebec side, for he reasoned, accurately, that the iron ore lay along the height of land that separates the two territories. The result was that Hollinger, a gold company, found itself with twenty-four thousand square miles of stick forest and some promising iron showings.

It was at this point that a shy, lantern-jawed millionaire with gold-rimmed glasses and a subtle, imaginative mind entered the picture. This was Jules Timmins, the president of Hollinger, and the scion of the most famous mining family in Canada. The name of Timmins is a legend in northern Quebec and Ontario. Jules's father, Henry, a storekeeper from the village of Mattawa, had in 1903 bought a quarter of a share of an unknown silver mine in the Precambrian wilderness of northern Ontario. His friends soon stopped scoffing, for it was this mine that turned Canada into a silver-producer and built the incredible boom town of Cobalt. Henry sold out for a million dollars. Six years later Jules's uncle, Noah, grasped the significance of a gold find made farther to the north by a nineteen-year-old prospector named

Benny Hollinger. He bought Hollinger's claim, and the two brothers parlayed it into the most lucrative gold mine on the continent. The town of Timmins, Ontario (population: 27,000), sprang up around it, and the mine itself has produced more than one hundred and fifty million dollars.

Jules Timmins was born with a gold-and-silver spoon in his mouth, but he worked as a mucker in his family's mine and studied geology at university. When Retty talked to him about iron in Labrador, he told him to find out how much there was and what it would cost to get it out. Retty and his crews spent eight years and six million dollars on this task. They proved up four hundred million tons of high-grade iron ore, but by this time Timmins knew it would cost him a quarter of a billion dollars before the first shovelful was mined. A lesser man might have been staggered by the immensity of such a project, but Timmins set about getting customers for the iron and money to produce it.

He chose a singularly propitious moment. The big steel companies in the United States had been caught napping at the war's end. The expected drop in steel consumption didn't come and, as a result, the great Mesabi Range of Minnesota began to show signs of exhaustion. Led by M. A. Hanna Co. of Cleveland, six large U.S. steel firms joined with Timmins to form Hollinger-Hanna Ltd. and develop Labrador's iron. The new company put up a million dollars; nineteen insurance firms loaned the rest. A small army of subsidiaries, of which the Iron Ore Company is the most important, were formed to build the railway, operate the airlift, open the mines, and produce the ore. Just six years after the first announcements were made, the shovels were munching into the red soil of the trough, and the ore trains were speeding to the sea.

We reached the new town of Knob Lake after dark and the following morning I set out to view the surrounding iron country. The community itself was still in crucible. Bulldozers were everywhere ripping into the soil and leveling out new blocks. Churches and schools were a-building. Telephone poles were going up alongside new three-bedroom homes of cedar siding. Plans were being laid to complete a television station by Christmas—the most northerly TV outlet on the continent. It was being designed to show films, but there was already talk of purchasing cameras and doing local production.

A guide drove me out a few miles through the gray stick forest, and then, suddenly, we entered a world of flaming crimson. We stood on the rim of a blood-red crater gouged out by some of the world's largest steam shovels, and for the first few moments it seemed as if we were on the lip of the inferno itself. But there were no embers here, only a brilliant expanse of high-grade iron ore stretching off almost to the horizon in a multitude of colors—alizarin crimson, burnt orange, deep purple, blue-black, oxblood brown, yellow, and scarlet. What we were looking at, mainly, was an enormous deposit of rust—as if a million steel girders had been allowed to oxidize for a century, and the deposit collected here in a mighty heap. Other deposits, darker red in color, consisted of hematite, which is simply jeweler's rouge.

The land about us was a monochrome of red. The hills in the foreground were red. The water lay in pools as red as blood. The men themselves were red, caked with the red dust that rose in clouds and permeated everything so that clothing, trucks, buildings, and foliage were layered in a thin veneer of crimson. It was a relief to look off beyond the craters at the blue Labrador skyline flecked still with small patches of snow, but even here one could see the red roads winding through the thin forests to the horizon.

Below us the great shovels were gouging into the soft red face of the crater in ten-ton gulps. Enormous Diesel trucks, belching clouds of blue exhaust, strained and groaned up the inclines, each loaded with thirty-five tons of ore. From the moment the shovel scoops it up, this ore scarcely stops moving until it reaches the steel mills of the United States. The trucks dump it into a hopper where it is screened, and from here an endless belt pours it into the waiting ore cars. The cars begin moving almost immediately down the railroad to Seven Islands. Here they are seized in steel jaws and turned turtle into another belt, which carries the ore to a freighter, which, loaded in a few hours, moves off at once up the St. Lawrence to the Lakes, or down-river to the Atlantic coast.

Jutting out into one of the scarlet craters (there are three large mines in operation in the vicinity of Knob Lake) was a small peninsula of land, and on it the remains of a log city. This was the original iron town of Burnt Creek, originally planned as the community around which the iron mines would be based. But a group of geologists, testing out a new drill on the main street, discovered that

Burnt Creek was sitting on a vast hoard of high-grade ore. The town was shifted to the new site of Knob Lake, and now the ore-diggers had eaten their way to within a few feet of the main street. Soon it would all vanish into the scarlet pit.

I spent two more days watching the swift human erosion of this richest section of the Labrador Trough. The ore is moving from the mines at the rate of ten million tons a year, and when the St. Lawrence Seaway is completed, this figure is likely to double. The four hundred million tons of high-grade ore already proved represent only a fraction of the total amount lying under the ashen soil of this bleak land. (There are literally billions of tons of low-grade.) All along the trough, especially on the northern coast, other companies are drilling for ore—and for other metals, too. Labrador's moment in history has arrived. Finally, after four centuries, it begins to look as if the land no longer belongs to Cain.

Postscript

One of the themes of this book is that the Canadian north is a land of boom and bust. Ghost towns litter the landscape. The hosannas that accompany each new mineral discovery are followed by dirges when the mines close and entire communities collapse.

That has been the history of the north since the days of the Klondike stampede, but few northerners absorb the lessons of history. It should be obvious that a vein of gold, iron, lead, or silver is finite; that world markets for minerals are notoriously unstable; that no boom can last forever. But it isn't. When Eldorado Mining pulls out of its company town, the five thousand residents of Uranium City are shocked and embittered. But uranium is not a renewable resource like wheat and hydro power, and the demand is fickle. Several towns have sprung up and died since I wrote this book. Schefferville, Quebec, is one of them.

I visited Schefferville in May 1955 when it was still known as Knob Lake. It was booming then; it is a ghost town today, all in the space of three decades. But the Grand Falls on the Hamilton River, whose potential I described in these pages, have become one of the great continuing sources of long-distance electrical power. The river's name has been changed to the Churchill River and the falls are known as the Churchill Falls. When they were harnessed, between 1966 and 1974, the project was the largest ever undertaken in North America. Since then, the contract that Joe Smallwood signed with Quebec has been the subject of a long, acrimonious, and (from the Newfoundland viewpoint) unsuccessful dispute. Newfoundland got taken when it signed a long-term contract to sell its Labrador power cheaply. Today that power, however, is not so cheap, and Quebec benefits. The contract will eventually run out; fortunately the falls won't.

When I travelled north on the new Labrador railway in May 1955, the development on the Hamilton River was still a dream. The railway had been completed only the year before, and the first carloads of ore had started to move south just the previous July. Between the two editions of this book the boom came and went. Iron prices dropped; markets vanished; the metal became too expensive to mine. Brian Mulroney, then president of the U.S.-owned Iron Ore Company of Canada, was forced to announce that the operations at Schefferville were at an end. The town, which had once held several thousand people, became another empty community like Pine Point, Uranium City, and Port Radium.

There is still iron in Labrador, but at the moment most of it is too expensive to mine. Labrador City, the Iron Ore Company's other boom town, which didn't exist when I wrote this book, has gone into decline; once it was home to fifteen thousand people.[39] And the various projects around Ungava Bay that I so enthusiastically described have come to nothing.

Perhaps the most significant change in the Arctic has nothing to do with boom and bust. The place names are being returned to the native people. Frobisher Bay is once again Iqaluit, "the place where the fish are." This name change, which took effect on January 1, 1987, heralds a new attitude. It is said that as many as ninety thousand place names and geographical features will acquire native names or have their present names changed. In *The Mysterious North* I wrote that the government was planning a new community at Frobisher Bay, the largest north of the Arctic Circle, large enough to hold a thousand people. That prediction has been exceeded. The population of Iqaluit has reached three thousand, half of it Inuit. The town continues to be the anchor point on the DEW line (soon to be

---

39 Labrador City weathered decline and now, thanks in part to a burgeoning market in China, the IOC's order books are full and the community is bustling.

replaced by the more ambitious Northern Warning System), complete with a native TV and radio station.

Pond Inlet, at the far end of Baffin Island, is now known as Mittimatalik. With a population of eight hundred, it is the largest of the thirty Inuit communities on the great island's east coast. Idlouk, whom I met when I landed on the ice, is dead now, but his family still lives in the community, not in a skin tent but in a government bungalow with electricity and a flush toilet. Appearances, alas, can be deceptive. "The people of the seal," as the early anthropologists called them, are faced with the extinction of their traditional culture. The villains of the piece are the foolish and unthinking activists of the animal rights movement, who apparently care more for the welfare of animals than that of human beings.

The adult ringed seal is at the core of the Inuit way of life on Baffin. The banning of the white pelts of the Canadian harp seal pups in Europe in 1983 and the popular disapproval of seal hunting in general caused a collapse of the European sealskin market. Yet the seal has been traditionally the mainstay of life for the Inuit families. The fat provides cooking and heating fuel in a treeless land. The meat, rich in vitamins, has long been their main source of nutrition (and the chief reason why the Inuit do not suffer from the scurvy that plagued the Arctic explorers). The hide is turned into boots, mittens, trousers, and parkas. More important, the sale of seal pelts provided the native families with a stable economy, allowing them to purchase flour, rifles, ammunition, and outboard motors.

The economic power that helped the Inuit move into a twentieth century world has dwindled. In just a decade their total annual income from the sale of seal pelts has dropped from $586,000 to a dismal $76,000.

The people of the seal still eat the meat, but the skins now largely go to waste. The hunt has diminished; there is less reason for it. With nothing to do, the hunters sit idly in their houses, their sense of worth dwindling. The future is predictable. When the culture goes, when the traditional way of life vanishes, alcohol and drugs take over; murder, suicide, and child neglect follow.

That is why I have no patience with Brigitte Bardot and her supporters in the animal rights movement. The ringed seal is not an endangered species. The Inuit of the Baffin coastline most certainly are.

CLOSURE OF HEBRON

In 1955 the Superintendent of the International Grenfell Association travelled north from Mission headquarters at St. Anthony on the northern tip of the Island as far as Nain to examine the communities whence came so many tuberculosis patients. He decided that most of the houses were unfit for habitation and was told that at Nutak and Hebron conditions were even worse. He recommended moving the Hebron and Nutak people south to new homes where there was a wood supply to heat them.

Evidently the Moravian Mission agreed with this course of action and some government officials argued that in the south better health, education and housing services could be provided. So in May 1955 the provincial Executive Council voted to close the Nutak depot and transfer the families to Nain or farther south.

Now the Hebron people were alarmed and wrote to their MHA, telling him they did not want to move at least until they could be assured of good jobs and good housing. A reply came back from the Deputy Minister that there was no plan to evict the residents and, if there were, they would be given a year's notice. But in the summer of 1958 the Moravians decided to abandon Hebron. The Government felt it had no choice but to close its store. The move was poorly planned and executed.

Elsewhere in the province a great deal of resettlement had taken place during the first two decades after Confederation. But in most cases there was consultation with the people. In the case of Hebron, the will of the people was clearly subordinate to the will of those responsible for their welfare. Walter Rockwood, the government administrator in northern Labrador, was opposed to the move and pointed out forcefully that the people had not been consulted. They had been promised a year's notice before any move; that promise had not been kept. They had requested houses and jobs before moving but housing provisions in the receiving communities was grossly mismanaged. Clearly the Inuit were the victims of the ethic of the day—that aboriginal people were not capable of managing their own affairs and were dependent on the state and associated patrons.

In *Reconciling with Memories* Carol Brice-Bennett says:

> *The removal of the entire Inuit population residing north of Nain from 1956 to 1959 was the largest exercise in social engineering that ever occurred in the entire history of the northern Labrador coast. With the elimination of residents at Okak and Hebron, a total of 418 people in 104 families were resettled and divided between five other communities. The relocation disrupted the traditional organization of the Inuit population along the entire northern Labrador coast, and also disturbed the customary economic and cultural order of community life for everyone. Families already living in southern communities had to adjust suddenly to the arrival of new residents, while northern Inuit had to adapt to places and environments and people that were radically different to their previous homeland."* (p. 13)

In August 1999 almost 160 Inuit from communities in northern Labrador and Ungava Bay, Nunavik, returned to Hebron to share memories of a village that was abandoned in 1959. For most of them it was the first time in forty years that they saw their native home and reunited with original village residents. The reunion was sponsored by the Labrador Inuit Association, Labrador Inuit Health Commission and Torngasok Cultural Centre as an initial step in assisting relocated Inuit to heal. The apology was given by Premier Danny Williams at the historic signing of the Inuit Land Claims Agreement in January 2005 prior to the inception of the new territory of Nunatsiavut.

In the following excerpts from *Reconciling with Memories*, the excellent account of the move by Carol Brice-Bennett is followed by the voices of some of the former residents and their descendants.

Carol Brice-Bennett

Excerpts from *Reconciling with Memories*

The closure of Northern Communities

This remarkable movement of people to Hebron was the reverse of a dramatic departure from the community which occurred in the summer of 1959. The entire resident population of the Hebron region, including 247 people in 60 families, packed their belongings and left their original homes after they were told by the Newfoundland Government that the village's only commercial trade store would be closed. The Moravian Church also announced that it was abandoning its station at Hebron, in operation since 1831, and transferring their minister to a southern coastal community.

Hebron Inuit were informed of these drastic changes at a meeting held in the church, although a community hall existed where these decisions could have been discussed. No one reacted to the announcement because people had been taught not to speak out or argue in the house of God, and so Hebronimiut were never able to express their feelings about the loss of their homes and hunting territory. Families were promised new houses and jobs with a regular salary to replace the income they earned from fishing, trapping and hunting at Hebron. But people quickly discovered that there were no houses or jobs waiting for them at any community along the Labrador coast.

Most of the Hebron families spent the first winter crowded into temporary shelters at Hopedale, and a year or two later, many of them moved farther south to Makkovik when small cottages were built there for northern Inuit. Some families remained at Hopedale, and others went to live at Happy Valley in the upper

Lake Melville area, but only a few families settled at Nain. This community had already expanded three years earlier when most of the population living in the OKak Bay area moved to Nain.

As at Hebron, OKak Bay residents were compelled to leave their homes after the Newfoundland Government decided to close the retail store at Nutak in the summer of 1956. A total of 44 families, including 171 people, lived at isolated homesteads scattered throughout OKak Bay and depended on goods supplied at the Nutak store. They were considered to be part of the Moravian congregation attached to the Hebron Church, and were visited on seasonal tours made by the Hebron minister. With the promise of new houses and jobs, 29 families moved to Nain while other families went to Makkovik, North West River, Happy Valley and also Hebron.

People settling at Nain could easily return to their former hunting, fishing and trapping grounds because the distance to OKak Bay was short, involving only about 80 miles (130 kms). However, families moving in 1959 from Hebron to Hopedale and Makkovik had to travel twice as far, or more, to reach their previous hunting grounds. The expense and additional time were major obstacles that prevented them from having access to familiar resources.

Hebron Inuit were isolated in many other ways from their former lifestyle. Wooden cottages built for families at Makkovik, Hopedale and Nain were clustered together in a separate area away from the rest of the community, so Hebron people were segregated immediately after they received new houses. In addition, northern Inuit did not have a language in common with other community members, since they spoke neither English as did the majority of Makkovik inhabitants, nor the same dialect of Inuktitut as spoken by Hopedale Inuit.

Hebron people also tended to have darker skin tones, and were more accustomed to a diet of fresh game than southern community dwellers whose lifestyle had altered due to greater contact with non-native cultures and goods. An abundance of seals, char with deep red flesh, and other wildlife in plenty around Hebron had given wealth in food to northern Inuit, but the few material possessions they carried to southern communities made them seem poor to other observers.

Carol Brice-Bennett

For the first time in their lives, adults and children were made to feel different and inadequate compared to established community residents. Youngsters were taunted when they walked to school and called avanimiut (meaning 'northerner'), exposing them to racial prejudice. This experience made children vulnerable and insecure, and led them to question their identity. Repeated incidents of discrimination occurring after individuals became adults further eroded their sense of self-worth, and reduced their confidence and pride.

Hebron hunters had to learn about new landscapes and search for wildlife that was less abundant than they were accustomed to seeing in northern areas. The heavily forested country around Makkovik was especially foreign to Hebron hunters familiar with harvesting in barren regions, and language prevented Inuit from gaining information about local resources from English-speaking hunters. In addition, prime fishing and trapping places around southern coastal communities were already claimed by established residents, which further reduced opportunities for newly-arriving hunters.

The result, as William Andersen III observed in his report, was that

...many experienced and aspiring hunters failed in their efforts at subsistence activities in the new and foreign environments. In a few short years this failure led to loss of respect by their peers and loss of self-esteem for themselves.

The shortage of fresh food caused another previously unthought-of experience for many households—hunger—which increased people's despair and helplessness. Reliance on social assistance for meagre allowances further reduced Inuit self-worth and became the norm for northern families. Being on welfare made people feel even more inferior because they were no longer able to support themselves as they had done when they lived at Hebron.

Without a community and hunting places of their own, Hebron Inuit lost their social and economic security. Family networks were severed as married sons and daughters moved to different communities, and lived apart from their elderly parents and from aunts and uncles, cousins and childhood friends. Poverty, demoralization, and frustration led people to consume alcohol in excess which contributed to family violence, accidental deaths, criminal offenses and the further breakdown of family relations. Elderly people are believed to have died sooner from the heart-break of being exiled from their homeland, and from being humiliated in the communities where they ended up living. The last wish of many elders was to be buried at Hebron, but even this request could not be fulfilled....

Reconciling With Memories

The reunion stimulated a degree of social interaction among Inuit that does not often occur. William Andersen III described the powerful atmosphere in his report, stating:

> ...even the Inuit who don't necessarily socialize with one another in their present communities all of a sudden became a complete part of the social fabric in Hebron for those few days. People laughed together, cried together, shared the wild meat and fish brought in for them by the hunters. For four or five short days, social interaction in ones own language and culture became a reality...
> For those precious few moments, the pain, the anger, the hopelessness that have become the norm for the majority of relocated Inuit in their new settings had disappeared. Five or six days out of forty years are really only a few moments.

Now 69 years old, Sabina Nochasak and her family moved in 1959 to Hopedale. During the conference she recalled:

> They said the hills are too high and Hebron is too far away from the hospital, that is why we were relocated to Hopedale. When we were leaving on the 'Trepassey', I did not want to look at Hebron... it was very stressful for me because this is my land. I was baptized here. I didn't like it at all when we were moving... I was crying. We had three children when we moved and we tried to be happy...
> At Hopedale we were called 'avanimiugâluit' (old northerners)...

William Andersen III was amazed by the overwhelming social attachments that were expressed during the reunion.

> *Families, relatives and old friends began to renew the friendships of the past from which they had been torn with little, if any, choice. Just standing between the church and the former retail store, one could see it all happen: some going through the remains of their former homes rummaging for anything they could take as souvenirs or something that would help them remember what the good and the bad days were before relocation. There were others who visited the old grave and burial sites, while others picked berries on the hillsides. More sat around in small groups telling stories about life in Hebron and surrounding areas before relocation.*

Alice Pilgrim walked into the house where she was born and, under part of a ceiling that had collapsed, she discovered a number of personal family items. A small handwritten diary kept by her father in the early 1940s, a wooden toy truck, an arrow made for a child with a bullet cartridge at its head, and a leather wallet were left behind in the attic when her family moved to Makkovik. Finding these things gave Alice a special connection to her family and the community at Hebron that were a direct result of the reunion.

Sophie Keelan and her brother Paul Jararuse spent time exploring the mission house where they found old store receipts dating back to 1958 in the attic. Among the papers was a bill for groceries purchased on June 16, 1958 by their father Benjamin showing that he paid $3.42 (including 8¢ tax) for 5 lbs. sugar, 1 lb. lard, 2 cans of condensed milk, 1 lb. butter, 5 lbs. hard bread, and a pair of children's gloves. Sophie's sister Hulda Snowball also found a piece of a slate writing board in the area where the schoolhouse had been; slate boards were used by children for doing their exercises. These details are mentioned in a journal kept by Sophie of her experiences at Hebron which was published in the Fall issue of the Makivik magazine.

Rita Andersen found several articles around the ruined dwellings of her relatives that represented people's everyday life In the community. The objects included pieces of a teapot, over a dozen coloured glass beads, needles for knitting and sewing, one teaspoon, a section from a pit saw, and a wrinkled, dried-up rubber playing ball. Outside Sampson Andersen's house Rita also found an enamel mug and a hard plastic bowl. As well, she collected red sand and white sand from the nearby beach that was customarily spread on the floor of thechurch. All of these items were real treasures for her and keepsakes of life at Hebron. In addition, Rita brought something special to leave at Hebron, in order to honour the memory of her deceased relatives. She placed floral wreaths in the cemetery for her grandfather David Kajuatsiak, and her aunt Amalia Nochasak.

MAGGO

The Labrador Inuit had had regular contact with Europeans from the 16th century onwards. From the farthest northern reaches the Inuit moved farther and farther south, drawn either by a greater supply of wood and food or by easier access to European goods. Slate and soapstone were replaced by iron and skin boats by wooden whalers. But gradually relations between the Inuit and the Europeans became characterized by hostility and treachery.

In the late 1700s the British Governor Palliser attempted to contain if not eliminate the conflict that existed between the Inuit and British fishermen who frequented the coast. He struck an agreement with the Moravians whereby the Church was to convert the Inuit to Christianity and confine them to an area north of Cape Harrison. The establishment of the Moravians first station at Nain in 1771 started the process of displacing the market networks of the Inuit leaders and traders. The Moravians supplanted Inuit governance and set up new systems. They began their own trading operations which they expected the Inuit to use exclusively. They started the first schools in Labrador and did their best to keep the Inuit healthy. Indeed, it is fair to ask how many Inuit there would be north of Hamilton Inlet today if it were not for the Moravians. But there is no doubt they brought about permanent change. With the increasing presence of the Europeans Inuit settlements were moved and their lives changed forever.

Paulus Maggo was born in 1910 when the Moravian Missions were well established and spiritual and economic life revolved around the village Mission House. Paulus was in Nain in 1926 when the Moravians leased their trade operations to the Hudson's Bay Company for 21 years. He was there when the Bay withdrew from operating stores on the Labrador coast, forcing the Newfoundland Commission of Government to manage the commercial outlets and to bring government to bear on the lives of the people in a very real way. He was there in 1949 when Newfoundland with Labrador joined Canada with all the social benefits that that entailed. When radar sites were constructed along the Labrador coast in the 1950s as part of the DEW Line Paulus went to Hopedale and learned to operate a jackhammer for drilling rock. But he returned to Nain where he saw new community facilities created and experienced the influx of new people as a result of the closure of Hebron.

Paulus experienced massive social and economic change in his life. He went from the age of the dog team to the age of the snowmobile, from the age of the kayak to the age of the speedboat, from the age of the inukshuk to the communities of today linked by satellite communications. In the last chapter of this book on his life he reflects on the present and the future. Carol Brice-Bennett has faithfully and sympathetically presented his memories and his reflections.

Paulus Maggo

"Reflections on the Present and Future," from *Remembering the Years of My Life: Journeys of a Labrador Inuit Hunter*

We Inuit in Labrador are not very numerous but we are one people and we are united. We have had the Moravian Church here for over two hundred years. We have the same belief and we have been given the privilege of living together. I am humbled and made happy for all of this. Sometimes it may not seem easy because we do not have a full-time minister here. We do the best we can and I feel sympathy for people who have to wait when they want to get married. The fu-ture looks much brighter. Inuit seem to really want to go back to helping and caring for each other, and people are showing greater concern for each other both within and outside immediate families. I'm much more optimistic about a lot of things than I was before.

I have not seen everything by any means. Many of the meetings that I have attended at places like Iqaluit and Greenland have reminded me, time and again, how wonderful it was in earlier days. The meetings involved discussions, co-operation, coming to terms and agreements, and helping each other. This is the way we did things around here in the old days. One of the meetings is held once every three years and is attended by Inuit from every community throughout the North. Delegates talk about traditional and cultural matters, and about wildlife, as well as many other subjects of common interest and concern among Inuit. They speak about holding on to their traditional customs and about their desire to help each other. After all, they are one and the same people. The last time we met in Greenland, Russian Inuit were present for the first time al-though they had always been invited to attend previous meetings. They had the same concerns and lifestyles that we had, and they wanted to hold on to their customs and traditions, too. They wanted control of their own resources and wildlife. They are Inuit. They also feel that they deserve and want the same things that all Inuit want and feel they deserve. Those were meaningful and helpful meetings. We discussed everything.

The Inuit and other people living in Nain when I first arrived in the village are outnumbered now by people who came after us from Hopedale and Okak. All of the Inuit who were adults when I moved here have died off. The Dicker and Harris families have the greatest number of offspring from their grandparents who were alive when I came to Nain. There were quite a few people in the Hunter family living here, too, but they have all moved to Hopedale. Their grandfather and father were both born in Nain.

It seems ironic, and I guess fate has a lot to do with it, but if the first Harris and the first Dicker whom I knew were here now, they would see the work they did in the church being carried on by their descendants today. The church work is back in the hands of the Dickers and the Harrises, people with the same family name from the same family tree. I think it was meant to be. Those people who wanted to settle here have passed away but their children are now taking over many things and carrying on the family name. Their grandparents must have had a guiding hand in helping them to choose to live here.

People have moved and settled here from all over the place. Many Hebron Inuit were forced to move to Nain, and there are more of them living and working here now than the original villagers. I am thankful, even though they were made to move here, that they came to live with and help their fellow Inuit. I'm grateful for this because we are all Inuit, and we should help each other. Although we originated from many different places, we have come to settle at this one place and we are all involved in some way in keeping the community functioning.

I often think about the many customs and traditions that we no longer have or follow. We no longer have a brass band due to lack of instruments, and the church choir may cease sometime in the future because fewer practices or rehearsals are being held, and no new or young singers are being trained. When we had a full slate of choir members, organists, trumpeters, and fiddlers, we always recruited young people to teach them whatever interested them most. If one person or another had to leave for any reason, we were able to replace them from the people we had trained. We always encouraged young people and a lot of them had natural talents. Some took a little longer to teach but they eventually learned when they kept at it with a lot of encouragement. We were always able to recruit enough people to keep everything going. No one was forced to participate. Now newcomers don't stay very long and quit before they finish. We will run out of singers and no longer have a church choir, and we may not have organists or fiddle musicians because no one is being trained for any of these positions. It worries me but I hope that I will be proven wrong.

We learned to use and repair many new articles as they arrived. Some things were awesome at first but we eventually accepted and used them all. When I heard the ministers talk about television, I was flabbergasted and could not imagine what it was. I never thought that I would own a television. Now our radios and record players are all run by electricity, and we even look at images on TV. We also have VCRs and cable TV so you can watch any channel you want. We can know the name and time of programs in advance so we select shows to watch. All of these things that we never even thought about, or ever imagined, are taken for granted now.

We also learned to repair equipment when parts happened to break down, but now people have to go outside for long periods to learn and get certified for operating this and repairing that. This requirement is an obstacle for a lot of capable people who are not able to go out and attend schools. There are many people without university education and they, or at least some of them, are just as capable as ones with training. Some people learn about things at universities and schools, and some people learn from experience, by hands-on-effort and actually doing something. They can repair and replace parts just as well as those who have certificates.

Some demands that we have to comply with today are contrary to the usual way that we handled matters in earlier days. Some of the new regulations may not be specific or of direct concern to us. Going away to places of higher learning for long periods seems necessary now but doing this requires a lot of money. People have to borrow if they don't have readily available cash. I don't think this requirement should apply to each and every person. Some people have acquired skills that are not gained from attending outside schools, and they are just as capable and should receive equal treatment. They are self-taught and have both earned and natural skills gained through the experience of actually doing things. I am just saying what I have been feeling and suspecting for some time. Obviously some people can take care of themselves and do well without having attended universities. I sometimes don't like the idea of forced education.

There have been many changes. We didn't think so many houses would exist as we have at present. There was only one narrow footpath through the trees, with little bridges built across the streams, that was always maintained and cleaned up in the spring. The min-isters, storekeepers, and Inuit kept the footpath maintained and clean. The trees were protected with signs posted at both ends of the path warning that no tree was to be cut down anywhere between them. There was one sign at the beginning and one at the end where Julius Saimat lives now. Not even a grave was to be dug anywhere between the two signs. Anyone caught cutting trees was dealt with harshly at a meeting with the Elders and minister, but people could go beyond the signs and cut trees for firewood. The ministers in-spected the trees and if they found any rotted or dead ones, they would mark them and have them cut down for firewood to be given to the elderly, disabled, or anyone who was sick and needed wood.

This patch of forest was used for leisurely walks especially by the ministers and their wives on Sundays. They would catch white butterflies with a kind of flycatcher dip nets and they seemed to love doing that. They put the butterflies in glass containers and I think that they sent them somewhere south to other people and places collecting them. They gathered other insects, too, put a little pin through them and placed them in glass containers.

When I was ten or fifteen years old, people from Europe were sent to various communities to learn to become ministers and were taught by the minister stationed at a particular village. They were taught the Inuit customs, traditions, and language. Some of them were quick to learn how to speak Inuktitut, but I don't know if they received other training elsewhere before being sent here. Those trainees were a great help in classrooms and they always visited Inuit houses. They would pick up objects and ask what they were called in our language, and do other things that helped them to learn Inuktitut.

The main language of communication here at that time was Inuktitut and very few people spoke English. The Europeans would often visit to listen to Inuit speaking, and while many of the conversations would be one-sided, in time they started picking up the language and some of them became fluent. When Mr. Peacock[40] first came here for training, he was young and single but the first Mr. Hettasch[41] was already an old man and he taught Mr. Peacock to speak Inuktitut. Mr. Peacock didn't take that long to learn to speak our language but I don't think that he understood some of the meanings. When I'd be walking by his house, he'd call me into his office to show me something written in Inuktitut and ask me what it meant. I really got to know him and he got to know me, as we paid each other many visits. He was always honing his newfound language and tried to improve it by asking all kinds of questions and writing down answers in both languages when he understood. Mr. Hettasch spoke Inuktitut well and was a good storyteller. He told stories when he visited us or we visited him at his house, or when he was working outside around his house. He was inclined to tell stories whenever he had an audience. We enjoyed his stories because, through them, he made us aware of many things that we knew very little or nothing about at all.

It was the same way with the Hudson's Bay Company store managers. They learned the language quickly because they always had an Inuit cook who was

---

40 Reverend Bill Peacock, later Superintendent of the Moravian Church in Labrador.

41 Reverend Paul Hettasch, Superintendent of Moravian Missions at Nain.

the late Jim Webb's daughter. She's living in the United States if she's still alive, and her name was Eliza. She spoke both languages and was a good teacher for the managers. One manager who learned from her when he was in Nain is Mr. Mercer,[42] who I heard recently was living in Goose Bay. He was speaking Inuktitut by the third year of his stay here. He became fluent and would often go hunting with Inuit. He went on many seal-hunting trips on his own by borrowing dogs from Inuit, and he always delivered seal meat for dog food to whoever loaned him dogs. Having Inuktitut as the main language of communication made it easier for people to learn it.

The ministers are different today. We have gone for long periods without a minister here. We've been abandoned for a year, two years, and as many as three years at a time. The ministers come and then leave before they can properly read or write in Inuktitut. When they are here, they speak only in English to everyone, even when they are talking to unilingual Inuit. I think this is why they do learn so little Inuktitut, but this is my personal feeling because I really don't know the reason. The earlier ministers visited often and mingled, they made visible attempts and were interested in learning the language, and did everything to get better at it. If the present ones did the same, they would achieve the same result. It goes for me, too. I can learn to speak English only if and when I have someone to teach me, and if and when I want to learn it.

Some languages can be forgotten and I know of examples when this happened. Mike Dyson from Hopedale was adopted and lived here after having spent some time at an orphanage in St. Anthony. He spoke only English at the orphanage but when he was adopted by Boas Obed and his wife, he learned to speak only Inuktitut. By the time he was sixteen or seventeen, he could not speak or understand English. He and Jacko Obed once went on board a schooner, and Jacko told Mike to ask one of the fishermen how many tubs it would take to load the schooner. Mike refused and Jacko got mad at him. They

---

42 Hayward Mercer, store manager with HBC and later with Northern Labrador Services Division, the brother of Frank Mercer, Nfld. Ranger, later Labrador Section NCO with RCMP and Director of Labrador Affairs.

were almost brawling when Mike shouted "How many tubusik?" He mixed the two languages. Jacko started laughing and Mike got mad in turn. Another case involved Sam and Miriam Brown's daughter Maria,[43] who was sent to St. Anthony [Hospital] as a young child speaking only Inuktitut. Before she left, my late daughter Regina and she would play and speak only in Inuktitut, since neither of them could speak English. By the time Maria returned, she spoke only English and she had to point to things and make signs to try to make herself understood. This can and has happened, which is how I know that languages can be lost.

All of my children learned to speak Inuktitut and my grandson Roland can speak it fluently because he has spoken Inuktitut with us ever since he was small. Hardly any of my other grandchildren can speak Inuktitut now. Amos's oldest son is the only one who can speak it and some of my daughter's children can understand a little but they cannot speak our language. They can only say grandfather and grandmother in Inuktitut. Many young people don't speak or understand Inuktitut now and we are losing our language because it is being used less and less. If some of them could realize how important language is, then maybe it would return.

If at all possible, we should never forget our language and we should be thinking of ways and doing things to help our younger generation retain our language. We should be teaching our children and they should be teaching their younger ones. Only in this way will our language not be lost. I am sometimes afraid our language is disappearing because all I hear coming from our younger people is English. It should never have come to this stage. It's sad because we still have a few unilingual Inuit who, when they ask questions, have no one fluent enough in Inuktitut to interpret what is really being said. Those older ones, when they speak Inuktitut, are not fully understood by some of the bilingual speakers. The situation is critical and more Inuktitut should be used by more of our people.

---

43 Now a translator in Ottawa.

A few of us still speak only in our language to our families. My little great-granddaughter is bilingual, and she talks to me just in Inuktitut because it is the only language that I use when I speak to her. Some Inuit don't think she speaks Inuktitut so they talk in English to her, but most of them are discovering that she can speak both languages and they speak to her now more in Inuktitut. All of my kin speak it, because after all they are Inuit and so am I. It is normal and expected, or it should be at least. I'm just saying this but I am not preaching. I have tried, and I am using the language with my children and grandchildren to see if this would work, and it is working. It can work when properly promoted at home. This makes the young people happy to learn it and makes them proud to be able to speak their own language, which is Inuktitut.

I have a lot of grandchildren and great-grandchildren. My grandson Roland is my only caregiver in every way now because I don't work any more either around the house, chopping firewood, or anything else. He can hunt for food and takes care of us, and I am very proud that he is with me. I used to hear that grandchildren can be more lovable than even your own children, and I believe that because I love my grandson's youngest child very much. I am also very proud of my late daughter's children because since she died, they have been able to take care of themselves. They still live in their own house and take good care of themselves, and I am very proud of the way they are growing up.

At one time Inuit had no surnames. They chose a surname and informed the ministers of the name by which they wanted to be called. According to Michael Atsatata, his father chose their sur-name and he lived to be an elderly man. I remember a very elderly man with white hair, Natan Illiniartitsijok, who got his surname [meaning "the one who teaches"] because he was once a teacher. At times he couldn't remember where he was and would get lost on one of his walks but he would be found in the evening, none the worse for wear.

The surnames were chosen and should not be changed now. In the case of a female who marries, they are given the surname of the male. The surnames of all married Inuit women have been changed through marriage. When their husbands die and they happen to re-marry, they change their name again. Should they happen to get divorced, they can go back again to using their original surname. There seems to be a lot of attention being paid to surnames today, and maybe people want to hold on to the past, hold on to their own father's or grandfather's side of the name. There is more need for personal identification today by those who keep records. Inuit becoming eligible for Old Age Pension have to have their names traced back to their relatives. That's why I think it's important to have and retain surnames.

I am often awed and surprised by our younger single women of today. We don't have that many more single women than we had in former days but they have a lot more children. We have more and more single women having babies, and either they are having babies more often, or more of them are having babies. Most of them don't seem to care what name they give to their children. They show no regard for their own mother's or father's names. They seem to take whatever name they happen to come across for their children, giving them non-Native names and calling them after people with no ties to the family. This is the way it appears to me.

I think Inuit should respect, retain, and be known and traceable by their name. I just mention this as it's been a concern of mine because at one time we had to approach and inform the minister when we married couples had or were having children. We were asked who the child will be named after, and we also had to explain why we wanted a particular name, why we wanted the child named after a particular person. The child might be named after a close and respected friend, or for someone who wanted a namesake. This is just a personal concern of mine and I don't want to get in the way.

It would be helpful now if we could return to the days and ways of helping each other as we once did. In the past people who could no longer move around freely because of old age were cared for and helped by anybody and everybody. Children with parents and orphans did not do anything on their own. They would be provided with food and ammunition and whatever else was needed when they went on a hunting trip. People had to try to survive in any way they could, and we, the older generation, did that by providing for our family from morning until night. Our parents did the same for us. Today this tradition still continues, but our younger generation can go on their own because they are able to earn their own income and get what they need. It seems better now because they have an easier way to earn a living. In the past we were always given things for our use and nothing that we needed was refused to us. Our forefathers looked after us, not only their younger folks, but they looked after married people as well.

We no longer help each other freely in our communities. We used to fetch water for the elderly, carry things for them, and assisted them in many other ways. Now they are abandoned in their time of most need, and we just leave them to fend for themselves. There should be more concern and care shown to our elderly and to those less fortunate, but the question is, who should be responsible? We, the elderly, talk about this subject amongst ourselves. The church elders were involved, as were all residents of the community, on matters that affected our elderly. Responsible groups and organizations have multiplied over the years. I think that the organization most responsible for looking after the affairs of the elderly should initiate a program directly aimed at them. As I've said, there are all kinds of groups and organizations holding meetings and discussing all kinds of subjects today. I think that the Inuit Women's Association is best suited to look after the affairs of our elderly. They seem to be the most qualified group and were initially involved. Maybe they'd be interested if they were asked. They even had a skidoo for use by or for the elders at one time but I think it broke down. I heard them talking about getting a taxi service, too. I think the problem of acquiring adequate funding prevents them from doing this and other things. Bearing this in mind, I'll save some money when I can, and make a donation at their next meeting or go to the executive and tell them the intention of my donation.

It's uncertain what the future holds. There have been many changes in the present compared to the past. Everything costs money and everybody wants to be paid. There is no volunteerism like before. We are all too used to receiving payment for whatever we do. We really have to get together to discuss, agree, and be willing to help each other about the way that we would like to see things handled, and do it collectively before I can predict what the future holds. Although much of the way I remember life is gone now, I want to see people getting along with each other and helping each other as they used to do in all the communities. Inuit and Kallunângajuit got along very well and always helped each other in working, with food, and in many other ways because money was not used as it is now. They treated each other well and helped each other in any way when someone needed help. Their lifestyle was good because they got along well and helped each other, but now Inuit and Kallunângajuit[44] seem to avoid each other. Although they should treat each other in the same way as they did before and should really support each other because they live in the same land, it seems in my mind that they want to be separate.

I know that being able to get along well is the best thing that can happen so I hope it can be this way again. We don't spend time together as we used to, perhaps because we don't leave the community as much and we spend too much time in one place. Maybe the problem causing us not to get along as well as we once did is that people don't spend time outside the communities so they could miss seeing each other. What I would like to see happen is for everyone to get along well in their communities because this was the way it was everywhere here.

Everything, our way of life and our land, is different from what it once was. I think the future will show that the land will just keep on changing, especially if we don't mind whether or not it's taken care of. Our land and beaches are shifting all the time through erosion, waves, and landslides. Land where some houses once stood is no longer there, and some existing houses are now perched on top of pretty high places because the land has eroded as much as five feet or more. What will be done about it in the future is uncertain. We used to back-fill areas using logs at one time, which helped a great deal and prevented erosion and landslides before a Town Council was created. We also worked at and maintained our roads using only wheelbarrows and shovels when I was a member of the Elders. I was even put in charge of our roads before the days of the Council.

---

44 People of mixed Inuit and European ancestry, commonly known as "settlers" in English. The Inuit term literally means "resembling a white person."

There is some work being done by the Town Council but they always run out of money before any project is complete. At times it seems that the season is too short, with cold weather setting in too soon, to complete some projects. I think most of it is due to lack of planning, lack of preparation, and lack of the required tools and material. No doubt it will get better. They've been working on a water and sewer system for many years now. The material seems to have been available and ready for some time, but the water supply is too low and the dam is too small to hook up all of the houses.

We had no water this past winter because there wasn't much snow. Even if we had a lot of snow and if all of the houses were hooked up, the water source would dry up in no time because it's too small. It will become more difficult as more houses are built, but if they built another dam, there would be lots of water. Even now with just a few houses on line, the water dries up and the pipes freeze in winter creating a lot of heavy and difficult work for the Council and hardship for those of us who depend on it. The problem is with the rock and permafrost underground. In some places the permafrost below ground is four feet thick and the route they have to take to get to the water source is full of permafrost. They just laid the water pipes on top of the permafrost, which guarantees frozen pipes each and every winter. The solid rock just below ground level is a big prob-lem, too. I just mention this subject as I am aware of how hard it is to work on our land. I don't envy the Council workers and I'm even thankful that they have this duty. They're responsible for many other things, too, but I don't think that they will conquer the water problem anytime soon.

The last group of arctic char fishermen were dissatisfied with the char stocks in nearby areas and the way they were discouraged from going further north where they knew that lots of char could still be caught. The char farther north go out of the rivers much later than around Nain, and they return to the spawning grounds much earlier and much more suddenly, at a time when some char can still be caught around here. All of the char fishermen knew this and were sure of being able to catch a lot more char, if they had been allowed to go further north and return to Nain at proper intervals.

The problem centred on the collector boats that were operated by government authorities, who refused to send the boats to collect char from areas they considered were far north, even at the time I was still working on one of the collector boats. There were two boats stationed at Saglek but they were always sent back close to Nain as soon as the authorities felt that the char would be going into the riv-ers around Nain, although they were still plentiful in the north. The fishermen couldn't keep catching fish because they had no means of getting them to market before the char rotted. There were not many people fishing as far north as Saglek, although some of them originated from Hopedale. People were also fishing at places closer to Nain like Napartok Bay and the Okak area. The collector boats would not have been able to keep up with transporting char had there been more fishermen. When the char were returning to their spawning grounds, the fishermen were barely able to keep their nets clear of char when I was working on one of the collector boats.

All of the negatives in combination now cannot come close to describing the difference between the past and the present. The comparisons are too far apart. There is very little or no fish to catch, no animals to hunt, seals are not in demand, boats and engines are in need of repair or broken down altogether because of neglect or lack of use, and all of the equipment and necessary tools are worn out, rotten, corroded, or too old to use. Even the few fishing crews that are still trying to eke out a living from char do not have enough fish being picked up by collector boats to pay for their food. They are not making enough for food and nothing at all for repairs and maintenance. Isaac Zarpa had his boat almost paid for when his engine broke down. His boat was left on land all last summer and the summer before.

There is a feeling of hopelessness for the future. How will someone purchase food when there is not enough fish, and no equipment so that a person can try to make money if they don't have a place of employment? There are no alternatives and no way of purchasing food or equipment on credit because of too much uncertainty about whether or not enough will be caught to payoff accumulated debts. A few people work for wages and have no worries, but there is no hope for the hunters, fishermen and others for whom there is no alternative here.

Today my life has changed dramatically. I do not get around so much because of my age and wind bothers my eyes, bringing tears to them. They are not very good for reading, even when I am wearing my spectacles. When I lost my daughter, it took a lot out of my life and ever since then the strength in my legs has not returned. I find it difficult to walk now and I can't do much any more, but I know that there is nothing I can do about it. I envy those who can go off hunting as I can only travel now in my mind.

RICH

The Innu are perhaps the oldest of the peoples who have lived and moved in Labrador, and yet today they are clearly the least comfortable, the least happy, and the least prosperous. The descendants of thousands of years of aboriginal occupation of Labrador, today's Innu are found in two villages at Sheshashiu, about 20 miles from Goose Bay, and Natuashish, where the Davis Inlet people moved, just south of Nain and the Voisey's Bay nickel mine. Before the coming of the Europeans, the Innu inhabited the Labrador Peninsula, including portions that are now parts of both Quebec and Labrador. They called their territory Nitassinan, "our land," as they do today. It was the ever-increasing presence of the Europeans and the expansion of the Thule Eskimos along the coast of Labrador that forced the Innu to move deeper into the interior. When the caribou herds were plentiful the Innu were self-sufficient and there was little need for European goods, but the coming of the fur traders had a profound effect on their lives. Hunters who had previously tracked caribou were now enticed to trap enough beaver to satisfy the demands of the European market.

Until the beginning of the twentieth century, the hunting grounds of the Nascapi, the northern Innu, had centered around Indian House Lake on the George River. There the Innu who used the trading post at Davis Inlet had contact with the Nascapi from the Fort Chimo area. Around 1916, after the caribou herds changed their migration route, near-starvation drove the Innu to depend more heavily on the trading posts, but their situation continued to deteriorate.

At Davis Inlet, a Catholic priest had made annual summer visits since 1927, and one was posted there permanently after 1952. After the fur trade collapsed, although there was improved health care, there was greater dependence on food from the government store. Despite good intentions, settlement brought a tragic decline to the Innu lifestyle. Houses lacked running water and electricity, and, incredibly, there was no water supply at the site chosen for the community—a major factor in the later decision of the community to move to Natuashish (Sango Bay). Fundamentally, the Innu had never made the transition from the life of nomadic hunters to that of nine-to-five wage earners in the cash economy in which very few, if any, real jobs existed. From a different culture, speaking a different language, forced to become dependent on European goods and materials, the Innu sank into dependency and despondency. The young got caught up in drug and alcohol abuse. Later, young Innu people switched to glue and gas sniffing, as the dramatic TV footage of the tragic fire of 1992 recorded. Now at Sango Bay a new and modern community has arisen, but the old evils remain.

In *Struggling With My Soul*, George Rich describes the challenges faced by the new community and by himself. In his moving personal testimony Rich describes his struggle against the effects of sexual abuse and the drinking that led to his marriage break-up. Only after he found the strength to break the hold alcohol had on him did he find the way ahead. Many of his fellow Innu, both young and old, still struggle.

George Rich

George Rich

EXCERPT FROM *Struggling With My Soul*, 2000

A Boy Between Worlds

In places like Natuashish,[45] the Innu world went on as before. But in the new settlement of Davis Inlet, the children would be educated in English, a language foreign to them. The Innu would struggle to keep their own values and beliefs and way of life. Already their spiritual beliefs had been mocked by the missionaries. Their fundamental rights as people had been violated—how and where they lived and how they governed themselves had been taken over by another culture. The promised land became a shambles of despair and poverty.

I sometimes wonder what would happen now if Innu people entered a foreign land and tried to make the rules and regulations, and tried to impose their cultural and spiritual beliefs on other people. What would happen if the Innu tried to force others to speak their language? People of European descent need to take the time to think of how hurtful and degrading that can be. Maybe then they will understand why there is so much anger and suicide among Labrador's aboriginal peoples.

As a young boy, I watched, fascinated, as the world of my people changed. Snowmobiles quickly replaced dog teams; outboard motors replaced canoes and paddles. All the new conveniences cost money. But work was scarce and there were few ways to get money. People also needed to learn how to manage the money they earned. All of a sudden, money was important in Innu culture in ways it never was before.

When food was scarce in Davis Inlet, my parents walked all the way to the hunting grounds. Even though they now lived in houses, families still prepared for their fall hunt when they would camp near the mainland and near the rivers. There, they caught the winter supply of Arctic char, small game like porcupine and small birds. They would leave the community that had been built for them behind.

In the late 1960s my parents and five other families traveled to hunting grounds where caribou usually were plentiful. This may be the last time I know of that people traveled quite a distance by dog team to hunt caribou. The area was known as "Border Beacon" because of the new weather station there. The caretakers of the weather station would always share when the Innu ran out of grub like tea or sugar. It was fiercely cold on those barrens. I remember now how the five of us children were tucked in and bundled up in canvas. I am lucky to have this memory.

I also remember the day my younger brother was born in the country. I don't know how my mother survived the ordeal of harsh cold and all the pulling and shoving of the komatik. My father was pulling the sled with the help of three cranky dogs. There were blizzard conditions that day, and on the barrens wood was scarce. It must have been hard for my mother to keep warm through her labour.

We were sent to my uncle's tent to wait for the baby's arrival. We didn't know what was happening. All my father told us was that our mother was sick and we had to behave ourselves. This brought back fear and bad memories of the time she had to go away to hospital in North West River with TB. What was going on in our minds brought our usually energetic spirits to a halt for the day. My uncle told us not to worry because she was in good hands. Three midwives were taking care of her.

Late in the afternoon we had a little brother. As any child would do, we asked our father how the baby had arrived in our tent. He told us the baby was found crawling up to our tent that afternoon. Being curious, we set out to look for tracks and couldn't find any.

Because of the birth, my parents were forced to stay behind while other Innu families headed home. We had to wait until my mother started to gain her strength back. On the way home, I had to walk beside the komatik. I started to dislike my little brother. I told my mother quietly that she should have left him there where they had found him. He was taking my space where I would have enjoyed being bundled up against the cold.

---

45 One of the locations inland from Davis Inlet, which the Innu frequented on their sorties to the country. It is now the name of the relocated community of Davis Inlet.

As we settled into the new community, we had to get used to new neighbours. There were teachers, nurses, store managers, and other new people to work with the Innu. These people were all white. The only jobs available to Innu were as janitors in the school and as relief workers for the hydro generating plant. The lucky ones who had been obedient to the missionary got the first chance at these jobs.

Many other people suddenly became dependent on welfare and family allowance cheques. Parents were told that in order to receive family allowances, they would have to send their children to school. The Innu were not supposed to take their children out of school to go in the country, although this was an important part of our way of life. Few people struggled against the new rule. One missionary tried to find a way around it. He encouraged the families to camp about a mile outside the community.

The missionary and the new leaders that had been parachuted in to look after us had begun to realize something. The restless Innu could not easily turn away from their way of life and move to a more permanent settlement. Almost immediately, they began to turn to alcohol.

The new school opened in the late fall. There were nuns and brothers to supposedly educate us children. From the beginning, the new language and the outside world sidetracked our way of thinking. We had to learn quickly about Prime Ministers of Canada. We had to be patriotic like any Canadian child and learn to sing O Canada.

But we had our own culture. I remember hearing as a child the legends about the Tshakapesh. He is a folk hero who destroys Atshen, a mystical cannibal who hunted down the Innu. Eventually, Tshakapesh and his sister went to live on the moon. Now when we heard about men landing on the moon we were confused. When the teacher asked one of the Innu students who was the first man on the moon, the Innu child replied "Tshakapesh."

In religion class, our beliefs clashed again. I remember a priest asking a student who created the earth. The student answered without hesitation, "Kuekuatsheu." There are comical legends about Kuekuatsheu, a man who deceives everyone who comes across his path. He is also known as creator of the earth with the help of the animals. This was another of our beloved legends that soon went down the tubes.

Of all the things we were taught during our first year of school, religion was the greatest torment. The missionary had graphic pictures of the devil and demons that looked so horrible, they stayed in my mind late at night. His thundering voice preaching about hell and fire left us with the impression that he was the saviour of our people.

Despite the demons, I always enjoyed school, and I was eager to learn about other things and other places around the world. I stayed in that school until grade eight. We had to do grade nine outside the community. It would be my first time ever on the island of Newfoundland. At first it was culture shock. I didn't understand what was going on in my new surroundings. The first day of class I was surprised to come face to face with Brothers again. I was frightened and concerned about what they would do to us. It took a while to adjust. The new teachers weren't so bad, but I could not really trust them. I had been sexually assaulted by the Brothers in Davis Inlet in the late 1960s.

I never did finish the second semester. I had trouble keeping up with other students in the class. During one of our English classes, the teacher told us to write an essay on Pontiac, the car. I had no idea what a Pontiac was. If he had suggested writing about the snowmobile, I would probably have gotten a good mark on the essay. I didn't do a lot of the assignments because I didn't understand them.

At the age of fifteen, I'd had it with school. My friends and I went back to Davis Inlet. For a few years, I just hung out. There weren't many opportunities for work or training.

Our summer youth employment in Davis Inlet was make-work projects, hauling the store goods from the coastal boats to the warehouse. Almost every summer, I worked in community cleanup. The sale of a catch of Arctic char to the nuns brought enough money for a round trip to Nain on a coastal boat. Either of the two coastal boats was a chance to get out of the community for a night, a quick getaway. A lot of times we would go without paying the fare and we would share with others who paid for a room. We used their tickets that were already punched by the purser. Sometimes they didn't even bother to look for stowaways. No wonder Marine Atlantic is in trouble now.

Our one-night vacations in Nain, the most northerly community in Labrador, put some variety in my boring teenage life. We eagerly awaited the first boat of the year, which usually got in around mid-July.

A boat expected was always excitement. When we knew a boat was coming that day, we would climb the hill at the back of the community and use it as a crow's nest. If we saw the boat on the horizon, looking south heading towards Davis Inlet, we would yell down below that the boat was coming. Those who heard us sometimes climbed the steep hill just to see what all the fuss was about. Adults would climb up with their binoculars and stay for hours, looking for wildlife or just passing the time away. The hill was a good place to play cowboys and Indians or war games or to escape from the mosquitoes.

With the first boat of summer, new store goods would arrive, including cans of pop and chips that would be a treat for the next few months. When nobody was around, those of us who unloaded it would reward ourselves with a soft drink and bags of chips after a hard day's work. Sometimes the coastal boats anchored out in the harbor, and collector boats brought the goods to be unloaded at a small wharf. The store manager and stock handlers of the government store marked down everybody who worked, and how many hours we worked. The next morning we had to wait in line to collect our wages. Sometimes our wages disappeared again before we left the store.

In the summer, the store had a new stock of fishing supplies—rods, reels and spinners. We fished daily, and it was the one thing I loved to do.

One time I tried to enlist in the army when a recruiter came by. I was told to travel to St. John's and meet certain people. I made my way up to Goose Bay and stayed in a hotel for the night. It was there I met with my stepbrother and his friend from Davis Inlet. They were working in Sheshatshiu at the lumberyard and were traveling back to Davis Inlet on a coastal boat the following morning.

After a few beers, they asked what I was doing in Goose Bay. At first I didn't want to say anything, but after a few beers, I told them about my plans. They laughed. They asked me how I could be in the army when I couldn't even shoot a caribou. How could I defend myself in a war when I didn't know how to use a gun? After a lot of beer, my wish to be in the army had flown away. After chatting with these supposedly wiser role models of mine, I decided to go back with them the next morning on the coastal boat. It was not long before I was caught up in my community's struggle to survive.

Coming Apart

The new way of choosing leaders went against the old traditional ways by which the Innu ran their affairs. The Innu had always relied on the elders in the camp, and they had their way of selecting camp leaders. There were many kinds of leaders. There was a camp leader and leaders for hunting. Almost everyone in the camp had a role to play. The election system created division and took away the elders' traditional role. It also brought all the kinds of corruption elections can have. In our small community, people with large families can control band council elections and government. Also, anyone who has a lot of alcohol can win a seat on council. Now every year we have elections in Davis Inlet, mainly because people crave influence or business contracts or good employment from the council. People think of community government in terms of what power or favours they can get. Petty politics grew from a spark into a blazing fire that divides the community today. The only way to extinguish the flames is to create a new way of electing community representatives. We need a way for everyone to have their say.

I loved the elections for all the booze brought in by the people who wanted the chief's job or councilor's position. When it was my turn to run, I used every trick I'd learned to get elected as band councilor. I had a lot of tactics. Once I went out for the Liberal leadership convention when Len Sterling was elected leader. I quickly imitated the use of campaign buttons in the next band council election. I ordered the buttons and distributed them to my supporters. I once wore the campaign buttons as earrings when I was drunk and crazy at a party. I did it to get votes and laughs, but you can imagine how I felt the following morning.

The thrills and excitement lasted until I turned sober at the age of 29. After 17 years, I reached a point where I felt guilt and shame that I was serving only my own self-interest. I could see my own people struggling to survive on $500 a month on welfare for a family of five. Yet some elected leaders wouldn't even attend meetings unless they received an honorarium of $500 a day. It began to keep me awake at night. When we attended outside meetings, we received a per diem of $60 a day for expenses. We would stay for a number of days to get the full amount. I once took my wife to Halifax for a quick holiday. We checked into a nice hotel. After a few days, she told me that no wonder we elected leaders loved to travel all the time. This was another stab to my inner soul. There we were, staying in five-star hotels, while our own people didn't even have water and sewer in their homes. It hit my conscience hard. It was time to quit this imaginary life.

Perhaps I should have listened to my father. When I decided to run for election, I turned to him for support and advice. My father said I should go hunting caribou instead. I should have realized by now that my father never bought all the changes happening around us. His beliefs and principles as an Innu gatherer and hunter were all he knew.

When the thrill went out of politics for me, it seemed we weren't achieving much of value. We were not doing enough for people who needed new homes. Alcoholism had rapidly increased. The band councils couldn't do a thing with their budgets; the governments of the day turned deaf ears to us. They ignored our pleas for the funding and resources we needed. We tried so hard to answer the needs of the people, but what could we do if nobody was listening?

Over the years I would chat with the elder on the council about the way things were going. Once I asked if he was going to run in the next election. He just laughed lightly and told me that if I wanted to create any image for myself, I should know by now it was all an illusion. He said he ran in the elections for fun, something to do. He knew nothing was going to change. He told me that if things were going to change now, then it was in the works already; it would happen so fast that we young leaders wouldn't be able to handle it. Looking back at it now, I realize he was right. When the federal government announced the relocation of Davis Inlet, all the things he told me were right there in front of our noses. We could not handle it.

The public meeting was held in the basement of the community bathhouse. The big question was: in what direction are we heading? We had a public forum on where we could have water and sewer, the topic on everybody's mind. The engineer the band council had hired to do studies on where we could get water still had no answers. The drilling had lasted for three years and the engineers had drilled everywhere; the cost of the studies was sky-high. We were running out of ideas. The community joke was that we had so many drill holes in Davis Inlet, the whole island would sink soon. It was then that the elders spoke of the first resettlement from the mainland 25 years ago. Water and sewer had been promised then, but had never been delivered. The elders urged the young leaders to talk to the federal and provincial governments about the current conditions of the houses and the skin diseases of the Innu in Davis Inlet.

It was time to listen to the elders. We organized a meeting for federal and provincial representatives to come see first-hand how our people lived. We organized the public meeting in a tent setting, and we invited the media. The elders were very outspoken; they were not satisfied to get their water and dump their honey buckets outside in the freezing winter. We asked the bored bureaucrats: what other Canadians live in such conditions? Is it a Canadian standard to live like this? The questions from the elders were very powerful and touching. The federal and provincial officials told the Innu they would listen to their concerns and take them to their bosses in Ottawa. But the ongoing meetings were postponed and we never did receive the answer we wanted to hear.

With encouragement from the elders, the leaders didn't give up. Somehow in the next few years, things seemed to fall into place. But first there had to be tragedy. The accidental burning of six children and the suicide attempts of teens created an uproar throughout Canada. People wanted to know what was going on in Davis Inlet and who was responsible for this mess. It wasn't a difficult decision to make when our crisis worker called to say that our teenagers were shouting and damaging the crisis centre. Apparently our tribal police spotted them just in time before they hurt themselves. Then on the spot we made a decision to release the video to outside news agencies. We had to get the children out too. With the help of the Innu Nation president, we chartered an aircraft in the early morning after the RCMP turned us down when we requested more back-up. It was then that the images of Davis Inlet scattered around the country.

We got a few hours sleep before hearing that the children we escorted out in the early morning were in a safe place. Now the real work began. All the media attention turned toward the social illness that had existed in our community for so long. A few months later the announcement was made: the Innu would move to the mainland site of our choice.

Good things were happening but we were left with the fact that six children had died in a house fire. My sister's grandchildren were burned. I believe the federal government decided to do something about Davis Inlet then, after it felt the heat from the Canadian public. It was certainly a turning point and eye opener for us to start to think about our children.

We asked the federal government to do an inquiry into why this pain and suffering was happening to Innu people. In the end, the Innu Nation and band council had funds to do such a study. All the frustrations and grievances were told in Gathering Voices.

The reality of relocation should be credited to the children who lost their lives in the fire, and to those who lost their lives in suicides. Now some Innu leaders want very much to take the credit, but I believe it was a team effort and the elders with their wisdom should also take credit. As for me, I once heard a man say in the news: it doesn't matter who takes the credit, as long as the job is done. And I know it was those children who turned the world's eyes toward us.

Crossing the White Line

In 1995 I moved with my family to Goose Bay. I had decided to enroll in ABE to try to finish my education. In Goose Bay, I could no longer do the things I loved—no more fishing and hunting and traveling on the land.

In the more urban setting of Goose Bay, there were cultural differences and lots of expenses. With a family of seven (and maybe I can count myself as two persons because of my size), it was very hard to keep food on the table. There were car loans and insurance for the car. Everything the children did I had to pay for—minor hockey, soccer, games, swimming. They all required money that I didn't have because I was on a fixed income. Going back to school at the age of 33 brought a lot of gray hairs. It was hard to live up to family responsibilities with the sudden difference in income. For 17 years, I'd worked for the band council and Innu Nation. I was used to making a decent living.

The second hard part of the transition was crossing the line to living in a white society. Perceptions of the Innu were different here. My children faced racism in school; they brought home new, racist names they wondered about. It was something I was familiar with from my years of traveling back and forth to Goose Bay. Each time I encountered racism, it sent shock waves to my spine. Racism towards the Innu is as bad as anything you might hear in the media in the United States. If nothing is done to fight racism in Goose Bay, things will only get worse, and the situation will go from name-calling to more destructive acts.

The first year was the hardest for my family We met up with the racist idea that anybody with black hair has lice and is a carrier of diseases. My two boys were playing soccer and at the end of the game the players were lined up to shake hands and at least five children wouldn't even touch them.

Sometimes, their report cards had comments from the teachers that they lacked oral and written English skills. Some of those teachers realized that our first language is Innu-aimun and we use it at home all the time.

I would often hear that aboriginal people had everything free—free education, free housing, no taxes. If the people who say this could see the houses we lived in, they would be ashamed. When CBC showed the deplorable housing conditions in northern Labrador in the late 1980s, the Canadian public was ashamed. Today the same conditions exist. Shortages mean that sometimes 10–15 people share a two or three-bedroom house. This is not acceptable by Canadian standards, but for the Innu it's always been the same. Every year, government officials question housing repairs: why do you have to repair houses every year? Why don't you learn to keep your homes from breaking apart?

White society often forgets that the Innu are different. We used to live in tents or teepees made of caribou hides; these are our homes and we know how to build and repair them expertly. Like whites, we know how to take care of the kind of dwellings we have traditionally lived in.

Free education is another scam. I have yet to see an educated Innu with a university degree working in Davis Inlet. Formal education was not a priority for the Innu, but that may be changing. When I went to do upgrading, a lot of people in the community followed my path. Then the band council set up a program for adult learners in partnership with the college in Goose Bay.

My experiences in Goose Bay changed my attitudes towards white people. I'd always thought people in Goose Bay were all racists, but I was wrong. There are a lot of good people who will remain my friends. I still see and talk to my classmates at the college and the others at the entrepreneurial courses I took. They had to get past racist attitudes toward the Innu, and they tried.

My own thinking changed in other ways too. I had believed that all Innu should live in the country and live the traditional way of life. But now I had chosen to live in this white, urban culture. I wanted my children to be ready to face whatever challenges may come along. I wanted this to be one of the experiences that would prepare them to face the difficulties that I struggled with when I was growing up. I knew that, like me, they would be caught between worlds.

Now I was also caught between responsibilities. When I decided to enroll in ABE, I felt I was deserting my duties as a community leader, neglecting the needs of the people, leaving the files I had been working on unresolved. The decision I faced kept me awake at night; questions kept pounding me. What sort of person am I? Why am I doing this? What do I have to gain in doing this? The questions would not let me rest the first few months in Goose Bay. Am I running away from my friends? Do they feel deserted by me?

We, the young leaders, took on a lot because we had few resources from the outside. We had to do everything ourselves, and we were expected to do a lot. Nothing we did could be enough to solve Davis Inlet's problems. We were under a lot of pressure. Sometimes I blamed myself for contributing to the social illness that haunts Davis Inlet. Sometimes I wondered whether we were making the right decisions for our own people.

I needed a change, a break from all the sudden changes we lived with in the community. I needed a new way of thinking. And I knew that the problems and the negotiations with governments—all that struggle—would still be there whenever I returned.

I am constantly in struggle with my inner soul to overcome the barriers that I am about to face. I know that education will be rewarding and will help me in my work. I want to write fluently. But I always question the path I am taking. I tell myself I can always go back. But will I?

GWYN

During the 1970s, there was political and social change in Labrador, which was helped by scheduled air service and progress in electronic communication. The feeling of alienation from and the dissatisfaction with the government in St. John's had been present in both the old and the new Labrador. In the nineteenth century, the relationship between the Newfoundland fishermen who came to the coast for the summer and those who lived there permanently was bittersweet as the former would often occupy the best fishing berths. Fish caught off the Labrador coast was not processed locally but rather shipped in a raw or semi-processed state to the Island or elsewhere.

Health and education services had been put in place by non-governmental organizations such as the Grenfell Mission, and other services in the law and in transportation and communication were slow in coming; when they did arrive, they appeared to be put in place for the primary benefit of the transient summer visitors. Those who came from the coast to work for wages during and after the construction of Goose Air Base were left without services or even rights for the early years.

In western Labrador, the iron ore companies provided first rate services to the communities; in later decades when the companies withdrew, government was slow to respond and to provide the services and facilities it claimed it could not afford. The most accessible paper in Labrador City was not the St. John's *Evening Telegram* but the *Montreal Gazette*, and until the late 1960s there was no direct CBC feed from the Island to Labrador. For decades after Confederation, the two parts of the province—geographically and culturally separate—existed in splendid isolation. Of course, the most controversial issue was the Churchill Falls power project, where, although some Labrador people received employment, the power was shipped elsewhere. With the exception of the provision of hydro to western and central Labrador, the territory that contained the resource saw little benefit. Labrador was a remote northern territory—inaccessible, expensive, and more often than not, out of sight and mind. At the root of the feeling was the question of identity. Labrador was not on "the Rock," and Labradorians were not Newfoundlanders just because some felt it should be that way.

This feeling of alienation and dissatisfaction came to a head in February 1969 in the Wabush Recreation Centre. There Tom Burgess, an Irish union leader who had left the Liberal Party two years after his election in 1966, fired the resentment of his audience with his passionate denunciation of the provincial government, which was ignoring him and his Labrador agenda. Catching the mood for change, the meeting proclaimed it would fight to put Labrador "on a co-equal basis with the rest of the Province." The New Labrador Party was born.

While the other New Labrador candidates lost, Burgess received 80 per cent of the vote in his area and became the lone NLP representative in the House of Assembly. However, his love of the good life and his procrastination led him to squander the balance of power he held in one of the most dramatic elections in provincial history. While the New Labrador Party lost battles, it continued to wage political war and does so to this day; the spirit that was set afire in Wabush still flames from time to time.

Richard Gwyn married Sandra Fraser, a Newfoundlander and herself an outstanding journalist and author. He therefore writes not simply with the superior knowledge and style that he has brought to all his work but also with the deep understanding of one who has been there—and who captures provincial reality not just with his head but also with his heart.

Richard Gwyn

"THE LAST HURRAH,"
FROM *Smallwood, the Unlikely Revolutionary*, 1968

Ever since the weekend immediately following the election, Smallwood had known, via his well-tended grapevine, of the missing ballots at Sally Cove. Well aware of the possibilities their absence opened up, he had carefully maintained his lines of contact with Burgess. Dealing with Burgess, as all who attempted it discovered, demanded an endless supply of patience and good humour—though not necessarily of cunning. The real problem was, there were two Burgesses.

One of these was best described, by a cabinet minister, as "an Irish soldier of fortune," slim, good looking, with a gift for oratory and a refreshing lack of pretension about his motives who had bounced around the world from Australia to Africa, landed in Labrador as a carpenter's mate, married a trapper's daughter and then risen to become an international organizer for the Steelworkers. He had skipped from the expectant arms of the NDP to those of the Liberals, left them to become an independent, then formed and led his own New Labrador Party.

The other Burgess was a confused populist. He had been elected in the affluent but isolated mining towns of Labrador West, where talk of "special status" helped while away the long winter evenings. Elsewhere in the territory, the party had drawn its support (one candidate came within 83 votes of winning) from the poorest communities in the province, the tiny fishing hamlets strung along the length of the coast. Burgess was dazzled by the press attention, as much national as local, given him, and by the reporters' continued description of him as a "kingmaker."

In the wake of the election, heady talk bubbled of a new left-of-centre party that might sweep together the New Labrador Party, the Fishermen's Union, co-operatives, organized labour and the remnants of the NDP. What this hopeful movement lacked most obviously was a leader—a Smallwood, in fact. Instead, as spokesman, it had Burgess. He caught the idealistic mood in his first post-election statement. "The doctors, the lawyers, the big fish merchants, the owners of big construction companies are the people who have been getting the most out of Newfoundland. They have the biggest incomes in Canada. The rest of the people have the smallest."

The movement never got out of the living rooms and hotel rooms where it was endlessly discussed. Yet Burgess never forgot that the possibility had been there. His wanderings around the political map were to be erratic beyond belief. They were made more so by the constant tug of conscience.

Immediately after the election, Burgess had taken the advice of his idealistic friends and had refused to commit himself to either party. He quickly wobbled off that virtuous course.

After Sally Cove, the bidding between himself and Smallwood became intense, and so complicated that Smallwood at one point told reporters, "Newfoundlanders should get down on their knees and pray that Burgess does not hold their fate in his hands." That was precisely where Burgess held Smallwood's fate. One of Burgess's demands was that Smallwood promise not to run Liberals against NLP candidates. Smallwood could hardly accede, since this would have meant junking the two Liberals elected in the other Labrador seats. One of these, Joe Harvey, became so suspicious that Smallwood might do just that, that, "to make the old man sweat, he was making me sweat," he arranged a meeting with Moores[46] which the press conveniently heard about. Smallwood hastily reassured Harvey of his fidelity. Those who needed assurances now were the NLP's own candidates. Burgess at one point proposed to Harvey that he join the NLP, which would have meant abandoning Burgess's own man in that seat.

By Christmas week, when these initial manoeuvrings ended, all the players were back in their original places—except that Burgess, without the public's knowing it, had moved considerably closer to Smallwood. He spent a weekend

---

46 Frank Moores, leader of the PCs and subsequently the second premier of Newfoundland and Labrador

in Montreal with a prominent Liberal businessman. Late in December he flew to Florida for a holiday, his expenses paid by a Liberal supporter.

Smallwood, meanwhile, had made even quicker progress on another front. The district of St. Barbe South where, it seemed then virtually certain, a by-election would have to be called, was a stronghold of the Fishermen's Union. And the Union was in the market for favours. (The Burgeo plant had been closed for more than a month since Lake's departure, putting a heavy drain on the Union's resources.) On December 17, he announced that the government would nationalize the plant and reopen it; in return the Union's attitude towards the Liberals changed markedly.

The Conservatives, having knocked impatiently at the door for nearly two months, were becoming uncomfortably aware of a shift in the political climate. They knew also that as many as four of their own members had been in direct or indirect contact with Liberal emissaries and that one of these had even telephoned Smallwood himself twice to discuss, in blurred tones, the best party in which to seek his fortune. (The Conservatives knew this for the uncomplicated reason that the member told them.) Trouble in the ranks was compounded by disharmony at the top. John Crosbie[47] upstaged Moores by an endless stream of public statements. Roberts[48] took to calling the pair "co-leaders" and Burgess, after one meeting, told reporters, "I couldn't tell who was in charge."

By late December, Smallwood had a half-dozen irons sizzling merrily in the fire. On the 22nd, aboard a jet chartered by Doyle, he flew south to Florida where he owned a condominium apartment at Clearwater. Nearby, also enjoying the southern sun, was Burgess. There, a firm schema began to be developed. Burgess would join the Liberals and, after a few days, he would announce he planned to run for the leadership with Smallwood's support.

Before leaving, Smallwood had settled one other affair. Since the election, the common barroom gossip had been that Smallwood was delaying his departure

---

47 Then PC MHA, later Minister of Finance in Moores's administration, still later Minister of Finance in the Mulroney administration in Ottawa.

48. Ed Roberts, then a minister in Smallwood's government, later leader of the Liberal Party, and subsequently Lieutenant Governor of Newfoundland and Labrador.

because he needed time to clear out sensitive documents. What he really needed, was time to create some new ones.

Since late October, *habitués* of the Holiday Inn in St. John's had grown used to watching the comings and goings of the portly resplendent figure of John Christopher Doyle. Not for many years had the mining promoter graced the city with his presence for so long a period—not, in fact, since the last time Canadian Javelin had been under attack.

Since the mid-sixties Doyle had also stayed pretty much out of the headlines. The heady days of developing iron ore mines and the harrowing days of battling the D.S. Securities Exchange Commission were far behind him. His style, though, was much as ever, his apartment on Sherbrooke Street in Montreal encompassed three kitchens and eight bathrooms. So also was his intimacy with Smallwood. Ray Guy, in one of his deftest shafts for the *Evening Telegram*, wrote that the Premier, whenever he was in trouble, phoned "Doyle-a-Prayer." It was not far from the truth. Late in 1969 Smallwood had said, in heated exchange with John Crosbie, "I wish I had one hundred, one thousand John Doyles to help develop Newfoundland."

For numbers of Newfoundlanders, one John Doyle was more than enough. At times it became hard to tell where government began and promoter left off. Of Canadian Javelin, *Barron's Weekly* commented in April 1971, "In effect it has been the chosen instrument of provincial economic policy, a role in which it has pledged its own resources, plus whatever it can borrow, to grandiose and chancy development schemes."[49]

The latest such scheme, Doyle's giant linerboard mill at Stephenville, was certainly chancy and grandiose. Even so, as critics of the Smallwood-Doyle partnership tended to overlook, it would also develop the province. The mill would be the third-largest in the world, it would provide a use for Labrador's endless

---

49 The problem of distinguishing between province and promoter was made more difficult by such circumstances as that in the summer of 1971 when Smallwood's long-time Justice Minister, Leslie Curtis, resigned from the government. He joined a law firm whose principal partner, until then, had been handling Doyle's accounts. The partner promptly joined the government as Justice Minister while Curtis took over on behalf of Doyle.

stands of spruce (on which Doyle held concessions for some sixteen million acres) and, when completed in mid-1972, it would employ close to two thousand people. Originally, the project had been expected to cost $120 million. By the end of 1971 this figure had escalated to around $200 million, the precise figure depending upon a number of factors, notably the purposes for which estimates were made, and by whom.

Smallwood's original pledge had been $53 million of provincial funds. Later he raised this to $58 million. In June 1971 he pledged a loan of another $24 million. Three weeks after the election, giving scarcely a thought to the propriety of such an act by a government almost certain to leave office shortly, he advanced the last $9 million of the June commitment. (Smallwood gave as little thought to the post-election propriety of appointing Liberal faithful to the public service.)

Now Doyle needed another $30 million, of which all but $6 million would be used to enable him to pay back the $24 million loan of the previous summer. But this time the cabinet, more precisely its two youngest members, Roberts and Bill Rowe, balked. Both members of Smallwood's inner team, the pair had long been rivals for the leadership. Now, far from unaware how the record might look once the Conservatives arrived, they forged a close alliance. Enraged by their obduracy, Smallwood called them "The Bobbsey Twins." Day after day they argued that the loan should be given only if it were accompanied by a back-up agreement which would prohibit its being used without the province's approval. Unable to drive a cleft between the Roberts-Rowe twins, Smallwood took matters into his own hands. On December 10, Doyle's son came to the Premier's Office carrying in his briefcase the papers covering the provincial guarantee of the bond issue. Unbeknownst to any of his ministers or civil servants, Smallwood signed the documents—without any backup agreement. Shortly thereafter, Doyle left for Germany.

It was not until a fortnight later, on December 24, when Smallwood was in Florida, that Roberts and Rowe discovered what had happened. From financial sources, they learned that Doyle had raised $30 million in Germany on the strength of the province's guarantee, and that he had deposited the money at the Banque Nationale in Paris. Immediately, the two got in touch with Doyle by phone. Threatening to quit the cabinet and thus bring the government down, they demanded that the money be placed in trust, to be used only with the province's authority. Several hours later, Doyle phoned back and agreed to the terms. The bulk of the money was deposited in the security of a St. John's law firm, the balance in a Montreal bank.

Smallwood was furious about the erosion of his own authority, and embarrassed by what he considered a grievous insult to Doyle. From this point on he became an implacable opponent of Roberts as successor. It became almost as important to him to block the man who had once been his closest confidant as it was to extend his own term of office. (Oddly, though Rowe had fought the loan as vociferously as Roberts, scarcely any of Smallwood's wrath was directed towards him. Smallwood in fact at one point urged Rowe to run, promising him the same $100,000 campaign fund offered to Burgess.)

Many of the details of Smallwood's last favour to Doyle were uncovered after he had left office and the new government had taken over. John Crosbie, the new Finance Minister, secured a return of the $24 million guaranteed loan under threat of legal action. During the subsequent election campaign Crosbie announced that the government would buy up Doyle's holdings in the mill and operate it itself, and this step was taken shortly after the Conservatives were returned in March.

In the palmier reaches of Florida the progress was a good deal smoother. There Burgess, as a friend later put it, "was taken to the top of the mountain." If he jumped, the Liberals would have a majority, 21 to 20 pending a settlement in St. Barbe South, and could remain in office at least until the legislature assembled.

The plan the two agreed on was for Burgess to return to Newfoundland the first week of January, and to time his announcement before the Supreme Court ruled on St. Barbe. This timing was critical. The point was that if Burgess jumped before the Supreme Court decision, the Liberals would have enough members, 21, no matter how the court ruled. If in fact, as everyone expected, the Court ordered a by-election in the contested district, Smallwood counted on picking up the seat. But even if the by-election were lost, or the Court awarded the seat to the Conservatives, the Liberals, with Burgess, would still have enough members to remain in office, call the Legislature into session, and put the onus on the Conservatives to defeat them and force a general election with the Liberals still holding the advantage of being in office.

For Burgess, the chief problem was how best to explain his switch. Smallwood coached him carefully and, aware that the best plans go awry, wrote out his explanatory statement. It said that Burgess, after a month's association with the Conservatives, had come to realize that the party was incompetent to govern. He therefore had decided to rejoin the Liberals, whom he had left three years before because of a disagreement with the Premier. Since the Premier was now stepping down, the way was clear for him to return home. As Smallwood said later, "I rather liked the last part. I thought it up myself."

Early in January, Smallwood flew back to St. John's. Burgess was due to return a few days later. In Smallwood's mind, the prodigal son was cast for two roles; he could certainly give the Liberals enough members to justify their remaining in office and he might possibly mount a strong enough challenge to halt Roberts's bid for the leadership. But during Smallwood's absence, that bid had gained momentum. Though he had still to announce his candidacy, Roberts had now the vocal support of Bill Rowe and the tacit support of Jamieson. Given his formidable drive and tactical skill (Roberts, who won over 80% of the vote in his district, was the only Liberal to increase his majority since the last election), this combination would almost certainly prove too much for Burgess, no matter how well coached. As reassurance, and in the event that Burgess, at the last moment, failed to deliver his side of the bargain, Smallwood set out in search of an alternative. By the second week in January, he had found him.

On Monday, January 10, Richard Cashin, President of the Fishermen's Union, telephoned Smallwood on routine union business. Smallwood asked Cashin to join him for lunch at the Confederation Building. On the other side of the table were Roberts and Rowe. A politician of proven skills, possessed of Celtic charm and oratorical powers few of his contemporaries could match, Cashin was a considerable power in the land. Why not, Smallwood proposed, as the "Bobbsey Twins" looked on impassively, run in St. Barbe South? With his union background, Cashin would be certain of victory there; after that he could storm into the convention as the man who could win the next election. Cashin promised to think it over, and began to map out his strategy.

That evening, January 10, Smallwood stood on the brink of one of the most remarkable political comebacks of his career. The Supreme Court was due to hand down its decision on St. Barbe South the following day. If the Court ordered a by-election to be held, as both Liberals and Conservatives took for granted, Smallwood had an unbeatable candidate in Cashin. He also had Burgess, although the maverick was taking an unconscionably long time wending his way back from Florida.

At the same time, his opponents, the Conservatives, were on the verge of collapse. Two days before they had staged a putsch against their leader. While he waited impatiently for Burgess and for the St. Barbe by-election, Smallwood knew that his opponent Moores was close to being finished.

Moores had been in trouble with his own party ever since the election. Twice he had flown out of the province on vacations. Whether he was absent or present it was John Crosbie who grabbed most of the headlines. Many in the ranks felt his leadership lacked decisiveness, not a few showed it by their readiness to parlay with the Liberals. Shortly after the election, Moores's position had been damaged further by a story in the *Daily News* of November 10, which linked him to an alleged scandal involving the bankruptcy of a Toronto brokerage firm, Malone Lynch Securities. The story claimed that Moores, the day before the company was delisted, had withdrawn from the firm $200,000 of his own funds. In reply, Moores explained that the money was a trust fund for his family, which, dissatisfied with the firm's performance, he had moved elsewhere.

A worse blow fell on Moores on January 7th, while he was on vacation in St. Lucia. The press reported that his wife Dorothy had filed a divorce petition before the Newfoundland Supreme Court claiming grounds of adultery and mental cruelty. In a province where religion and the family still anchored society, the political impact of a divorce would be devastating.

That weekend, with Moores still out of the province, a group of dissident Conservatives met to consider the party's and their leader's political future. Led by John Crosbie and John Carter, both later to become cabinet ministers, they concluded that with Moores in charge the Conservatives could not hope to win either the by-election in St. Barbe or a succeeding general election. The next day, Sunday, January 9, the rebels forced a meeting of the full caucus. A vote taken at the end of the long heated meeting showed ten of the twenty elected members demanding Moores's immediate resignation. Only four stood by him. (The others were neutral or absent.)

On the Monday, while Smallwood wooed Cashin, Moores flew back to St. John's to fight for his political life. That afternoon his wife withdrew her position. "I am not divorcing my husband," she said in a formal statement. "I believe as I always have that he is the best man to be Premier of Newfoundland." The rebels, though checked, were far from beaten. A second full caucus was scheduled for the following day.

A week behind schedule, having made a slow passage northwards via Montreal, Burgess now reappeared in the province. He telephoned Smallwood early Tuesday morning to report that he was ready to make his announcement. But to Smallwood's dismay, Burgess said that he first must go to Labrador, to convince his New Labrador Party executive to support him. To Smallwood's remonstrations, Burgess replied, "I must do it." He promised to call back late that same evening.

The two Burgesses, the soldier of fortune and the populist, were warring that day within a single man. On Tuesday evening, he spoke to his own executive and won their support. But he did not telephone Smallwood until well after midnight. All was going well he reported, but added, this time to Smallwood's barely concealed fury, that before he could make a public announcement he would have to secure the approval of the party executives in the two other Labrador ridings. He would, he promised, phone back in the evening (Wednesday).

That day, January 12th, spent waiting for Burgess's call was perhaps the most frustrating Smallwood had ever spent. Time and again he jumped up when the telephone rang to find it was only a journalist or a cabinet minister on the other end of the line. And they were all demanding to know when he planned to announce his resignation. The reason was that the Supreme Court had handed down its decision on St. Barbe South. In one stroke, the two judges had virtually settled Newfoundland's political future.

The decision came down at 5:30 p.m. on Tuesday, January 11—just as Burgess was making his rounds of Labrador and as the Conservative rebels waited to challenge Moores in full caucus. The opinion was unanimous: "to declare an election void under these circumstances" as one of the judges put it in his written statement, "would leave the door open to the possibilities of practices which could invalidate any future election." The Conservative candidate in St. Barbe South, the winner by eight votes on election night, who was ahead by just two votes when the recount was halted, was formally declared elected.[50] The decision restored Conservative strength to twenty-one, and gave them a clear majority once Burgess's vote was added—an addition that no one, at that time, had any reason to doubt would be made.

For the Conservatives, the effect of the Supreme Court judgement was to puncture the putsch against Moores; its members recognized they were dealing now with a certain Premier. John Crosbie paid for his part in the rebellion. When Moores announced his cabinet line-up he placed Crosbie third in line behind Alex Hickman in the post of unofficial deputy premier.)

The impact upon the Liberals was as decisive. Ed Roberts had announced his candidacy for the leadership on Tuesday. To hasten things along, Jamieson issued a statement that since the Conservatives now had a majority, he expected Smallwood to resign, "if not on constitutional grounds, then certainly on traditional grounds."

Yet Smallwood would not give up. By Wednesday morning, he had received Burgess's first call reporting success with his own executive, and the promise of a second call that evening. Burgess was late, desperately late, but he was not yet too late. His belated defection would even the standings 21-21. Smallwood would have at least the constitutional right (which Senator Forsey, to the annoyance of the Conservatives, confirmed) to call the Legislature into immediate session and there seek a vote of confidence. While he could not win such a vote, or elect a speaker, he would be able to secure a dissolution and a general election with the Liberals still the government.

---

50 The Supreme Court based its decision on the interpretation that the election itself was valid, no matter what may have happened afterwards. Smallwood gave no thought to appealing the decision since, pending the inevitably lengthy outcome, the Conservative candidate would rightfully have taken his seat.

From the moment the Supreme Court decision was announced, Newfoundlanders hung by radios in cars, houses, offices, restaurants, waiting to hear Smallwood announce his resignation. Instead there was silence. On Wednesday evening, they found out why. Frank Moores told them. A New Labrador Party member had tipped off the Conservatives to Burgess's intentions, and Moores in turn attacked Burgess in a public statement.

The full equation was more complex in fact than Moores let on. The Conservatives had also discovered that one of their own members planned to make the jump in tandem with Burgess, a double jump that would give Smallwood not just parity but a majority. To ensure this member's loyalty until the tempting moment had passed, Conservative workers locked him in a hotel room and stationed one of their number as a chaperon during the critical twenty-four hours.

By midnight Wednesday, Smallwood had still to make any announcement. While he waited the pressures mounted. Among the public at large, disgust at Burgess had turned to blind fury at Smallwood. The next day, he was scheduled to speak to the St. John's Rotary Club. Memorial students planned to demonstrate at the hotel and the police feared an outbreak of violence.

Might-have-beens are for historians; politicians deal with facts, lucky or unlucky according to the breaks. Smallwood stayed up till one o'clock then turned in to sleep. He took for granted that the delay in the call from Labrador meant that Burgess had failed. He was right.

In his own riding, Burgess's charm had succeeded. In the coastal tidings of Labrador, seat of the populist wing of the party, his passionate pleas were met by equally passionate rebuttals. If he jumped, the party would not follow, but would oppose him on his own ground. A man almost broken, who in the space of forty-eight hours had managed to alienate every political party in the province, Burgess could not bring himself to report failure to Smallwood. Instead he called a journalist friend at Radio Station VOCM in St. John's, and through him spoke to Moores who in turn told the press, "Mr. Burgess has assured me he will stick by his commitments." At 3 a.m., the journalist phoned Smallwood at Roache's Line, woke him up, and told him that the last thread holding him to office was gone.

Richard Gwyn

POSTSCRIPT

Identity cannot easily be stamped out. It is possible to take away fish and wood and iron ore and waterpower and nickel. It is impossible to take away a name. So it is with Labradorians.

When I arrived in Labrador in 1963, I discovered that I was a Newfoundlander and that the people I had come to live among were not. If I had gone to Fortune Bay, where I was born, I would have been a Newfoundlander and so would those who met me. The same is true for Trinity Bay and Conception Bay, but it was not the same in Labrador. The people that my wife and I met in Labrador were Labradorians. We discovered that there is a Newfoundland identity and there is a Labrador identity. The Newfoundland identity is strong, borne of years of triumph and tragedy on and near the sea. It has been forged by a largely homogeneous population that, up until now, was mostly from the West Country of Britain and Ireland. It is expressed in songs and stories that are unique in Canada; it is expressed in the written word and in theatre. It defines a people and a place. To some in other parts of Canada, it is the Rock. And on the Rock live Newfies, a term pejorative or otherwise, depending on who said it and when.

There is a Labrador identity too. The Inuit do not live on the Island, and no one on the Island speaks Inuktitut. In fact, historically, the Labrador Inuit have had more in common with the Inuit of northern Quebec, Nunavut, and Greenland. Nor do the Innu live on the Island, and no one on the Island speaks Innu-aimun. Those who came from the Orkney Islands and took partners from among the Inuit women never lived on the Island. There were no Hudson's Bay Company posts on the Island until the Bay became a chain of retail stores.

The Moravian Church is virtually unknown on the Island even though it was the first Christian church in what is now Arctic and sub-Arctic Canada and has been associated with the Labrador Inuit since 1770. Labrador is nine miles from the Island across the Strait of Belle Isle, but those who live on the south coast of Labrador consider themselves Labradorians. Many Newfoundlanders settled in Labrador, first on the south and north coasts in the nineteenth century but later in all sections of Labrador, from the centre to the west; but their children born in Labrador consider themselves Labradorians. Phyllis Moore, a pioneer business-woman in Labrador West, contends, "Being a Labradorian is a matter of mind, heart and soul, not exclusively a circumstance of birth." For as Rilke has said, "One composes within oneself one's true place of origin." Labrador is that place for these people. They have felt its magnetic pull, witnessed its beauty, experienced its bounty.

The Labrador identity is expressed in the Labrador flag, which was designed in 1968 and is protected now by the Labrador Heritage Society. The blue, white, and green flies in all parts of Labrador. An inukshuk is emblazoned in these colours on the flag of the new territory of Nunatsiavut. These are also the colours of the flag of the Innu Nation. The Metis have adopted these colours as well. People use them on their fences, on their sweaters, and on their houses. No mat-ter what the origins of the people, all of them have embraced the flag. Unlike the Acadians, Labradorians do not share a common language, but like the Acadians, they have adopted a common flag. The "Ode to Labrador," composed by Dr. Harry Paddon in the early years of the twentieth century, is sung in Labrador to the tune of "Tannenbaum."

All of these are signs of an identity that is not fading. There is evidence that many people who live on the Island are recognizing the distinct identity of Labrador. Recently, the name of the province was changed from Newfoundland to Newfoundland and Labrador, and the constitution of Canada was amended to make it legal. This was significant recognition of Labradorians and the Labrador identity.

At the present time—in 2006—there are fewer than 30,000 people in Labrador spread over 154,000 square kilometres of land, sometimes rocky, sometimes forested, sometimes cold, sometimes warm, often rich and always challenging. They came from different places and origins. They brought different skills and expectations. They came for different reasons, yet they had common obstacles to overcome. They settled in different places, and Labrador is still a land of parts that needs putting together.

Beginning in the 1970s, transportation and communication in Labrador improved tremendously, as did health and education. Perhaps the most significant change was the coming together of the various peoples of Labrador, spurred on by the discovery and exploitation of the northern nickel resource at Voisey's Bay. Early Labradorians were always strong environmentalists; they had to be. But now there is an even greater appreciation of the environment in all parts of the territory; the birth of two national parks is evidence of this. All of the aboriginal peoples are searching for self-determination within the Labrador society: the Innu negotiating a land claim, the Labrador Inuit celebrating theirs becoming law, the Metis so far locked out of legal recognition but making progress through the programs of several federal departments. It is a land with a potentially exciting future, both with its southern neighbour, Newfoundland, and its northern neighbour, Nunavut.

The challenge of the future, as in the past, is how these different peoples in different places with different skills and expectations can find a way to live together. It was the challenge of the Inuit and Innu who only recently improved their dialogue because of the overlap of land claims and the realization that both could share in the good fortune ahead. It was the challenge of the ancestors of today's aboriginal peoples when they encountered the Europeans. The two cultures learned from each other, it is true, but the Europeans were the dominant society. It was the challenge of the early Labradorians who encountered the Newfoundland fishermen on their shores in the eighteenth and nineteenth centuries. It was the challenge of Canadians and people from other parts of the world as they came to work side by side with the settlers. It was the challenge of the French and English workers at Churchill Falls and Labrador West. Today, in the wired world and the global economy, Labradorians are better informed and confidant of their ability to articulate their needs and aspirations, and well equipped to meet the challenges that lie ahead.

Acknowledgements

This book would not have been possible without the help and cooperation of a number of people. First of all thanks to Pat Hayward of *The Downhomer* in St. John's, who put me on to Nimbus Publishing; then to Dan Soucoup, who bought me lunch; to Sandra McIntyre, who came to lunch and over the haddock at McKelvie's and gave such sound suggestions and guidance; to James MacNevin, who made sure I had chosen the right word; and to Heather Bryan, who made sure my pictures were up to standard.

Of course, this collection would not be possible without the permission of the authors and publishers. I am very grateful to all of them. I also want to thank the Library of Parliament and the Centre for Newfoundland Studies at MUN.

The assistance of Janice Marshall was invaluable. Not only does she have an honours degree in English, but I suspect she could qualify for an honours degree in computers. I am so thankful that she loves words and is diligent and creative about how they are presented.

Last, but surely not least, my wife, Carolyn, was constantly supportive. Her advice from time to time was always valuable because she has shared Labrador with me for over forty years.

Image Credits

1   From a painting by John Russell in the Royal Academy of the Arts.
2   From a painting by W. G. R. Hind.
3   Courtesy of *Them Days* magazine.
4   Courtesy of *Them Days* magazine.
5   Library and Archives Canada
6a Photo by Kate Hettasch; courtesy of *Them Days* magazine.
6b Library and Archives Canada.
7a Courtesy of "Ghandi" Coombs.
7b Courtesy of Environment Canada.
8   Photo by William Rompkey.

INDEX

komatiks, 100, 107, 109, 135, 240

Kyle, 4, 156–165, 170, 171

L

L'Anse aux Meadows, 9, 23

Labrador; boundary dispute, 15–16, 18; coast of, 64, 75, 147–155, 156–165, 166–173, 221, 222, 264; flag, 19, 264; governance, 14–16; identity, iv, 1, 7, 263–265; map, iii; naming, 9; relationship with Newfoundland, 11, 15–19, 250; Royal Commission on, 19

Labrador City, 6, 17, 197, 211, 250

Labrador Current, 201

Labrador Heritage Society, 264

Labrador Inuit Association, 19, 20, 214

Labrador Inuit Health Commission, 214

Labradorite, 197, 201

Labrador Metis Association, 264

Labrador Metis Nation (previously Labrador Metis Association), 19

Labrador Mining and Exploration, 197

Labrador Peninsula, 200, 204, 237

Labrador Shrimp Company, 20

Labrador tea, 200

Labrador Trough, 205–207, 210

Labrador West, 6, 17, 21, 122, 252, 266

Lachine, 81, 85, 93, 96

Lac Nascapis. *See* Ashuanipi

Lake Melville, 5, 12–16, 19, 20, 23, 78, 85, 97, 118, 175, 187, 189, 192, 216. *See also* Esquimaux Bay

Lake Michikamau, 126, 140, 188, 192

Lake Petitsikapau, 85

legends; Innu, 110, 189, 241; Inuit, 109–110

Lester's Point, 108

Liebisch, 74

Lister, 70–73

literacy, 4

livyers. *See* settlers

Lobstick Lake, 123

Lodge, The, 59

London, 34, 36–40, 43, 47–54, 65, 67–70, 80, 84, 91, 93, 94

Low, Albert Peter, 5, 193, 206–207

Lower Churchill, 197

Lucas, Francis, 33–46, 47

Lure of the Labrador Wild, 136

M

MacMillan, Captain, 131

Maggo, Paulus, 6, 221–236

Magnusson, Magnus, ii, 2, 23, 24

Makkovik, 163, 176, 215, 216, 217, 219

Mannock Island, 156

Maraval, 176–178

Marconi Station, 158

Marine Atlantic, 242

Maritime Archaic, 8

Markland, 9, 23, 25

Marten, The, 86

Martin, Mike, 19

McClintock, Leopold, 92–93

McGill, Peter, 81

McLean, John, 12, 185–189, 193

McPherson, Joseph, 88

medical care, 14, 16, 128–134, 157–162, 174–183, 213, 265. *See also* Grenfell, Sir Wilfred; Moravians; Paddon, Harry; Paddon, Mina; Paddon, Tony

Meeks, William, 105

Mercer, Hayward, 228

Merrick, Elliott, 3, 4, 97, 118–127, 156–165

Methodist Church, 104

Metis, 264, 265. *See also* Labrador Metis Nation

Michelin, Hannah, 100, 102, 107, 117

Michelin, John, 118–127

Michelin, Mensie, 102

Mikak, 2, 32–46, 47, 68; portrait, 39

minerals, 78, 93. *See also* iron ore; Iron Ore Company of Canada; Voisey's Bay

Mingan, 10, 82, 83, 87, 91

Moisie River, 199, 204

Montagnais, 9, 82, 110–111, 126, 136, 138, 141, 144, 145, 188. *See also* Innu

Montague, John, 190

Montreal Gazette, 17, 83, 250

Moore, Phyllis, 264

Moores, Dorothy, 259

Moores, Frank, 253–254, 259–260, 262

Moravians, 2, 10, 11, 12, 14, 17, 33, 35, 36–38, 39, 61, 78, 98, 174, 213, 215, 216, 221,   223, 228, 264. *See also* Beck; Brasen; Drachard, Christen Larsen; Haven, Jens; Lister; Liebisch; Peacock, Bill

Mountaineers, 101, 108, 115–116, 117

Mount Hyde, 191

Moutaineers. *See* Montagnais

Mulligan River, 99, 101, 104, 107

Mulroney, Brian, 211

Munn, W. A., 23

Muskrat Falls, 190

N

Nain, 10, 11, 69, 70, 73–74, 75, 131, 156, 159, 176, 213, 216, 221–236, 237, 242

Nain Bay, 43–45

Napartok Bay, 235

Nascapi, 237. *See also* Innu: Barren Ground; Nascopi, Naskapi, Naskaupi